MW01620679

SO SAID
THE RIVER
Life, Loss, and Pie
on the Colorado

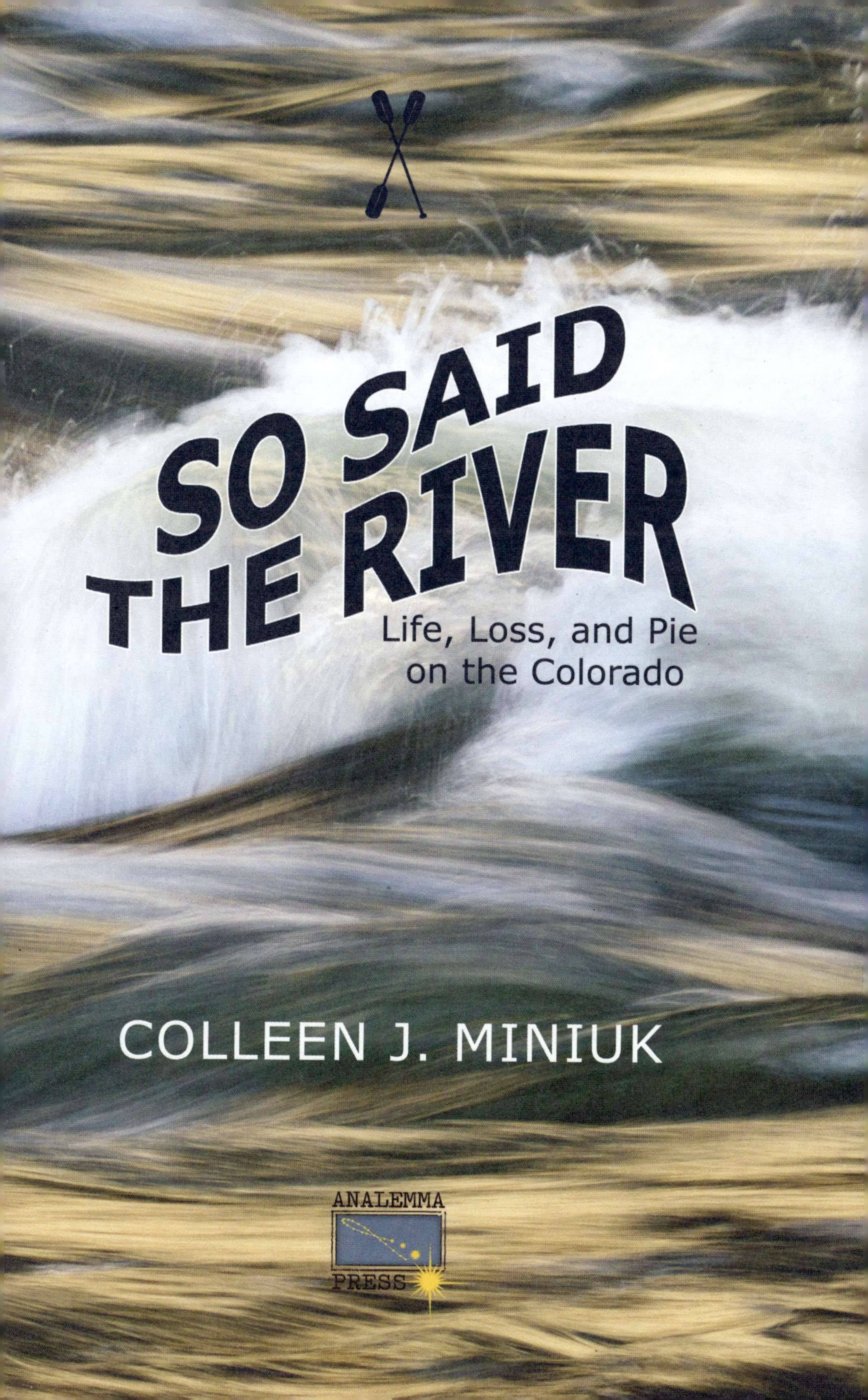
SO SAID THE RIVER
Life, Loss, and Pie on the Colorado
COLLEEN J. MINIUK
ANALEMMA PRESS

So Said the River:
Life, Loss, and Pie on the Colorado

www.analemmapress.com

Text: Colleen J. Miniuk
Photography: Colleen J. Miniuk, unless credited otherwise
Editor: Erik Berg
Proofreaders: Erik Berg and Lori A. Johnson
Layout and Design: Colleen J. Miniuk
Maps: Bruce Hucko (watercolor paintings) and Colleen J. Miniuk (design)

Hardcover ISBN: 978-0-9987857-0-7
eBook ISBN: 978-0-9987857-8-3
Library of Congress Control Number: 2024901040

Printed in Canada

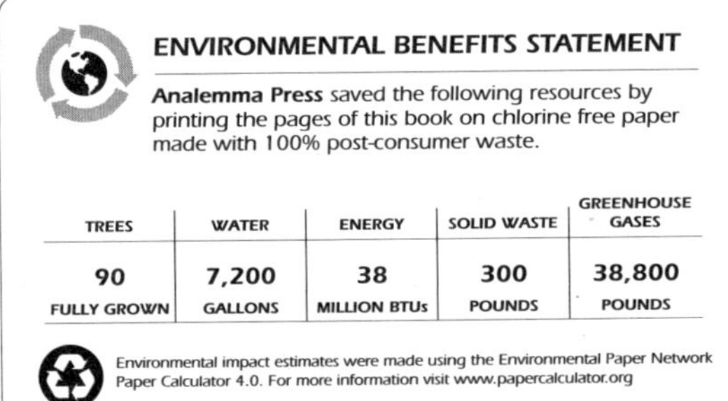

ENVIRONMENTAL BENEFITS STATEMENT

Analemma Press saved the following resources by printing the pages of this book on chlorine free paper made with 100% post-consumer waste.

TREES	WATER	ENERGY	SOLID WASTE	GREENHOUSE GASES
90 FULLY GROWN	7,200 GALLONS	38 MILLION BTUs	300 POUNDS	38,800 POUNDS

Environmental impact estimates were made using the Environmental Paper Network Paper Calculator 4.0. For more information visit www.papercalculator.org

COVER: Paddling in a rainstorm on the Green River in Labyrinth Canyon (north of the confluence with the Colorado River) in Canyonlands National Park, Utah, in April 2016. Photo by Guy Tal.

INSIDE COVER: A wave on the Brown Betty Rapid on the Colorado River in Cataract Canyon, Canyonlands National Park, Utah.

PAGE 6: Paddleboarding in Lone Rock Bay on Lake Powell, Glen Canyon National Recreation Area, Utah. Lone Rock is on the left. Photo by Guy Tal.

To my mom, Jacque,
for being a fearless Energizer Bunny and sharing this incredible journey with me

To my dad, Bob, and brother, Rob,
for always supporting all the wild things the two wild girls in the family come up with

"To be yourself in a world that is
constantly trying to make you something
else is the greatest accomplishment."
-Ralph Waldo Emerson

TABLE OF CONTENTS

MAPS

THE COLORADO RIVER WATERSHED

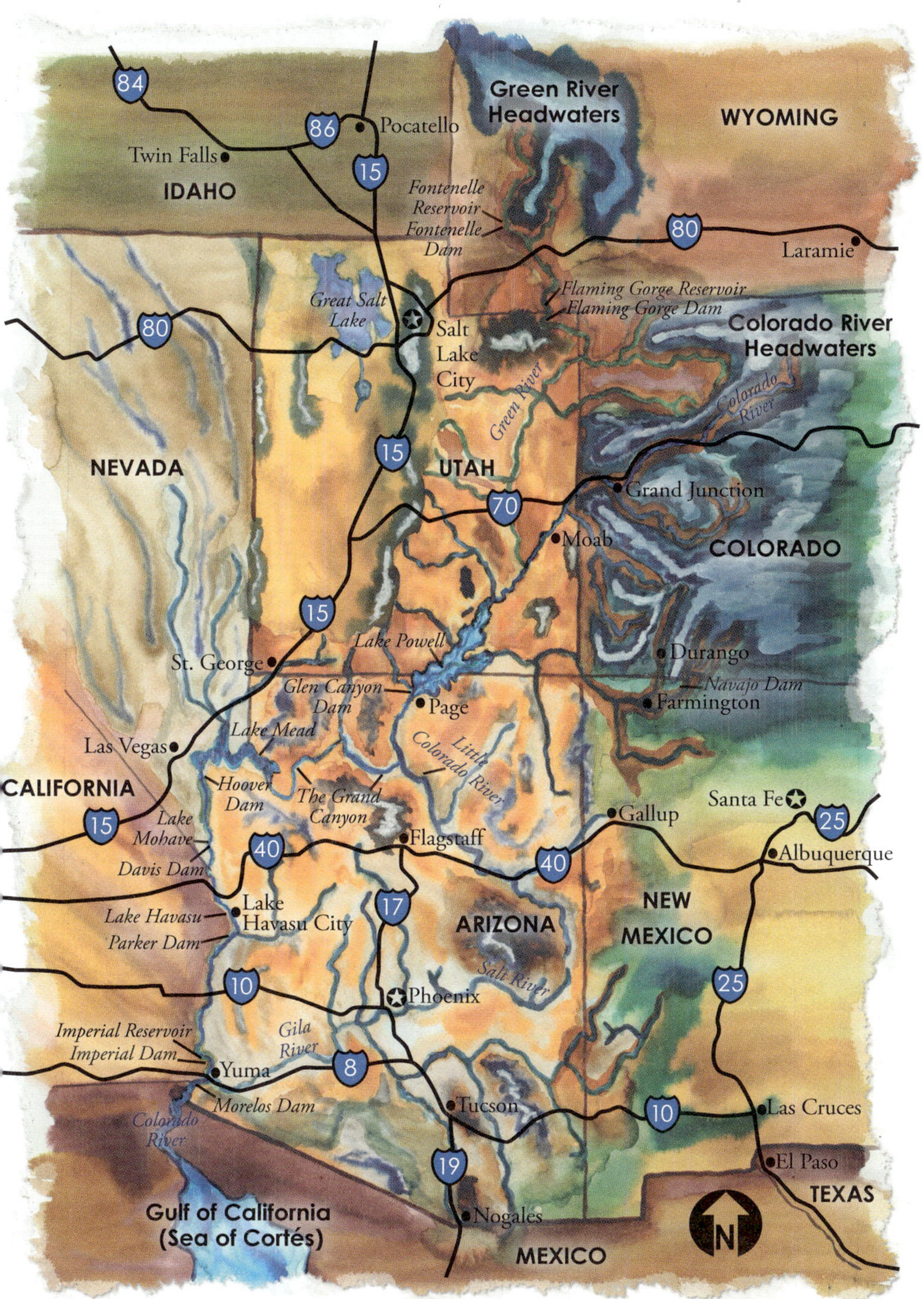

Artistic rendering only. Map not to scale and should not be used for navigational purposes.

AUTHOR'S NOTE

This work of nonfiction represents my own truth. I have striven to be faithful to the facts regarding the story, events, people, and conversations based on my own memories, my journals, email exchanges, newspaper clippings, voice recordings, and other reference materials. In times when I was unable to derive a complete picture of the original details on my own, I have clarified these situations with those who shared in the experience with me.

I have not received financial or other compensation for referencing company names in this book. I mention company names and products only for clarity in storytelling and not necessarily as a recommendation. Also, many of the designations used by companies to distinguish their products or services are claimed as trademarks.

The author and publisher acknowledges the Indigenous peoples on whose ancestral homelands we live and travel. The Colorado River watershed is home to thirty federally recognized tribes including the Ak-Chin Indian Community, Chemehuevi Indian Tribe, Cocopah Indian Tribe, Colorado River Indian Tribes, Fort McDowell Yavapai Nation, Fort Mojave Indian Tribe, Gila River Indian Community, Havasupai Tribe, Hopi Tribe, Hualapai Tribe, Jicarilla Apache Nation, Kaibab Band of Paiute Indians, Las Vegas Paiute Tribe, Moapa Band of Paiute Indians, Diné/Navajo Nation, Paiute Indian Tribe of Utah,

Pascua Yaqui Tribe, Quechan Indian Tribe, Salt River Pima-Maricopa Indian Community, San Carlos Apache Tribe, San Juan Southern Paiute, Southern Ute Indian Tribe, Tohono O'odham Nation, Tonto Apache Tribe, Ute Indian Tribe of the Uintah and Ouray Reservation, Ute Mountain Ute Tribe, White Mountain Apache Tribe, Yavapai-Apache Nation, Yavapai-Prescott Indian Tribe, and Zuni Tribe (source: Water and Tribes Initiative, www.waterandtribes.org). We thank these diverse native communities for welcoming us as they have.

Become part of the flow! To see additional resources regarding the Colorado River and this book, visit www.sosaidtheriver.com.

The milky turquoise waters of the Little Colorado River (left) on the Navajo Nation blend with the clear green waters of the Colorado River (right) in Grand Canyon National Park, Arizona. Numerous Indigenous tribes consider the confluence sacred.

FOREWORD

Little did I know, when I first met Colleen at a photography event, of the great friendship and experiences we would share in the years to follow. For a couple of years, our paths crossed professionally here and there, and each time, despite both of us being introverted and private people, we found it surprisingly easy to get into long conversations and to share details of our lives with each other. Being outdoorsy types, we soon started hiking and camping together, sipping tequila by campfires in the desert, talking into the late hours of the night, entertaining each other on long wilderness hikes, sharing banter and awe and beauty—and sometimes tears—in remote canyons, floating down desert rivers, and surveying grand views from the peaks of desert mountains.

Shortly before the Moab Photography Symposium in 2015, Colleen informed me of her separation from Craig. She and I were both scheduled to speak and lead workshops at the event, and I couldn't help thinking that if anything like that happened to me, I would not be up to the stress of speaking, teaching, and socializing. But Colleen was on her way to Moab. Not even a personal tragedy of that magnitude would keep her from getting on stage, putting on her bubbly positive persona, and inspiring her audience.

What do you do when your best friend tells you that her life is in shambles, that she is in pain and struggling for hope, and there is little you can do to fix it? Although described with humor and insight, there is no underestimating the struggle, the courage, and the fortitude it took to live through the events described in this book, let alone to emerge from them with such power, grace, and conviction. It is my sincere hope that readers who, for whatever reason, face doubt and despair in their own lives will find similar inspiration and motivation in Colleen's words and experiences.

Life, ultimately, is what you make of it—your experiences, your attitude, the hurdles you overcome, and the beauty you witness. And life is magnified a thousand times if you find it in yourself to pursue the meaningful path, to not always favor the easy road, to pull yourself up from the abyss, to acknowledge what is truly important and to pursue it with all you're worth, to love who you are and to make peace with all of it—your soul and your body, your gifts and your imperfections. More than anything, life becomes meaningful with the recognition that it is fleeting, that it is not predictable, that it comes with no guarantees, that we have less control over its unfolding than we would like to believe, that each of us is, as described by Hermann Hesse, "a bird in the storm."

When Colleen told me of her plan to paddle the length of Lake Powell, I felt happy for her. I thought it was a wonderful idea and a worthwhile endeavor. I never doubted Colleen's skill and ability to do it, and I hoped she could find the same solace in these canyons as I have. In fact, if instead she told me she decided to get an office job or to curtail her outdoor adventures in some way, I would have responded with, "Why would you do a stupid thing like that?!" But a couple of weeks on the Colorado River sounded like the best kind of medicine.

I received Colleen's message about having to end her trip early as I was walking out of a hike in one of the lower canyons of the Escalante. I headed to high ground where I could pick up a better signal and called her as the last light of the day was fading. She told me about the day's events and I felt both great relief and great pride in how she and Jacque handled the storm. This is wild country. Spend enough time exploring here and you'll learn that mishaps, sometimes life-threatening ones, are inevitable. At one point or another, you'll be stranded somewhere, be forced to deviate from your plan, to improvise, to survive, to seek help or to bail early. Mystery and unpredictability are parts of the adventure—very important and indispensable parts.

"So, you ran into a challenge, you made the right decisions and did the right things, and you survived to tell about it. And you still have a few extra days to enjoy the desert. What's the problem?" I asked half-jokingly, hoping to console Colleen, who was obviously shaken by the day's events.

As we have on many prior occasions, Colleen and I talked about life's unexpected setbacks and the importance of living fully and deeply. Having known Colleen in other challenging times, I knew that she didn't just have the skills to paddle a river; she also had the fortitude to deal with crises and emergencies. More important, she had the strength, courage, and clarity of mind to see through her pain and to find meaning in it. But just in case, I thought she could use being incessantly reminded of it.

"Come join me in Escalante for a few days," I suggested. "You're not done."

We live in a culture obsessed with accomplishment. We foolishly condemn as failure anything that did not work out as intended, regardless of how much we learn, grow, and gain by it. Oftentimes, even if failing to execute on an original idea, the lessons, transformations, and epiphanies we may experience eclipse whatever rewards the original plan could ever hope to offer.

Studies show that among the most important traits for success is grit—the capacity to dust yourself off after a setback and to keep going, to find the motivation to try again or to try something else.

Completing something according to plan is one kind of accomplishment, to be sure. But it is also a very poor measure of one's temperament and a very poor means to a truly profound experience. In fact, it is trying—not doing—something worthwhile that is the greater test of a person's mettle and the test of true heroism. To try—to show up, to jump in, to commit (especially when attempting a challenging act with no guaranteed outcome)—requires more courage, self-confidence, and spirit than to follow a prescription to an expected outcome. To do something is a test of skill, not of personality. To try, to improvise, to take charge when things go awry—these are the marks of a hero. To have proven, if only to yourself, that you are the kind of person who will step up, overcome doubt, and begin something just because you consider it worth doing—is the greater accomplishment; to finish—a lesser one; and to finish something predictable and devoid of surprises—a lesser one still.

Of all the parts of Colleen's adventure, the one requiring the greatest courage was simply pushing off into that silty fast-flowing river for the first time, knowing there was no turning back. I was proud to be there for that moment, and I am proud of my friend.

Guy Tal
Torrey, Utah

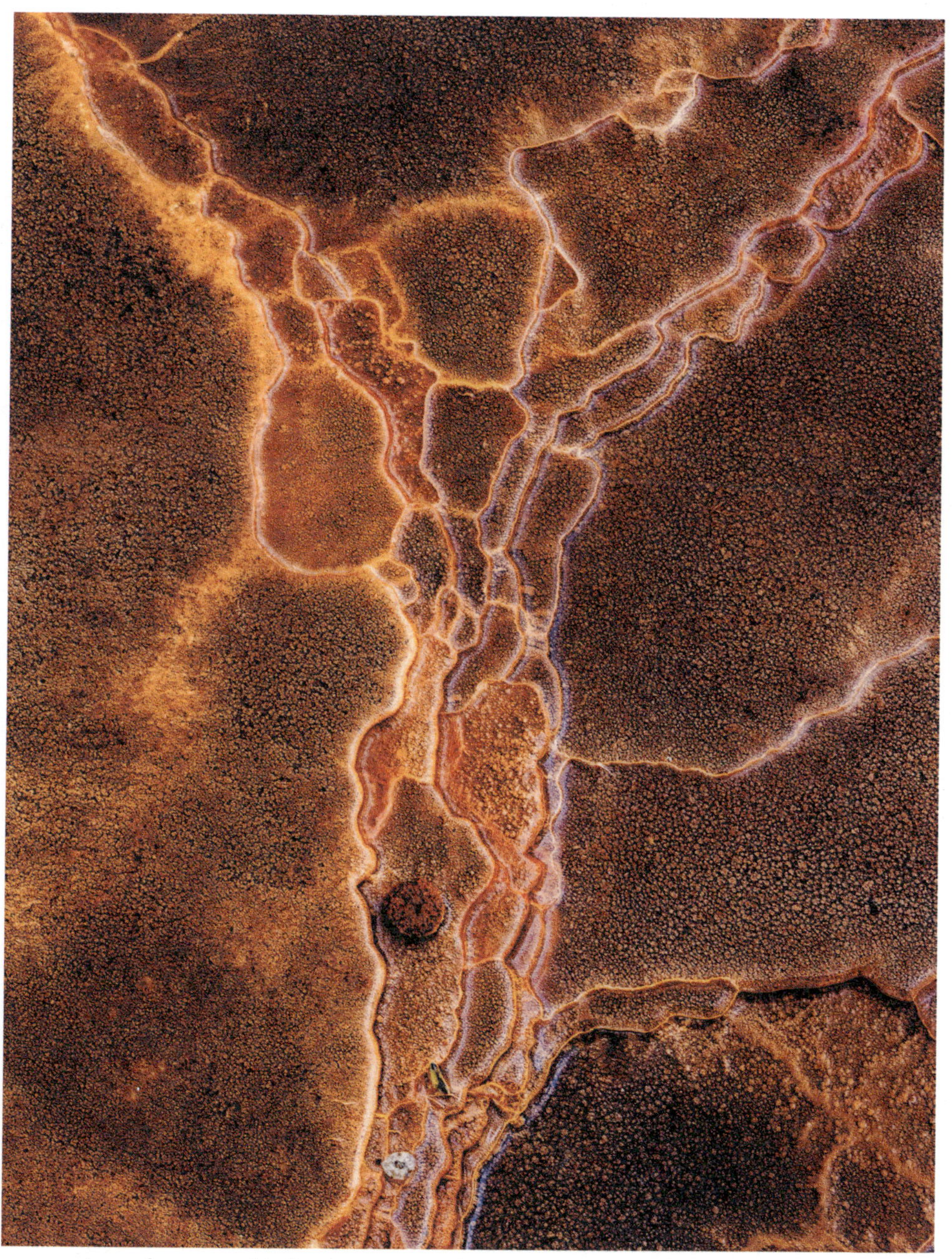

An anthropomorphic figure appears in the travertine surrounding Crystal Geyser, a human-caused geyser along the Green River north of the confluence with the Colorado River in Utah. I made this photograph in April 2016 while paddling through Labyrinth Canyon with Guy.

PROLOGUE: THE STORM

November 27, 2015
Near Knowles Canyon, Lake Powell, Utah

Water gives life. *So they say.*

I never had any reason to doubt them, whoever "they" were. Until November 27, 2015. On the fourth day of my attempt to paddleboard across Lake Powell, the Colorado River tried to kill me.

The wind raced around the winding walls of Glen Canyon. The gale's fury hissed through sandstone plateaus, buttes, and spires along the lake's snakelike channel. Whitecaps foamed all around me, churning, seething like a raging river rapid. I plunged into a haystack wave. My paddle bowed against what felt like wet cement. The crest of one wave tossed my inflatable standup paddleboard into the trough of another. Then another and another.

This was no longer Lake Powell. The Colorado River, blocked behind the Glen Canyon Dam and obscured beneath the reservoir for fifty-two years, had reappeared in the morning's sudden windstorm. The river was alive. And she was pissed.

The river spit in my face. I wiped splashes and specks of blowing sand and tears from my eyes. I didn't belong here. I was irrelevant here, a nuisance even, a piece of trash to be crumpled up, thrown out, and forgotten.

Is this the end?

Is this how I'm going to die?

I wasn't alone. My mom, Jacque, and her turquoise touring kayak vanished behind a four-foot swell. I scanned the base of the near-vertical sandstone cliffs soaring hundreds of feet over our heads. "Mom! Where are you?!" The wind hushed my cry as soon as it fell from my lips.

My board rolled to the top of a whitecap just long enough to spot her struggling thirty yards to my left. Her teeth clenched. Her paddle flailed. The river was trying to kill her too.

I pulled hard with my paddle on my right. I slammed into an oncoming wave like a bird crashing into a glass window. The force knocked me off my paddleboard's chair and flung me face-first into the neat pile of gear stacked in front of me. I reached for the bungee cords rigged behind me and tried to pull myself back onto my seat. The next wave pummeled me and brought me to my knees.

"Not so fast," the wind and waves howled in unison, two bullies banded together to pick on the new kids in town. "We aren't done with you yet."

I gripped the side of my board with both hands and looked up. She was gone. "Mom!"

She reappeared on top of a distant wave.

Thank god.

Until she disappeared.

Did she fall in?

Then reappeared.

Thank god.

Then disappeared.

What do I do? I don't know what to do.

We had set out four days earlier to paddle across the 141-mile length of America's second largest reservoir in southern Utah. Mom and I had struggled against merciless headwinds for the first twenty-eight miles of our trip. On our fourth morning, a heavy-handed tailwind woke us in our overnight camp near milepost 113 (113 miles from the Glen Canyon Dam, that is). We cheered our good fortune. As we passed Warm Springs and Cedar canyons, we had taken only a few strokes here and there to direct our course down the narrowing corridor. The wind did much, if not all, of the hard work for us.

If all went according to plan, this push from behind would carry us to milepost 106 and then into Forgotten Canyon where we intended to camp that night. If all went according to plan, our trip would conclude at the Wahweap Marina at the far southwestern end of the lake in ten more days.

But things were definitely *not* going according to plan.

When we rounded the corner at Tapestry Wall, an imposing 700-foot-tall, two-mile-long precipice near milepost 110, Mother Nature had changed her mind. Once-encouraging gusts shifted into a roaring crosswind. Playful whitecaps transformed into furious four-to-five-foot swells.

We had changed our minds too. Mom and I had crossed the half-mile-wide channel from north to south. We thought the tall, shadowed monoliths on the south side would shield us better from the storm than the exposed sunlit walls on the north side. We thought we could duck under the wind, avoid the waves, find an easier ride. We thought wrong.

A receding wave revealed a hidden alcove along the base of the southern cliff. An incoming surge pushed Mom toward the hole. She took two hurried—but strong—backward strokes as the gap threatened to swallow and crush her. Water from behind grabbed the nose of her kayak. The swell threw her against the unforgiving blank sandstone slab at the top of the nook. Then shoved her away. Then tossed her into the wall again. And again.

Mom lifted her paddle over her head and jabbed the cliff as if trying to slay a wild beast. She unleashed a petrifying primal scream, her fear and rage echoing off the rocks and into the wind. The lake ignored her and tossed her back into the cliffs. She too was irrelevant here.

"Oh my god, Mom! Don't give up," I screamed even though I knew she couldn't hear me.

My tears started to drip into the water like rain, first a drizzle, then a downpour. I scanned the horizon looking for an answer, a way out. Turning back and paddling upstream was not an option. Stopping here wasn't either. Seven-story-high precipices lined both sides of the canyon. There was no beach. No ledge. No lone rock to take refuge on. There was no escape. The winds wailed. The waves owned us. The river had trapped us in a maelstrom on the lake.

I had no idea how much longer Mom, or I, could last. Eight months earlier, I had lost my marriage. Now I could lose my mother. I could also lose my own life.

Dying wasn't part of my plan.

It's never a part of anyone's plan.

My breakfast climbed into my throat. I puked into the lake. I wiped my mouth with the back of my coat sleeve, then looked back at Mom.

"Please, please, make this stop!" I pleaded with the storm. "I'll do anything to make this stop. I'm begging. Please. Anything!"

One of the last photos I made near mile 111 before the waves started to gain height and changed directions. The Tapestry Wall, the illuminated rock cliff on the far right, looms on the horizon.

"There are many ways to salvation, and one of them is to follow a river."
~David Brower

PART I: UPSTREAM

1

THE UNEXPECTED BEND

We sat together at our kitchen table in silence. The noon sun filtered through the blinds and cast shadowed stripes across the wooden surface. After spending the morning fighting about who knows what, we poked at our sandwiches, searching for an appetite, searching for something, anything, to say to keep the peace.

"I can't do this anymore," Craig said without looking up.

"I can't either." I tossed my napkin onto the half-eaten food on my plate. "We must figure this out. We have to stop arguing all the time."

It wasn't like us to quarrel. We had fought little, if at all, in our twenty-two years together, first as best friends, then for almost fourteen years as husband and wife. I was an animated, tall, athletic gal of Irish descent who loved planning for the future. He was equally as tall as I but was a reserved, brawny lad of English stock who loved studying history. He liked to joke that we were proof the English and the Irish could, in fact, get along. And we did.

We were inseparable from the moment we met at Stanford University during our freshman year in 1993. We stayed connected even after I transferred from Stanford to the University of Michigan-Ann Arbor after my first year. While he remained in California to finish his studies, we talked and talked, first as friends. We became long-distance lovers before the start of our senior years. We racked up $300-per-month phone bills. Each. In our defense, this was before the invention of Facetime, Zoom, and cell phones with unlimited calling plans.

Much to the phone companies' dismay, we both landed jobs with Intel Corporation in Phoenix, Arizona, after graduation in 1997. We married in April 2001. Together, we shared our joys, despairs, and dreams while cooking chicken fajitas and dancing to Jimmy Buffet. And while sitting on our patio toasting glasses of chardonnay. And while watching dust storms thunder across the saguaro-dotted Sonoran Desert in late summer. And while hiking new trails and camping beneath the Milky Way in awe-inspiring places across the western United States. When his, or more often my, travels took us away from each other, we exchanged countless handwritten cards, lengthy emails, and yellow sticky notes scribbled with words of endearment, encouragement, and longing. We ended most communications with our trademark signature, "LYLM," an acronym we made up for "Love you. Love, Me."

But in February 2014, right before our 13th wedding anniversary, the winds changed. We no longer had much to say to each other, and what we did say often led to an argument. How I asked too much of him. Why he didn't call while I was away. Whether his new mentee at work was *really* just a friend. Neither of us saw it coming, but over time, Mutt and Jeff dissolved into oil and water.

"No, I mean…" Craig hesitated as if even he were afraid of the words that would follow.

Our eyes met. I knew what he meant. He had hinted at it in earlier fights. I didn't want to hear it then, and I didn't want to hear it now. I started to tremble. I could not bear to watch the words drip from the same lips that had kissed mine for over two decades.

"I can't do *this* anymore," he looked away.

"What do you mean 'You can't do *this* anymore?' You mean…you can't do *us* anymore?"

He nodded to agree.

I stormed from the table to hide upstairs in our bedroom. Still, I couldn't outrun the piercing sting of my best friend and husband not wanting to be with me anymore. I made it only halfway up the stairs before I collapsed face first into the carpet and started wailing. My hands clutched the wooden railing, desperate to hold onto the life we had built together.

What do I do? I don't know what to do.

Is this the end?

When we married, it was for life. At least it was for me. Craig and I had always worked well as a team. I was sure that we could—and would—work through anything the universe threw at us. Love conquers all. *So they say.*

Although nothing had tested our relationship like this, we could figure this out. We had to. I had everything planned out for us for the rest of our lives. We were going to be that adorable old couple who had stayed married for sixty-plus years, sitting hand in hand in our rocking chairs, sipping our coffee on our screened-in porch, and finishing each other's sentences until, as we promised one another, death do us part. Divorce is something that happened to other people. Not me. Not us. Marriage is forever. *So they say.*

A minute passed. Or maybe it was two hours. It's hard to say. Time stops when forever ends without warning. However long it took, I regained my composure and walked back into the kitchen. Craig stood and faced me when I entered the room.

"It takes two to make a marriage work. If you're done..." I said, pulling my wedding ring from my finger and slamming it onto the table in front of him. "Then I'm done too."

In early April 2015, two weeks before our 14th wedding anniversary and four weeks before my 40th birthday, Craig and I came to an agreement, the first one we had made in months: we decided to informally separate. By "agreement," I mean I finally caved into what he had wanted for almost a year. I regretted it the second I surrendered.

Darkness fell. Days later, he came home from work, stuffed some of his clothes into a duffle bag, and collected a handful of his personal belongings in a cardboard box. He paused in the dimly lit hallway. I looked into his tired hazel eyes. His shoulders and head dropped. "I'm sorry," he mumbled before the door closed.

I reached my hand out to the cold, blank back of the door. Blood pooled into my feet. I couldn't move. Eventually, I turned back into the house we had shared for fourteen years and drifted from room to room. Cheerful but tainted memories haunted me from every direction. His playful curly brown hair running through my fingers. His warm bear hugs on the couch. His running shoes at the base of the stairs. His dress clothes hanging in the closet. His leftovers in the freezer. All frozen in time.

I ran my hand across several of my framed landscape photographs from various national parks hanging on the walls in our foyer. These photographs reminded me that I knew how to enjoy solitude. I had spent much of each year traveling across the country, mostly on my own, as a full-time freelance photographer and writer.

This felt different.

The one person who promised never to leave my side in life was imposing solitary confinement against my will. I felt irrelevant, a nuisance even, like a piece of trash to be crumpled up, thrown out, and forgotten. In the punishing silence, I became a ghost in my own life.

In the days that followed, I alternated between staring at my ceiling fan spinning against the white ceiling above my bed and making love to glass after glass of sauvignon blanc while soaking in lavender Epsom salts in my bathtub. That is, if I birthed myself out of the protective womb of my down comforter by noon and into the nakedness of my bathroom without stopping to sob on all fours on the tile and whirl through all five of Elizabeth Kübler-Ross' stages of grief.

And that was on good days.

At night, while drowning in the empty space of our king bed, I closed my wet eyes and watched every plan, dream, and plan to achieve our dreams unravel from my grip like a tornado carelessly ripping trees out of the ground. The 5,000-square-foot timber-frame house I had sketched, gone. The thirty-five-acre rolling green meadow where it would sit, gone. The rocking chairs on the screened-in porch, gone. Happily ever after, gone.

One night, at three a.m., I woke up in tears and screamed, "Please, please make this stop! I'll do anything to make this stop. I'm begging. Please. Anything!"

I sat on the edge of my bed, wiping drips of confusion from my red puffy eyes and staring at the pile of crumpled white tissues gathered at my feet. Stopping the demise of my marriage was not an option. Restoring the perfect life I had planned for was not either. Despite every grain of my being resisting changing my course without Craig, I had to do something. Anything. But I had no idea what to do.

All I knew was that I couldn't do *this* anymore.

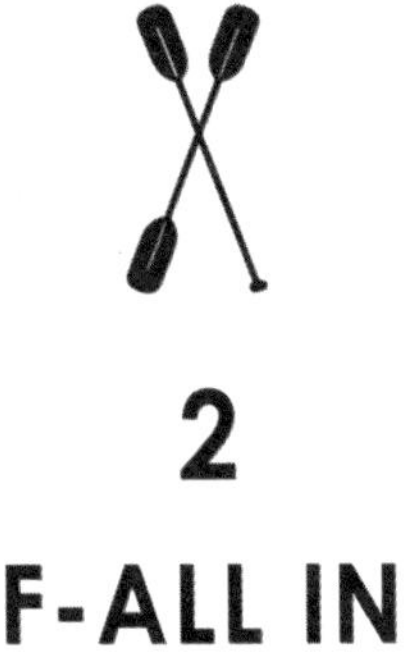

2
F-ALL IN

"We require a two-person minimum for private trips," the manly voice said sternly but politely from the other end of the telephone.

I suspected there was a catch. Minutes before, I had tried to book a half-day, guided standup paddleboard trip on the Colorado River online with Paddle Moab. I had begrudgingly called the outfitter when their "Book Now" page would not allow me to select "1 adult" from the pull-down menu. The introvert in me disliked talking on the phone.

"But…I'm in Moab alone," I said. I tried to sound not too desperate, but just desperate enough, in hopes he'd cave on his condition. "And… it's my 40th birthday."

An awkward silence buzzed.

Money. It's just about money. They can't cover their time and expenses with only one participant.

"What if I pay for two spots and only I show up?" I rolled my eyes. That definitely sounded desperate.

"You mean…you'd…pay double?" Confusion rode on each of his enunciated words.

"Yes, but only I will show up. My 'friend' will get sick overnight. Whatever you need to do to get it to work for you, I don't care. I want to paddle the river tomorrow on my birthday."

"You're sure about this?" he asked.

"Here's my credit card number," I said.

He took my payment and booking information. "We'll pick you up tomorrow morning at 8:30 in front of your hotel," he said. "See you then. And…happy birthday."

"See you tomorrow." I set my phone down. I felt pleased that I had finally scheduled something for my big day. Even if it came together at the last minute in a place I never thought I'd be.

~ ~ ~

Years ago, Craig and I had made a deal. We'd save up and celebrate our respective 40th birthdays with a special trip of our choosing. He took no time at all to decide. For his November 2014 birthday, we visited Belize. Despite things being tense between us, we laughed while exploring Mayan ruins. We fly-fished for bonefish. We sipped on frou-frou drinks while sitting next to waterfalls. As the locals liked to say, we "took it Belize-y." Between the tiffs, that is.

I could not, for the life of me, decide where I should commemorate mine. Photographing icebergs and penguins in Antarctica? Sipping chardonnay in France? Seeing the Maldives before the world's rising oceans swallowed the country whole? So much to see, so little time. My wandering soul wrestled with building angst. I wished on occasion, can't somebody pick somewhere—anywhere—for me, please?

As the yarn of my marriage started unraveling, so did the idea of spending my 40th birthday somewhere exotic with Craig. I received an invitation to present at the Moab Photography Symposium which was scheduled for late April 2015. I had presented there once before as a photography instructor, in 2014, so I knew what to expect. I'd get to meet up with several of my friends at one of the country's most inspiring photography events of the year. More importantly, I wouldn't be alone. I accepted even though I'd have to work on my milestone birthday.

Moab, Utah, isn't exactly what I'd call exotic. Beautiful, for sure. Striking, no doubt. But Antarctica, France, or the Maldives it ain't.

The desert oasis sits in the Moab-Spanish Valley, an eleven-mile-long, mile-wide graben on the Colorado Plateau. It's where an anticline of a soft, salt-rich layer called the Paradox Formation collapsed between two parallel faults eons ago. The now-exposed geology represents a time span of 750 million years. Rock formations from the Jurassic and Triassic periods (dating from about 150-250 million years ago) created a rampart of red cliffs on the western edge so stiff in their repose the chiseled vertical rock faces now look like a platoon of army soldiers standing at attention, shoulder to shoulder, in a single straight line. Curvaceous and bulbous white-and-orange-swirled domes made of Jurassic Navajo Sandstone form the shorter rim to the east in the shadow of the nearby La Sal Mountains.*

What made life possible in this seemingly inhospitable landscape was the Colorado River. Precipitation and snowmelt birth the river on the west side of the Continental Divide in the Rocky Mountains in north-central Colorado. From there, she wiggles down the western side of the divide, then pulses diagonally across the Colorado Plateau—the largest plateau in the United States—through Utah and Arizona, then trickles along Arizona's borders with Nevada and California through the Mojave and Sonoran deserts. Minor and major tributaries feed her as she travels through narrow canyons and lush valleys and past a patchwork quilt of agricultural fields and towns.

The river pools into a series of tightly managed reservoirs behind concrete dams. But when she flows through the northern and western outskirts of Moab, her silty, mocha-colored waters act wild and free.** The river cuts perpendicularly through the Spanish Valley, poking her head out of one canyon, passing a decommissioned uranium processing site, and ducking into another canyon in less than three miles. On a map, the crisscross between the exposed river and the ancient rock forms an X. As in "X marks the spot."

Native Americans, including the Ancestral Puebloan, Fremont, and Ute cultures, have lived off the bounty of the river and the surrounding lands for thousands of years before Spanish explorers, Mormon missionaries, and miners of uranium, potash, salt, oil, and natural gas

---

* *"La Sal" means "the salt" in Spanish.*

** *The word "colorado" means "colored red" in Spanish.*

arrived in more recent times. Today, over 5,000 year-round residents call Moab home. Every summer, over a million tourists scour through the small town like a flash flood. The fantastical formations of rocks, hoodoos, and rocks waiting to become hoodoos attract all flavors of visitors: hikers, bikers, trail runners, rock climbers, river rafters, BASE jumpers, Jeep lovers, motorcyclists, antique car fanatics, and more. Wonderers and wanderers from across the globe come to frolic in nearby public lands, including Arches and Canyonlands national parks.

I had driven over the river and through Moab on many occasions. I had passed by the string of hotel chains with waterslides, local coffee shops selling cricket protein bars, and gift shops touting "2-for-1 red dirt shirts," but only on my way to somewhere else. I'd gas up my truck, then fuel myself up at the Moab Brewery. They served not only the expected beers and bar food but also heavenly gelato. After my fill, which usually took no more than an hour or two, I'd continue on my way to my destination.

Working in a tourist town wasn't the last place on Earth I'd thought I'd be on my birthday, but it sure wasn't the first. Instead of running through airports trying to catch connecting flights across skies and oceans and dreams, I arrived in Moab the day before my birthday after an uneventful eight-hour drive from Phoenix. I unloaded my luggage in a darkened hotel room, trying to avoid hosting a pity party. I mean, eating Italian ice cream in Utah and visiting Italy were almost the same thing, right?

I opened the drapes and stared out the window at the parking lot. Here I am. Now what?

I had a free morning before the symposium began. I started mulling over ways I could spend my time. I pulled out my laptop and sifted through websites touting the run-of-the-mill, touristy activities.

Off-road jeep tours. No.

Jet boat tours. No.

Zip lining. No.

Guided standup paddleboarding on the Colorado River. Yes!

~ ~ ~

I had my first experience with standup paddleboarding in July 2013 when Craig and I moved to Hillsboro, Oregon, to support his temporary job assignment with Intel. A mutual friend from Stanford, along with his wife and young son, were vacationing in nearby Bend. Chris and Susan invited us to join them for a few days. One afternoon, we all ventured to the Deschutes River to cool off. They suggested we rent standup paddleboards, or SUPs.

I had never seen or heard of standup paddleboarding before. But from the moment my legs wobbled on that board, ecstasy took hold. I dipped the body-length paddle into the river, then again, then again. The rhythmic pull mesmerized me. I melted into the waving evergreens, the kissing breeze, the hopeful sun. Instead of controlling my surroundings, the surroundings had control over me. I belonged to the river. To nature. To myself, my nature. I often enjoyed outdoor activities like hiking, skiing, and fishing. None of those activities had yielded such connection, such bliss, as I found by being on the water. I had never felt so free.

That said, it was odd for me to have taken a fast and passionate liking to standup paddleboarding. I say odd because I feared at least four things. One, being a burden on others. Two, being taken advantage of. Three, accidentally dropping my car keys into a pit toilet. And four, swimming in water where I could not see my feet. Bathtubs and swimming pools are fine. Small, shallow creeks—or more appropriately, "cricks," like the one I grew up on in Arkansas? Also fine. Muddy lakes, murky rivers, and—god forbid!—the dark abyss of the ocean? Not fine. I could be on the menu in those places, and I was not going to plunge my toes into the void only to become some critter's dinner.

I had tempted the man-eating creatures of the underwater kingdom only a handful of times in my life. Any time I swam or snorkeled in shadowy water, I hyperventilated and bolted back onto the boat like a panicked seal darting away from a hungry great white shark. To make matters worse, once I took refuge on a ship, I was prone to violent bouts of seasickness in even the smallest of waves.

Standup paddleboarding offered an alternative to swimming in scary, turbulent waters. I could stand on the wide surfboard-like platform and float on top of the surface while the carnivorous sea monsters remained hidden beneath my board. As far as I was concerned, so long as I couldn't see them, they didn't exist.

Since that first paddle in Bend, I had braved small unnamed lakes in Utah, calm bays in the Atlantic Ocean in Maine, and even the tranquil and oh-so-blue Caribbean Sea off the coast of Belize during Craig's birthday trip. With each stroke came more ecstasy. So when I found myself in Moab, no longer belonging to my husband or the life I once knew, I thought paddling on the Colorado River might comfort me. If nothing else, I could belong *somewhere,* if only for a few hours.

~ ~ ~

The dawn of my birthday arrived under a radiant and crisp cerulean sky. I stood on the curb of the hotel parking lot fifteen minutes before my arranged meeting time with the outfitter. My hands fidgeted with a recycled plastic baggie stuffed with my phone, sunscreen, and a wadded bundle of cash for a tip.

A few minutes before 8:30, a grey van with a Paddle Moab sticker on the side pulled up next to me. A bearded thirty-something-year-old guy jumped out of the driver's seat. He greeted me with a cheery bouquet of three handpicked red-dome blanketflowers. "Everyone should get flowers on their birthday," he said with a smile.

"How kind of you. Thank you!" I pushed my nose into the yellow petals and inhaled the buttery aroma of thoughtfulness.

Josh introduced himself as the owner. I recognized his voice. He and I had spoken on the phone yesterday.

A tanned woman with an athletic build popped out from the other side of the van. "Happy birthday," she said, extending her hand to mine. "I'm Alicia, your guide for the day."

She invited me to climb into the passenger's seat and away we went. When we reached the northern edge of Moab, pleasantries exchanged, I took the last sip of my hotel-brewed coffee. I slipped the stems of my flowers into the empty cardboard cup and positioned the arrangement in the van's cup holder as if it were a prized trophy on a shelf.

"Will you keep these for me?" I asked Josh. "I'd like to take them with me once we're done."

He tapped the dash. "You bet. They'll be waiting for you when I pick you up."

He turned onto Highway 128, a two-lane, paved road designated the Upper Colorado River Scenic Byway. Locals called it River Road. The reason why, the Colorado River, came into view on our left.

Turrets of burnt-orange cliffs guarded the canyon's mouth, where muted chocolate-colored waters in shadow stretched no more than 500 feet between the rock towers. Two unbroken, rounded ridgelines overlapped in the distant horizon, both tilting down and reaching for the river as if to embrace her. Sheer walls comprised of carrot-colored Navajo, Kayenta, and Wingate sandstone towered into the sky. Streaks of blackened desert varnish—a thin patina common in this arid desert landscape that naturally forms after clay, oxide, manganese, and iron mix over thousands of years—dripped down their exposed faces like spilled paint. Underneath, older Triassic rocks from the reddish-purple Chinle and Moenkopi formations sloped to the riverbank. Scattered sage and scree dotted the declivities. Tamarisk, Russian olive, willow, and an occasional Gambel oak with showy spring green leaves formed a brushy hemline along the shores.

The road ahead twisted into the folds of monoliths and disappeared in the golden haze of the morning sun. We sped past Matrimony Spring and Grandstaff, Drinks, and Jackass canyons on the right and a few primitive campgrounds along the river on the left. I scooted to the edge of my seat, stretching the seat belt taut, and leaned over the dash to get a clearer view through the windshield as we hugged the curves of the waterway at the base of the gorge. My shoulders relaxed. My jaw softened. After a relaxing fifteen-minute ride, Josh pulled into a small unmarked pullout called Sandy Beach.

The three of us gathered around the back of the van to unload our gear. I shuttled handfuls of paddling and safety equipment between Josh and Alicia who was already at river's edge scoping out the scene.

"You've paddled before, right?" she asked. She rested two rigid inflatable paddleboards side by side and perpendicular to the shoreline.

"Yeah," I tightened my life jacket. "But never on the Colorado."

"Good. Then I'll breeze through the basics."

"I've never had a formal lesson, so there's no harm in giving me your spiel as you normally would," I said, watching her lay a paddle next to each board. She looked exactly as I later read on her blog, like "a spunky rendition of Annie Oakley in a string bikini, braids, and a trucker hat."

She organized other accessories into two piles (one for me, one for her) as she talked through different paddling techniques. The basic CPR, or the Catch-Power-Release, stroke. The J-stroke. The cross-bow sweep turn stroke. The self-rescue, in case I messed up any of those strokes and fell in the water. She moved with poise and spoke with confidence. This wasn't her first ride down the river.

"We'll be going about six miles today," Alicia explained as she fussed with the rudder on her board. "Now, when we go through the rapids, look for the smooth tongue and…"

Wait. What? Rapids? That wasn't in the trip description. I didn't see any rapids on the river on the drive here. My eyes widened.

You can standup paddleboard through rapids?

Exactly how big were these things?

What if I fell in?

What if Jaws or the piranhas were hungry?

"I'm sorry," I interrupted her. "Did you say…rapids?"

"Yeah, there's three of them between here and our take-out point," she said, standing with her arms akimbo.

"When we get to one, angle your board at a forty-five-degree angle on the tongue." She continued while motioning with her hands. "Then straighten out and hit the waves head on."

Oh boy. I rubbed my forehead. Here I am. Now what?

We had just waved off Josh, who planned to pick us up downriver later. Bailing and hitching a ride back to town with him was no longer an option. Neither was standing here all day. I wanted to run away, run miles down the road to our pick-up spot.

Instead, I picked up my paddle and reminded myself that I liked running as much as my cat likes taking a bath. And that I had just paid double the price to paddle this river. Three or 300 rapids, I was not copping out of this.

I turned to the turbid water and looked downstream. The river crawled by without a sound and vanished into a narrowing chasm. I shrugged. How bad could these rapids get anyhow?

"Keep your knees loose," Alicia advised, unfazed by my nervousness. She collected her paddle from the ground. "Whatever happens, keep your paddle in the water when the waves hit. It'll keep you balanced."

I nodded my head and bounced my knees to confirm I understood her instructions. It seemed simple enough—at least, it did on land. I hadn't a clue how I'd do on a board bouncing in moving water. I shoved doubt into my plastic baggie, which I stuffed into a dry bag and tied into the bungee cords on my board.

She paused, looked at the river, then at me. "Ready?"

"Ready," I said, not certain I was.

We slid our boards into the silky brown water and propelled ourselves upstream fifty feet or so into what she called an "eddy," a feature along a river where water turns on itself and circulates in the opposite direction of the main current, where water goes against the flow, against gravity, and travels upstream. In the relative calm of the side pool, she watched me practice the techniques she just reviewed. Once I performed to her satisfaction, we angled toward the main current. The river pulled the noses of our boards downstream.

"Here we go," I mumbled.

For the first hour, we paddled side by side on the flatwater. We pointed at swimming river otters, dodged sand bars tracked by mallards and geese, and skirted around car-sized boulders rooted in the river. Sticks swirled in whirlpools, and boils bubbled in front of our boards. The canyon walls reflected into an upside-down V-shaped image on the water's surface. No matter how hard I tried to paddle out of it, the reflection moved with me, keeping me centered, keeping me in the light.

Between quiet moments of awe and wonder, Alicia spouted thoughtful questions. She chipped away layer after layer, like the water, wind, and gravity had eroded the rugged stone around us for eons.

Nature's anonymity protected me at first. Then words of my struggles first dribbled, then dumped, into the river.

My guide and the Colorado River were among the first to hear of my separation—and my shame. I had kept my marital troubles hidden from the outside world, even from my own family, for almost a year before we split. My failure embarrassed me, and I was reluctant to burden others with my pain. I also did not want to wear a scarlet "D" for divorce on my paddle skirt. Above all, I held onto a shard of hope that this was a temporary, short-term arrangement. That "today" would be the day Craig would decide to come home.

"Been there, done that," Alicia said in so many words. It was both sad and comforting to hear that I had company in my sorrow.

Like many river guides, Alicia was 100% wild and free, part mystic and part therapist. "Life is like paddling on the river," she said without breaking her paddling rhythm. "We have three options when it comes to navigating life. One, paddle upstream and fight the current. Two, stand on your board and let the river take you wherever it wants. Or three, dip your paddle in the moving current and direct your path in life as it flows. Which one are you going to pick?"

I straightened my back and stopped paddling. When she put it like that, I realized that I had been swimming upstream to go with the flow of what I thought society expected of me for most of my life.

~ ~ ~

My parents claim that I—their first born—came into this world feisty and determined. Being birthed under the ambitious and stubborn Taurus astrological sign probably didn't help. As a full-blooded Type-A personality, I believed from the get-go that I would not get anywhere on the river of life unless I played by society's rules, excelled, and impressed others with my abilities.

My parents, Bob and Jacque, were card-carrying members of this American Dream ethos. By insisting that my younger brother, Rob, and I strive for perfection in everything we did, society would view us as better than everyone else, which would get us more opportunities than everyone else, which would assure more success than everyone else, which would pay off one day with our everlasting happiness. But first, I had to please them, whoever "they" were, by doing whatever "they" say.

My mom, a devoted housewife, made sure I arrived at pre-school every morning as a mirror image of the young actress Shirley Temple. My long blonde hair, curled into tight ringlets, bounced across the puffy sleeves of my frilly white dress. I skipped to the front of the class so that my teacher and my classmates noticed me. And they did. You are your looks. *So they say.*

During my first—and only—two years in Catholic school, Dad drove me each morning, en route to his corporate management job, in his flashy white Corvette. I appeased the nuns in first and second grade by being the first to raise my hand when they asked a question, earning A's on my assignments, and completing extra credit homework. Boys are smarter than girls. *So they say.*

Years later, I cheered for the boys anyhow. As the co-captain of the junior varsity cheerleading squad, I stepped out of my parents' different (but equally flashy) white Corvette and into the halls of high school, ready to shake my pompoms at the evening's boys' basketball game. Being popular raises your social status and increases your chance of finding a quality mate. One must be coupled to be happy. *So they say.*

Whether I set out to dazzle my teachers and classmates, ace a test in school, or make an athletic team, my early successes led me to believe I could strong-arm my circumstances to control—and all but guarantee—a positive outcome to any endeavor. If I looked better, studied harder, and trained longer than everyone else, I wouldn't just meet "their" expectations. I wouldn't be just good enough. I'd be the best. I'd stand out. I'd get the attention and approval I wanted.

And I did. Of course, I did.

Mantras encouraging this echoed through every classroom, locker room, and gym. "Push your limits." "No pain, no gain." "Winners never quit, and quitters never win." I never questioned these notions. Swimming upstream was what one needed to do to be successful. Getting to the crest of the wave was supposed to be hard. If it were easy, everyone would do it, and then it wouldn't be worth doing in the first place. Doing things half-assed was not in my DNA. Neither was giving up. After all, I hadn't surrendered when I was first told I couldn't SUP on the Colorado River alone on my 40th birthday. And look at where we were now.

Damn stubborn Taurus.

So, when it came to trying to save my marriage—and avoid the social disgrace of divorce—I had begged and cried, kicked and screamed, guilt-tripped, and maybe even asked nicely on occasion for Craig to stay. I did not want to abandon hope. Even if I wanted to, I couldn't. I didn't know how.

Yet, fighting against my separation had already, in just four weeks, deflated me. So had trying to reconcile living up to what society thought was appropriate—to stay married—when the reality of my situation seemed to be leading me elsewhere. Paddling upstream to do what "they" said required two paddles to work together. I only had one. Continuing to force that current, which was my inclination and Alicia's first option, would only lead to more exhaustion and more frustration.

Her second option wasn't viable either. No part of my personality would allow me to stand on the shore and watch my life float by. I was not a dead fish. I was not detritus either. I was still alive. I had to do something.

Alicia's third option remained. I could dip my paddle into this new flow, one I didn't ask for or want, and direct my path, even if it led me into unexpected rapids I did not yet know how to navigate. Like it or not, I was already paddling in this current. Only the river could say where she would take me on this journey.

I turned to Alicia then slapped my paddle on top of the water's surface and yelled, "I'm all in!"

~ ~ ~

Alicia led me through two Class I rapids. I trailed her like a baby duck, mimicking her every stroke, angle, and route. Even the smallest waves made my knees quiver. My board rocked from side to side. With a lot of swearing, splashing, paddle thrashing, butt clenching, and praying to the river gods, I stayed upright and dry in the minor undulations. Alicia didn't bobble.

Afterward, she explained how the American Whitewater Association rates rapids using the international scale of river difficulty. Classifications range from Class I to Class VI. Class VI whitewater is generally considered unrunnable due to the extreme dangers involved. Class I rapids are small ripples in the water's surface that usually weren't significant enough to warrant a name.

We came to our final rapid, a Class II named Big Bend Rapid because of its location on a horseshoe-shaped curve in the river. Its roar made itself known long before we saw the river tossing her water into the air like confetti. Alicia encouraged me to take the lead. "Come on, what's the worst that could happen? You fall in? No big deal," she said.

What's the worst that could happen? Monsters could eat me, and I could die. On my 40th birthday. Right. No big deal.

"Go ahead. I'll be right behind you," she smiled.

I had listened to her directions. I had tried my best to follow them too. But I hadn't paid enough attention to the river's movements to find and follow a clean line through submerged rocks and two-foot whitecaps. Resigning to the mercy of the river, one that had suddenly become much larger and more powerful than it looked a minute ago, seemed like a formula for drowning.

I shook my head and offered a sarcastic "Oooookaaaaay."

I bounced my knees and spread my arms to the side to balance my six-foot frame, then anchored my paddle in the water. My board angled to forty-five degrees. The soft hiss of the nearing rapid turned into a gulping, cackling cauldron.

"Remember, keep your paddle in the water," I whispered to myself.

The river's dark, glassy V-shaped tongue, one of the most beautiful things I'd ever seen, seduced me into complacency. Once the bubbling chaos lured me in, I forgot everything. I stood up and leaned back, away from the rapid. My paddle flailed out of the water.

The first wave splattered water droplets onto my calves. My board teetered. I took a hard stroke to the left. I slammed into the second wave. My board spun sideways. I swung my paddle. It caught nothing but air. The third wave curled its fingers around my ankles and yanked me into the underworld where monsters lurked. My board disappeared from under my feet.

My world went black.

The frigid water paralyzed me at first. I thrusted my arms down to drive my head toward the light on the surface. I bobbed in the turbulence like a piece of driftwood.

You're okay, I lied to myself.

Bubbles frothed and splashed into my gasping mouth.

Get back on the board.

My hands and my legs started going numb. I managed to reach down and catch my ankle leash, my umbilical cord to my board.[***] Hand over hand, I dragged it toward me.

Grab it. It's right there.

I reached across the board with both hands, and with a frantic and hard butterfly kick, I flopped across it. I folded my legs into a sitting position, bowed my head, and coughed. My skin reddened and tingled in the warmth of the sun.

The wave train faded into placid waters. The blur of crimson and orange and beige along the rocky shoreline came back into sharper focus. The river pushed me into an eddy on the right. I looked over my shoulder. Alicia surfed with ease through the rapid then paddled over to me. "You alright?" she asked with a smirk.

"I can't believe it!" I shook my head in joyful disbelief as if I had won a gold medal. "I fell in the water, and I didn't drown, and I didn't get eaten, and for the first time in my life, I didn't hyperventilate."

I leaned over the side of my board and dragged my fingers in the river. I turned to Alicia and flashed a goofy grin. "Would now be a good time to tell you that I'm terrified of water where I can't see my feet?"

She laughed. Before we reached our take-out point, she snapped celebratory pictures with her iPhone. I raised my hands and paddle up to the sky and said, "See? I really am all in!"

*** *After gaining more experience with rivers, I no longer wear an ankle leash while standup paddleboarding due to entrapment concerns.*

3
THE POWER OF PIE

Back in my hotel room, I smiled into the bathroom mirror, clinging to my yellow bouquet of flowers like a bride walking down the aisle. I looked like a drowned rat but, no doubt, a proud one. I snapped a few selfies and sent them to my parents and a couple of close friends.

I showered and slipped into my favorite black dress and the black ballet flats I had packed. While shaking my shoulders and hips to "Ladies Night" by Kool & the Gang, I curled my hair and pushed rosy blush to my cheeks. I had a lunch date with myself at the Eklecticafé, one of my favorite restaurants in Moab (which has sadly since closed).

I sauntered into the quirky café, a refurbished 1930s tan stucco house capped by a silver metal roof. Without looking at the menu, I ordered my usual, a chicken curry wrap and an iced tea. The woman behind the counter swiped my credit card. I glanced at the baked goods in the glass display to my right.

"Wait! I forgot to order pie," I said, bending down to study the mouth-watering options. "It's not just my birthday. It's my 40th birthday. Of course, I must have pie!" I straightened up with a hint of regality, uncharacteristically oversharing personal details of my life with a stranger.

"What can I get you?" Smiling, the young woman handed me my credit card and a receipt for me to sign. "It's on the house."

In my hotel room with my birthday flowers after paddling on—and falling into—the Colorado River in Moab, Utah, on April 30, 2015.

I pointed to the strawberry pie. She nodded. "Good choice. I'll deliver it with your meal."

I set my tea down on an out-of-the-way table on the shaded patio and took a seat. Traffic hummed on Moab's main drag. Golden flowers in wooden planter boxes swayed in the cool breeze. I let my mind drift to the bliss of floating on the Colorado River, to the gift of my guide's wisdom, and then suddenly to why do I go so bonkers about celebrating my birthday?

Regular holidays did not mean much to me. They gave me an excuse to commemorate a moment in time—or history—with my family. But oftentimes, I forgot they existed. The only day I anticipated the entire year, every year, was my birthday, April 30.

Throughout my adult life, I had celebrated my birthday every year in a similar way, albeit often in different places depending on where my travels took me. I started the day by putting on my favorite clothes. I danced to my favorite songs. I treated myself to my favorite foods and desserts for all three meals. I spent the entire day doing activities I loved and, in some fortunate instances, with people I loved. I tried to make it the most glorious day of my life, getting drunk off all my favored delights and on every moment—just as I was doing today.

I took a sip of tea. As I chased ice with my straw, I made a wish: I wished that every day of my life could be as amazing.

I choked.

I set the sweating glass down and grabbed my napkin, coughing into it while tears beaded down the side of my face. I dabbed my eyes. I looked around to make sure I had not made a spectacle of myself in public. No one seemed to notice.

"Oh my god, the reason I love my birthday so much is it's the only day of the year I'm actually nice to myself," I said aloud.

It was true. I only needed to look at how differently I had reacted to the morning's events as proof. Had I fallen in the river on any other day of the year, I would not have praised the river gods for sparing my life. Oh no! I would have berated myself for days, weeks, or months even, with a flood of internal negative talk like: "You suck at paddleboarding. You can't even make it through a Class II rapid. You're pathetic. What's wrong with you? You're not strong enough. You're too heavy. You don't belong on a paddleboard. How embarrassing that must have been for your guide."

Exactly as I had reprimanded myself every day of my life in the relentless pursuit of perfection. I had never questioned the origins of these sentiments. Until now. Memories from my childhood started spilling onto the table.

~ ~ ~

I stood on the stage in my sparkling yellow-sequined leotard, fluffy tutu, and silver tiara. Chin up, shoulders back. Ready to show everyone in the audience what I, a three-year-old, could do in my first dance recital.

The curtains parted. The darkness disappeared. My feet tapped to the staccato rhythm. Out of my peripheral vision, I noticed that the other girls were following my lead. I wanted to be the queen bee. And I was. Of course, I was.

The voice in my head said, "Don't mess up."

The curtains closed. The lights dimmed. I scurried off the stage and into the arms of my doting parents. A crowd of people, including my dance teacher, my fellow dancing bees, and nameless grown-ups, showered adoring praise on me.

"You did so well tonight, Colleen."

"You were the best one out there."

"You're going to be a star someday."

So they say. And what they said fed royal jelly to my developing ego. I wanted them to bring me more.

"Just wait," I thought. "If you thought that was good, I'll show you I can do better."

My parents introduced me to gymnastics when I was four. It seemed like a natural progression, a symbiotic relationship even, to extend simple movements of arms and legs into more complicated routines. Instead, the nature of gymnastics only seemed to embolden my drive for excellence—and the self-degradation and condemnation that came with it—in ways shuffling, sashaying, and shimmying across a hardwood floor hadn't.

See, in dance, a routine has no specific value assigned to it before it begins. It is an expressive art aimed at entertaining. No one measures your merit. Critics might write a review about a performance, but that is nothing more than an opinion. An audience of people still clap for a dancer whether she twirled the wrong way, bent her leg at the wrong time, or missed her cue with the music.

Gymnastics is a competitive sport where judges scrutinize every move and assign performances a score. A gymnast's routine on each of the four apparatus used to start at a 10.00-point value.* A judge, or a panel of judges, sit at the ready with a pen in hand, eager to record your screw-ups and deduct points for your flaws. The 211-page Code of Points outlines a definitive right way for twirling. Bent knees? Up to 0.5 in penalties. Missed your cue with the music? A 0.3 deduction. At the conclusion of your routine, the judges tally a final score and flash it on a scoring pole for everyone in the gym to see. You—and everyone around you—know how deficient the judges thought you were.

A perfect score was unheard of at the amateur level at which I competed. It didn't matter. I knew perfection, at least in the eyes of others, was possible.

I won plenty of ribbons, medals, and trophies at various meets across the country. But it only took one fall on the balance beam—on a turn, a backflip, or a no-handed cartwheel called an aerial—to tumble from the podium and the good graces of society. It sounds absurd, given all the suffering and atrocities I now know occur in the world, but I believed when I was ten years old that my coaches would kick me off the team, my parents would disown me, and the sun would stop rising if I didn't win my meet. So when my coach shook her head and walked away from me in disgust, I chased after her, begging her to not give up on me. "Just wait. I'll show you I can do better."

A people-pleasing perfectionist couldn't imagine a more tragic fate: to be judged by people I didn't know and then ostracized by the people I did. The voice in my head said, "You're such an embarrassment."

By the time I turned eleven, I had won enough competitions to try out for the elite program—the feeder to the national team. The deciding coach said, "Gymnastics isn't your sport. You're going to

---

* *In 2006, the International Gymnastics Federation modified the scoring systems such that gymnasts could earn bonus points for attempting more difficult tricks and combinations. These offset the deductions. Since each gymnast could attempt different tricks than their competitor, final scores had no upper limit. Earning a perfect score at the Olympic Games is no longer possible. That said, the 10-point scale currently remains intact for amateur and collegiate levels.*

be too tall." I was already five feet tall—taller than the average post-pubescent Olympic female gymnast. And I hadn't hit puberty yet.

I ignored reality, switched gyms, and continued competing. I grew. Then fell. My scores fell too. My naïve twelve-year-old brain started to grasp that training harder, longer, or better would never allow me to overcome my genetic disposition.

Even still, as I closed the gym door behind me for the last time, the voice in my head said, "You're a quitter. You're a failure." Chalk it up to immaturity and an inability to mentally process such an overwhelming disappointment. I shoved my frustration into my gymnastics bag, zipped it up, and tossed it into the back of my closet. "Just wait. I'll show you I can do better. At something else."

That something else was volleyball, a sport I had never played before, not even at family picnics, but one where my height would work for, not against, me. I picked it because it was what all the popular girls were signing up for at my junior high school. The cute boys in my class thought I was "so far out" for making the team even though I had no concept of the game. One even invited me to pizza and a movie.

At first, balls accidentally bounced off my head, an act that led to, not surprisingly, me cheering for my teammates from the bench for most of my seventh-grade season. After a string of less-than-impressive performances in eighth grade, my coach said the magic words: "Maybe volleyball isn't your sport."

Hearing that "they" thought I wasn't fit for two different sports in less than two years was too much. It turned my naiveté into unfettered fury. Once again, I rejected this rejection by swimming upstream and did the opposite of what he advised: I tried harder. I ate, drank, and slept volleyball from that moment on. "Just wait, I'll show you I can do better."

By my sophomore year in high school, I topped out at six feet tall. Balls stopped bouncing off my head, and I earned a starting position on my high school's varsity volleyball team. The accolades poured in after the first game and continued throughout the season. The newspaper named me a special mention for the all-area team. I started getting recruitment letters from colleges. I wanted more.

One night after practice, I asked my parents, "Can I try out for Sports Performance next year?"

Sports Performance Volleyball Club was one of the premier private programs in the country. Their teams were notorious for their strict, disciplined approach—and, most importantly, for being the best. They rarely lost a match, and when they did, I watched the girls run extra wind sprints to make sure it never happened again. Less than half of those who tried out made their team, but every senior who graduated from their program earned a college scholarship. In my eyes, Sports Performance was perfection incarnate. I wanted—no, *needed*—to be perfection incarnate.

Ahead of tryouts, my parents moved our family into a new house across the Chicago suburbs so I could be within a twenty-minute drive of the gym. Thankfully, I made the team.

Oh, how I reveled in the new, demanding environment. The repetitive, regimented drills. The wind sprint contests. The weightlifting sessions. The blisters and bruises and stitches in the webbing on my hand. The charley horses in the middle of the night. Giving up most of the social rituals of a young teenage girl: pajama parties, parades, and proms. Nothing else had stretched me as far physically or mentally. I reassured myself that these sacrifices would pay off someday. "This is just what champions do."

During one of the first scrimmages at practice during my junior year, my team scored our first point together. We rushed to the center of the court with giant grins on our faces, slapped hands, and congratulated each other.

"STOP! STOP!" our coach yelled as he raised one hand and walked onto the court toward us.

I don't recall his exact words, but I'll never forget the message: "Don't ever do that again. Winning is the expectation here, not a reason for celebration. If you aren't winning, you're failing. Are you committed to excellence, or do you want to go home?"

Finally! Someone other than me understood this. Thank you, coach!

We resumed our positions on the court, turned into well-oiled, emotionless robots and did exactly what was expected of us: we won. We won match after match against the best teams in the United States.

And yet I still told myself it wasn't good enough.

Nothing in my childhood ever was.

Despite being named first chair in the band for flute in elementary school, I wasn't musical enough.

Despite going undefeated in track in four events in junior high school and qualifying for the state championships in hurdles in high school after being on the team for just three weeks, I wasn't fast enough.

Despite being elected the co-captain of my high school cheerleading squad during my sophomore year, I wasn't popular enough. (And given my poofy bangs and frizzed permed hair in my school photo, I sure wasn't stylish enough either.)

Despite earning a 5.1 GPA on a 5.0 scale, I wasn't smart enough.

Despite being named the Illinois Player of the Year and an All-American in volleyball during my senior year in high school, I wasn't strong enough.

Despite earning a four-year athletic scholarship to play volleyball at Stanford University, and later at the University of Michigan-Ann Arbor, I wasn't talented enough.

Sure, each accomplishment brought a temporary moment of pride and happiness. After a quick hit of dopamine, though, I jumped back onto the hedonic treadmill to chase something more, more, always more. Because I could have done better. Other people were doing more than me. My standards were too low. Even when I won, I still couldn't win.

I lived in a world of contradictions, churning in a paradox where I excelled and earned shelves and shelves of trophies, medals, ribbons, and newspaper clippings while trying to covertly overcompensate for my so-called inadequacies and insignificance. The more I pushed myself with negative rhetoric, the more I achieved. The more I achieved, the more attention and praise I received from "them"—my parents, peers, teachers, coaches, anonymous onlookers, and newspapers. The more attention I got, the more my starving ego craved to counteract the self-doubt gnawing on the smallest of my imperfections. The self-fulfilling cycle became an addiction, one that influenced, unknowingly at the time, most of my actions and decisions. "Perfectionist" became my middle name.

This quest to feel significant turned me into an overachieving control freak with high expectations, imposter syndrome, and a cat-o'nine-tails in hand for incessant self-flagellations. Any self-worth I had was wound tightly around external validation. In hopes they—whoever "they" were—would notice me, think I'm successful, and one day grant me the magic keys to the kingdom of happiness, I worked myself into the ground and treated myself like garbage. Except on my birthday.

On this one holier than all holy days, I put up an indestructible defense shield around myself. I let go of all the outside pressure and expectations. I shut out any judgments of whether I was a success or failure, of whether I was inadequate. I spoiled myself rotten with as many pleasures as I could shove into twenty-four hours. Indulging in my own interests and desires provided a momentary reprieve from the onslaught of overwhelming guilt and selfishness I otherwise felt for taking a break, albeit a short one, from chasing achievement and approval from others on the exhausting 364 days that had preceded my birthday—and on the 364 days that would follow.

"That's total crap." I took another swig of tea to drown these ludicrous notions.

Without missing a beat, the voice in my head said, "Stop bullying yourself all the time. Why can't you be nice to yourself?"

~ ~ ~

A server slid a steaming chicken curry wrap and a generous slice of pie in front of me. I raised my glass and made a vow. From now on, I would try to make every day the most glorious day of my life. I would try to get drunk on all my favorite delights and in every moment. I would try to treat every day like my birthday. Because, in a sense, every day was. So, I ate my pie first.

Then I wondered, what could I do to celebrate my 40th without Craig? What gift could I give myself? I couldn't let the "Over the Hill" milestone pass without pomp and circumstance. *So they say.*

I shuffled bites and crumbs and thoughts around. The morning events had inspired me. I could paddle like that all day and all night if given the chance. I wanted more.

I put my fork down. What if I kept following the course of the Colorado River?

From Moab, the Colorado River moseys through Meander Canyon for fifty-one miles before it marries the Green River in Canyonlands National Park. From there, it roars another forty-six miles through Cataract Canyon, through Class III and IV rapids where boat-flipping hydraulics take on names like Little Niagara and Satan's Gut. I had surprised myself with my morning performance in riffles, but no part of me believed I could navigate that level of whitewater and live to tell about it. I'd skip Cataract. One can only take so much chaos at one time.

What I needed was something more relaxed. Like a long, calm stretch of flatwater. Like Meander, only longer. Up next? Lake Powell.

America's second-largest reservoir stretches across south-central Utah and northern Arizona. On a map, the artificial lake slices through the Colorado Plateau like a blue lightning bolt starting near Hite, Utah, and ending near Page, Arizona. Its waters follow the Colorado River's original path through Glen Canyon, then branch out like a stepped leader into the dendritic canyons of even more dendritic canyons. Twisted and tapered side chasms—over ninety-five of them, each with their own name, length, and personality—branch off on either side of the 1,960 miles of shoreline and eventually dissipate into rock, rock, and more rock. A mostly treeless collection of hardened buttes, chiseled bluffs, and crusty, petrified sand dunes gives the body of water its form.

I brought up Google Maps on my iPhone to measure the distance from Hite to the Wahweap Marina near the Glen Canyon Dam. My quick measure of the main channel came to about 141 miles. Assuming I paddled four or five hours per day at a conservative pace of two to three miles per hour, I estimated I could easily make ten to fifteen miles a day. If I added a couple of rest days and time to explore some side canyons, I calculated I could make the run in about fourteen days.

Fourteen days of floating in the warm embrace of wildness. Where solace awaited. And rapids did not. And neither did hungry water monsters. Nor societal expectations. Where I could escape my reality. Where I could rub my hands raw along the sandpaper grit of sandstone until they bled so much that I had no other choice but to release my exhausting grip on the pain of my loss. Where I could feel alive again.

How soon could I go?

I pulled up my calendar. The only window of time I had for a two-week outing in the next year was in late November and December 2015. It would be cold then—cold, that is, for someone who had spent the past eighteen years in the desert. The high temperatures at Lake Powell averaged forty-five to fifty-five degrees Fahrenheit and dipped just below freezing at night. When I lived in Illinois growing up, we'd call that a warm front.

Cold weather aside, paddling in the off-season had its advantages. November would see far fewer biting bugs and boats than in the warmer spring and summer months. There was also a lower probability of brutal winds, ones that ushered in a new season in March through May and accompanied the desert's monsoon dust storms in July through September. No bugs, no boats, no wind? Winter arguably was the best time to be on the lake.

"Oh. Hell. Yes." I smiled like the Cheshire Cat. "Happy. Birthday. To. Me."

I pushed my pie plate aside and pulled my chicken curry wrap toward me. The voice in my head asked, "Are you sure you can paddle alone across a body of water for two weeks?"

Before I finished the last bite, my phone's sudden jingle startled me. My mom and dad's voices gushed in unison, "Happy birthday!"

I shared my morning paddle and then said, "Hey, so, I had this idea for a new adventure I'd like to take."

"Oh yeah? Where?" Mom said with insouciance.

"I'm going to standup paddleboard the length of Lake Pow..."

"I'm coming with you!" Mom blurted before I finished my sentence.

I laughed. "Sure, you can come with me, Ma. Let's talk details when I get home next week."

I hung up and realized I had a couple itty-bitty gaps in this grand plan of mine. I did not own a paddleboard. Could I rent a board? Could I buy one? How would I transport a ten- to twelve-foot-long board on my truck? Could I carry some of the gear on my board?

Also, Mom only had a small inflatable kayak. Craig and I had inherited a twenty-foot-long, ocean-going two-person touring kayak from his parents years ago. It hung untouched in our garage collecting dust and dead spiders. Could Mom use it and act as my support crew by carrying much of our gear?

I wiped the final morsels of lunch from my mouth with my napkin and smiled. Life hadn't gone according to plan, but I had a new plan. Mom and I would paddle 141 miles on the Colorado River on Lake Powell from Hite to Wahweap Marina for fourteen days in late November 2015. I wasn't sure how we'd do it, but I had the next seven months to figure out the details.

For now, it was enough to know that I'd start paddling in my own flow with my own paddle—even if I didn't have one yet.

4
WHAT FRIENDS ARE FOR

Later that evening, I stepped up to the podium on the wooden stage at the Moab Arts and Recreation Center at the start of the Moab Photography Symposium. Over one hundred amateur and professional photographers clapped. I waved to my friends and smiled at my new acquaintances. The spotlight felt familiar and comfortable.

A few seconds after the applause died down, as I shuffled my notes, the Beatles "Birthday" song started blasting on the sound system. I cocked my head. One by one, the crowd stood up. Most put on birthday party hats. Some blew bubbles. Others squawked on noisemakers. One attendee pranced to the stage and offered me a sparkling silver tiara. It looked like the one I wore when I danced as a child. I leaned over to accept my crown and cupped my hands over my mouth.

I had told only two people at the event about my birthday: my buddies and fellow symposium presenters Guy Tal and Bruce Hucko, who was also the event organizer. I turned to Guy, then Bruce, who leaned against the wall sporting a devious grin. I shook my finger, pretending to scold him, and mouthed, "You got me. You're in so much trouble!" I later learned that Bruce had distributed a note in the attendees' welcome packets. Everyone was in on the secret except me. The orchestrated—and appreciated—gesture rendered me speechless, which is not how anyone plans to go into a speech.

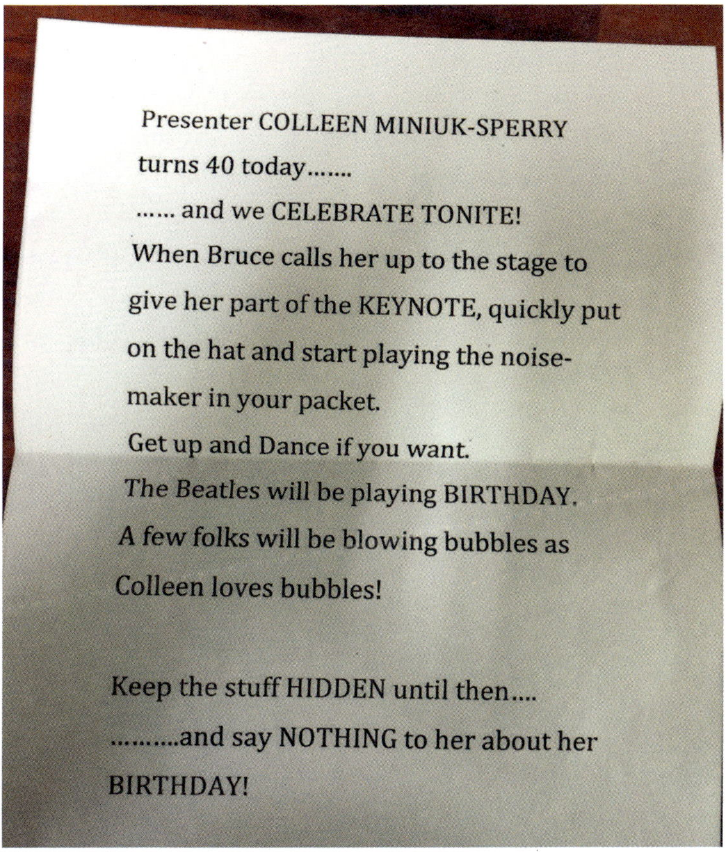

Presenter COLLEEN MINIUK-SPERRY
turns 40 today.......
...... and we CELEBRATE TONITE!
When Bruce calls her up to the stage to
give her part of the KEYNOTE, quickly put
on the hat and start playing the noise-
maker in your packet.
Get up and Dance if you want.
The Beatles will be playing BIRTHDAY.
A few folks will be blowing bubbles as
Colleen loves bubbles!

Keep the stuff HIDDEN until then....
..........and say NOTHING to her about her
BIRTHDAY!

The top-secret handout Bruce distributed in the 2015 Moab Photography Symposium welcome packet.

To open the event, Bruce had asked each presenter to spend six minutes sharing their answer to the question, "Who are you?" I had spent months preparing my talk. But Craig starting to build a dam on my river of life had hurled me into an existential crisis.

The lights dimmed. The hall hushed.

I took a nervous deep breath, straightened my tiara, and started: "Hello everyone, my name is Colleen. I am an ex-software engineer turned outdoor photographer, writer, publisher, instructor, and speaker. But that's not at all what I intended…"

~ ~ ~

"What do you want to be when you grow up?" they asked.

As a child, I despised it when grown-ups asked me this question. Because one, I didn't know. Two, I wasn't sure I wanted to grow up. And three, they almost always laughed at my answer, which was "rich and happy." Money buys happiness. *So they say.*

I daydreamed about becoming a doctor, lawyer, pilot, or architect, not because I found the work they did appealing but rather because those careers would help me make a ton of money, achieve high status within society, attract a well-to-do husband, buy a big house with a white picket fence, drive a fancy car, birth two children, get a dog, retire after putting in fifty years of service at the same company, and live happily ever after in my perfect fairy-tale life until I died in old age. I couldn't wait to be that polished, professional young lady, with her neat pin-striped suit, high heels, and long blonde hair waving in the wind, filled with exuberance by doing it all, having it all. Like Barbie, the doll I used to play with as a child. Only less plastic. And with a vagina.

In high school, I settled on pursuing international banking. During the recruiting process in my junior year, collegiate volleyball coaches rotated through my living room and offered to pay for my college education. I learned that one of my top prospects, Stanford University, did not offer an undergraduate business or finance program. It didn't matter. I applied, got accepted, and went anyway. No one in their right mind turns down a free ride to Stanford. Besides, the team I'd be joining had just won the 1996 Division I National Championship title.

It took only one semester on "The Farm" for me to feel unsettled with the idea of spending three and a half more years trying to force a major in economics, industrial engineering, or political science. So, I found the top undergraduate business program in the country at the time, the University of Michigan-Ann Arbor. Even though the school was no powerhouse in volleyball, I transferred there my sophomore year.

My accounting and finance classes during my first semester in business school proved that math and I did not add up. As my investment banking dreams washed up, Silicon Valley's tech boom—

and the demand for technical females—was rising faster than an incoming tide in the Bay of Fundy. I redirected my methodical and analytical tendencies toward computer information systems. It landed me a lucrative systems analyst job with Intel Corporation.

In September 1997, after graduating with a Bachelor of Business Administration with honors (of course), I packed my bags and headed for Arizona, a state I had never set foot in until my recruiting visit with the chip manufacturing company. My long-distance boyfriend, Craig, who had recently graduated from Stanford, had also landed a job with Intel at their Phoenix-based facilities.

I walked into the corporate world as a software test engineer—a job I didn't know existed until I sat in my grey-walled cube on my first day. My new manager put me to work writing and executing repetitive test cases in a windowless lab for a year. It bored me from the start. I eventually switched into software project management. As a project manager, I was paid to do what I was best at: organizing chaos into carefully constructed roadmaps and flawlessly executing to arbitrary deadlines. In other words, control. I made plans, remade plans, and then made my teams toil to the made-up plan at all costs.

I loved my co-workers, the Gantt charts, and tracking stock splits on a spreadsheet that suggested, if the tech boom continued, I'd be a millionairess by thirty-five. (It didn't.) I loved the gratuitous department awards for doing what I expected of us: deliver projects ahead of time and under budget with the highest quality. I hated the merry-go-round of weekly status reports, office politics, and hustling my weekends and evenings away to achieve someone else's vain goals. What I did achieve mattered so little to me. Unlike my time in school and in athletics, no amount of working harder, longer, or better filled that void.

In 2001, despite the highs of marrying Craig and moving into our new home together, I started complaining more often. I polished off a bottle of wine a night by myself. My lower back began to spasm, so much so, I was unable to get out of bed on most days. After standing out for much of my life, I couldn't stand up.

My immediate family moved from Chicago to Phoenix about a year after I started with Intel. After my parents gained a front-row view of my struggles, my mom handed me a brochure for an introductory photography class at the local community college. With it, she said in a loving way, "Colleen, you need to get a life." I walked into the traditional black-and-white darkroom without a camera or a clue. In one class, I felt the color returning to my life.

The Saturday sessions and weekly assignments were a welcome diversion from the grind. I hadn't spent much time outside before. But with my camera in hand, I found solace in western landscapes that Craig and I explored in our free time. Picking up a hobby helped me achieve what Intel called "work-life balance." It's the idea that employees should, once let out of their corporate cage, somehow find time and energy—between sleeping, eating, and taking care of family commitments—to experience enough happiness outside of work to make going back in the cage for eighty hours a week somehow more palatable. By developing a connection with nature, I had done exactly what Intel had told me to do. I had found balance all right. Meaning I wanted to spend none of my time at Intel and all my time outdoors.

Because my single-track, laser-focused, achievement-centric brain did not comprehend how to pursue an activity for pure pleasure, photography transformed into an obsession. I sold my first photographs at a local art show two years after my first class. Shortly thereafter, magazine editors, calendar publishers, local businesses, and private collectors began buying my work. By 2006, I had turned my pastime into a viable business. I mattered to others again. I had a good eye. *So they say.*

But back into the cage I went every Monday morning at eight. Despite having a creative outlet, I felt more and more disillusioned. By thirty-one, I had checked all the boxes I thought society wanted me to check:

A professional woman with steady job and a six-figure paycheck with bonuses? Check.

Married my best friend, a brilliant, kind, financially successful, and handsome man? Check.

A well-appointed two-story house with a three-car garage? Check.

A shiny white Mercedes-Benz sedan with a sunroof? Check.

I had made it in life by the strictest of societal and personal definitions. But the only thing my life made me was frustrated, unhappy, and exhausted. At times, it made me physically ill.

In late 2006, I sat in immense pain in a doctor's office. A sudden burning sensation in my chest made it impossible for me to lay down without feeling like someone was stabbing me in the sternum with a butcher knife. When combined with the lingering effects from the degenerative discs in my back, I couldn't move without feeling violent pain. The endoscopy revealed a hiatal hernia.

After my doctor read the results, I asked him if he thought that maybe, just maybe, stress might be causing my various ailments. He laughed and said, "You're too young to understand what stress is. Just wait."

I burst into hysterics in the parking lot. I had never contemplated suicide nor had I ever comprehended what would push someone to attempt it. On the drive home from that appointment, it occurred to me that my anxiety, sadness, and pain would disappear if I drove my Mercedes off the next bridge. I had it all. I had it easy. And I *still* wasn't happy. What in the hell was wrong with me?

At home, I sobbed to Craig, "I will give back every penny of my salary to make this pain stop."

We immediately planned my departure. On February 28, 2007, I walked—no, skipped—out of Intel. I consider the date my personal Independence Day and celebrate it each year like my birthday. I eat pie.

Photography was an escape hatch, not a long-time dream come true. Once I traded cube walls for canyon walls, I certainly had less to complain about. My health issues disappeared instantly after I handed in my badge. My body understood stress after all.

Still, swapping jobs didn't do anything to pull me out of subscribing to the arrival fallacy, the misperception that achieving certain goals will deliver enduring happiness. It also did nothing to quiet the nagging voice in my head or appease the ravenous type-A, overachieving perfectionist who craved attention to feed her self-worth. I simply pointed that lens in a different direction. And drank another bottle of wine.

Shortly after my departure, I asked a mentor what I could do to be successful in my new career. He suggested I'd never make it as a full-time landscape photographer for two reasons: one, the photography industry had changed so much that there were few decent paying jobs left; and two, I wouldn't be able to hack traveling alone as a woman. *So they say.*

So off I went to prove him wrong. I might have fled buzzword bingo in meetings, but I still knew how to swim upstream to gain approval from the outside world.

As my artistic career progressed, I started feeling a tug between two diverging personalities: the wild, carefree wanderer "out there" and the guilty, inadequate, absent wife at home. I also felt like I had let my parents, Craig, and society down when I couldn't cut it in the corporate world. So much so that I introduced myself to others first as an ex-software engineer—as I had at the start of my presentation—so people didn't look down on me as "just" a photographer.

After my six-minute talk, I walked off the stage smiling but questioning whether I had answered Bruce's question. Who was I? Not a software engineer. Not a lowly photographer. Not a traditional wife. Not a "Career Barbie." Not a millionaire. And really, not all that happy.

I realized knowing what you aren't isn't the same as knowing what you are. And knowing *what* you are isn't the same as knowing *who* you are. In the absence of titles on business cards, positions on resumes, and the opinions of others—all superficial external declarations—I could not tell you who I was.

I could tell you this, though: I was not going to be a divorcee if I could help it. I'd be damned if I'd become a reservoir of failure, loneliness, and unhappiness.

~ ~ ~

I sat in my truck in the hotel parking lot and called Craig out of habit. In sharing how my day had transpired, I hoped he would feel like he was missing out, that he would have some sort of magical epiphany and come back to me. He didn't.

We exchanged pleasantries. He wished me a happy birthday. I

shared my idea to paddle across Lake Powell and mentioned my lack of proper equipment.

He surprised me by offering to buy the standup paddleboard of my choice instead of scheduling my 40th birthday trip—one he and I were not likely to take together anyhow. He wasn't coming home, and I wouldn't get my birthday trip with him. Nonetheless, I hung up overjoyed by hearing his voice and receiving his charity. The gift gave me a glimmer of hope that he still cared about me.

As I walked into the hotel, Guy, my friend and fellow symposium presenter, poked his head out of his room across the hall from mine. "Time to celebrate?" he asked with a grin.

"You bet," I said. "Let me get out of this dress first."

I changed, then knocked on Guy's ajar door. He greeted me with a small wrapped present, the book *Reflections on the Art of Living: A Joseph Campbell Companion*, along with a lavender chocolate bar and an opaque plastic cup full of tequila.

"Happy birthday, Colleen," he said, raising his drink to mine. His piercing sandy brown eyes softened as he flashed a playful smile. "Here's to the big Life with a capital L."

"Thanks, friend. To the big Life." I pushed my cup into his.

Before interacting face-to-face with Guy, I, like many others, had drooled over his poignant photography and thought-provoking writings on the internet. Our virtual paths crossed in late 2011 in an online photography forum. Our actual paths crossed for the first time in California's Death Valley National Park in February 2012. There, over beers at the bar, I started to learn more about his story.

Guy began photographing while exploring Israel—his birthplace and home for the first twenty-six years of his life. After fulfilling his mandatory military service and graduating from Tel Aviv University, he pursued a job in the booming information technology sector in California. He taught himself to speak flawless English without an accent and became a U. S. citizen.

In his youth, he had read about the Colorado Plateau in Edward Abbey's book *Desert Solitaire*. Shortly after arriving in America, he headed to southern Utah, with his camera in hand, to see the sprawling landscape for himself. The never-ending vistas of sandstone buttes creased by canyons, the swirling patterns of iron in pillows of yellow-grey rock, the gnarled trunks of juniper and pinyon, the quiet, the solitude, and the big open sky all felt familiar to Guy from the moment he set foot in canyon country. When he decided to pursue photography full-time, he moved there and made it his home with his wife.

Guy and I kept in touch in the years after Death Valley, but our friendship seemed implausible to most people because of our preference for solitude and our apparent differences. His sensible, fervent, and profound—sometimes even morose—insights had earned him the nickname "Le Penseur," or French for "The Thinker," by our mutual friends. (He likes wearing a black T-shirt and jeans to encourage this reputation but does so in jest…I think.) My sarcastic, flippant, and more chirpy quips had also earned me a distinctive title by the same group of people: "The Velvet Space Monkey Queen of the Rubber Suit People." Or "The Queen" for short and, you know, more practical purposes.

(In case that isn't descriptive enough, Bruce started calling me "Bubbles" at the symposium.)

Despite our introverted tendencies, Guy and I enjoyed each other's company well enough to camp together a few times a year. Over campfires, we realized that, despite divergent upbringings, we shared a great deal in common. For starters, we were both about the same age. At about the same time in our lives, we had both thrown our individual computer jobs to the wind. We had escaped corporate America's safe golden handcuffs to pursue our individual passion for photography, writing, and the great outdoors. As full-time freelance photographers and writers, we were free birds—him, sharp like a raven; me, as persistent and clumsy as a pelican—soaring across the Southwest and exploring the natural world through our lens and pens. We also shared a propensity to overanalyze ideas, so we bantered for hours and hours about perspectives on the world, life, and photography. Oh, and we both loved tater tots too.

Each night after the symposium, we started spilling not only tequila into our glasses but also tears and details of our personal challenges.

His younger sister had died five months earlier in Israel. Our situations differed, but our struggle with loss didn't. Each night, we kept whacking at the piñatas of our lives, hoping one or both of us would crack into the sweet and juicy answers eluding us.

"You're uninhibited now," he said, pouring us each another shot. "Don't waste this chance you have to live the life you want, not the life you've been told to live."

He suggested I find a way to live the "big Life with a capital L" as he called it. Living free of expectations. Living beyond the meaningless minutiae. Living one moment at a time through curiosity and conviction. Living without fear of the future. Living deliberately according to one's own principles and desires. Living a life from which one doesn't need to escape. Truly living.

It sounded delicious. Real life. Real freedom. Real fulfillment. In other words, paddling in your own flow on your own river of life like Alicia encouraged earlier this week. Or, as I promised myself afterward at lunch, living as if every day was one's birthday.

I found it odd that the universe had echoed the same message to me in three different ways in one week. Maybe I should pay attention to it.

I liked the idea. I had even tasted parts of the big Life since becoming a freelancer. But I wasn't too sure of how to undo forty years of indoctrination, especially while wading through muck. I was still trying to understand the confusing details of my separation. I worried society would treat a middle-aged single woman as damaged goods. I was uncertain of who I was and where I was going without Craig. Could I really live a richer, happier life on my own without controlling my circumstances, chasing perfection and achievement, and seeking validation from others?

"Speaking of the big Life...I'm going to standup paddleboard the length of Lake Powell," I said, wondering if he believed me through my slurred speech.

"Awesome." He pushed himself out of his chair to toast my half-full plastic cup. "But don't just think about it. Do it."

"Oh, I'm gonna!" I laughed.

A few days later, at the symposium's close, I exchanged farewells with Bruce, Guy, and my photography friends. I mentioned my paddling idea to the group. Bruce teased, "Paddling the length of Lake Powell over two weeks qualifies as dumb shit to do in the desert."

I laughed as I hugged him and the others. Bruce might have been right. But doing "dumb shit in the desert" sounded much better than continuing to cry a river.

LAKE POWELL

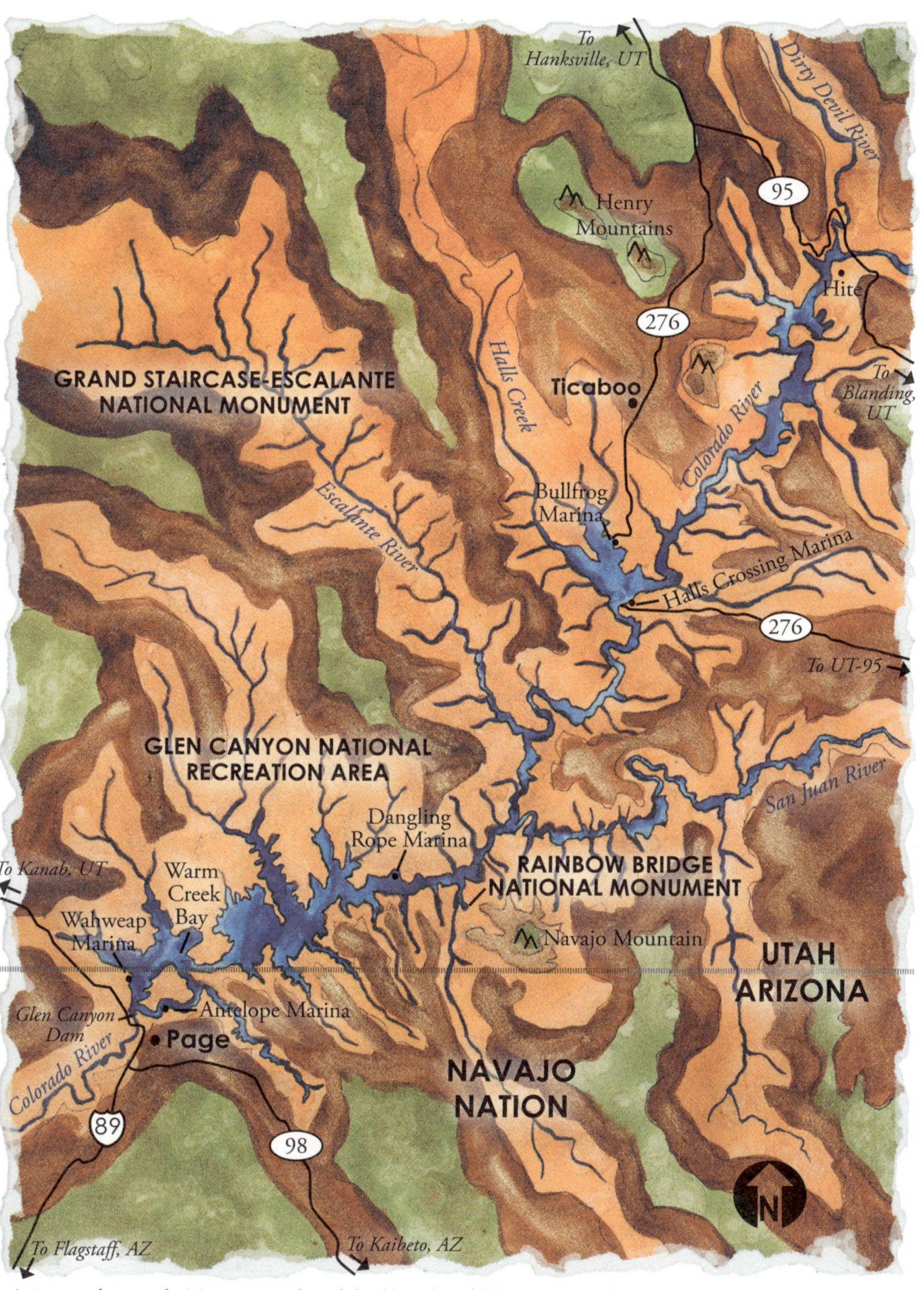

Artistic rendering only. Map not to scale and should not be used for navigational purposes.

5
THE EDDY OF UNCERTAINTY

Acknowledging you have a problem is the first step in resolving it. *So they say.*

Back in Arizona, I stared blankly out of my bedroom window for more mornings than I care to admit. Curled in the tangle of bedsheets, I massaged my ringless finger as if it were akin to shaking a Magic 8-Ball and asking, "What went wrong, and why is this happening to me?" The only response it gave was "Better not tell you now."

I hadn't a clue which direction to go with the bindle of bachelorettehood that had been thrown over my shoulder. Walking away from faceless institutions like Stanford and Intel had been easy to do, relatively speaking. In both cases, I stepped out of society's flow for my betterment. I couldn't—and wouldn't—abandon a person, especially one I had committed my life to, no matter how dissatisfied I had become. If I waited for Craig to come back, would we move forward together? If I started rebuilding a life on my own with the lessons I had just learned in Moab, would I leave him behind?

I tried pulling answers from the source. Craig and I attempted to reconcile our differences through joint and solo counseling sessions. To encourage communication between us, I created spreadsheets with two columns, one for him, one for me, to list what we each wanted out of our relationship. I took the Love Language quiz online. I developed a list of questions to help us reacquaint each other with our common interests, goals, and dreams.

It only led to more fighting. More counseling. More spreadsheets. More counseling. More lists and quizzes. More fighting about fighting.

In one drawn-out email I sent to him in between meetings, I apologized for all my sins, and even though I knew I had many, I wasn't exactly sure what they all were. Still, I promised to do better. I promised to do more. I even offered to give up my job as a freelance photographer and go back to an office job and be a "real wife" at home, whatever that meant.

"I'll do anything if it means you'll come home," I wrote. "What do you want from me?"

I waited and waited and waited. No response. Which meant I sent another email filled with more desperate promises, created another spreadsheet, and scheduled another counseling appointment.

I grew up believing that perfect people couldn't—and didn't—have problems. Whenever one appeared, I bludgeoned it quickly into submission with a spiked mace club and hid any kinks in my otherwise flawless armor. Heaven help me if anyone noticed the damage before I could cover it up.

Craig avoided conflict. So, the harder I swung, the further he retreated. Whatever I did in the name of reconciliation made the situation more hopeless.

For most of the summer of 2015, I spun in a slow-moving eddy where habits and old thought patterns held me back from the edge of a more constructive current. There was always something more, more, always more I could do—should do—to get us out of this. I had to. The word "failure" was not a part of my vocabulary. I attempted to spell it in my journal on several occasions. All that came out was "FUCK THIS."

Hey, at least I got the "f" part right.

I talked with my parents and my brother, who was healing from his own recent and unexpected divorce. I asked for advice from close friends who had navigated through the sudden deaths of previous partners. More frequently—sometimes daily—I'd fire off emails to Guy, my words soaked in depression. He would respond with a splash of sympathy and toss out paragraphs of personal insights and inspirational quotes by famous writers and philosophers.

He said Rainer Maria Rilke encouraged me to "...love your solitude and try to sing out with the pain it causes you. For those who are near you are far away...and this shows that the space around you is beginning to grow vast..."

Then Friedrich Nietzche warned, "It is the business of the very few to be independent; it is a privilege of the strong. And whoever attempts it, even with the best right, but without being OBLIGED to do so, proves that he is probably not only strong, but also daring beyond measure."

Lucius Annaeus Seneca offered the bluntest advice of all: "You are arranging what lies in Fortune's control and abandoning what lies in yours. What are you looking at? To what goal are you straining? The whole future lies in uncertainty: live immediately."

I sent back trite notes to Guy along the lines of "I got out of bed this morning. Would Seneca consider that living?"

Burdening other people with my issues made me feel uncomfortable, as if I could not get my own act together. These exchanges still served as my life vest. They didn't prevent me from falling into the churn of unwelcome and unfamiliar emotions, but they sure kept my head above water.

In the space between emails, spreadsheets, counseling sessions, and doses of philosophical guidance, I turned to The Almighty Library of Life Wisdom—the internet—for enlightenment. If Craig, my friends and family, and the universe couldn't give me answers, Google surely would:

How to get your husband back.
How to not feel rejected after separation.
What to do when your husband won't talk to you.
How to stop feeling like a victim.
How to be a better wife.
How to feel good enough.
What to do if he does not come home.

How to rebuild your life after your husband leaves.

How to grieve the loss of your husband.

How to not feel lonely.

How to be alone.

How to be happy.

My shoulders slouched and my knees curled to my chest as I read through each article.

"In time, you'll move on."

"Focus on making yourself better."

"Celebrate your new beginning."

This was all bullshit. I found the well-intentioned motivational advice woefully inadequate to address *my* problem. I closed the eighteen tabs I had opened on my desktop one by one.

No, I was not going to go to a meet-up for singles.

No, I was not adopting another cute pet. I already had a cat, my beloved orange tabby, Nolan, and he was definitely an "only child." A spoiled one too.

No, I was not going to leave Nolan behind to get lost in a foreign country so I could find myself in pasta, wine, and other men.

And no, watching a movie or reading fiction in the evenings, cozied up to the shadow of loneliness, wasn't going to do a damn thing to restore my marriage.

Hey! I know! How about my husband just comes back, and we live happily ever after like we're supposed to?

One afternoon in July, a loud knock at my front door startled me. I bolted down the stairs hoping to find Craig standing on the doorstep. My shoulders dropped, but only a little, as a deliveryman dropped a five-foot-long cardboard box on the landing. My new fourteen-foot-long, thirty-inch-wide Sea Eagle inflatable standup paddleboard had arrived. I squealed and clapped like the high school cheerleader I used to be.

Tape flew into the air. So did the Styrofoam and instruction booklet and any care I had about my separation. I unfurled the deflated board and pumped it to life in my living room. After inflating it to about twelve pounds per square inch (PSI)—a few pushes shy of the maximum recommended pressure of fifteen PSI—I stood and bounced on the diamond-patterned foam pad on top to test the board's rigidity.

"Rock solid," I said. "Impressive for a blow-up toy."

It was sleek, sexy even. Its long, racy blue and white body tapered into a sharp pointed bow, an exclusive design called a "Needlenose" which was engineered to cut through waves and wind. The blue snout looked more like the front end of a kayak than the typical rounded SUP head. I tilted the board onto its side and ran my hand along the small slit where the hand-sized fin fit in at the end of the plump stern.

"I love you already," I said, smiling as I turned the board upright on the carpet.

This new board was an answer. We—along with my mother—were going to Lake Powell, even if Craig and I were going nowhere. I raced upstairs to grab my pillow and blanket from my bed and tossed both on top of the board. I flopped onto my stomach and fell asleep with both arms wrapped around my new companion. I wasn't alone anymore.

~ ~ ~

Paddling alone is dangerous. *So they say*. What if you fall in and no one is around to save you?

I didn't know how to answer that. I hadn't ever lived alone except for one year, my senior year in college. Even then, if I wasn't in class or playing volleyball or hanging out with friends, Craig and I were chatting on the phone or exchanging emails. Other than a solo work trip here and there to places without cell service, I had never faced the shadow of myself unaccompanied. For forty years, someone had always sheltered me. Until now. The murky waters scared me.

Sinking into my own aloneness, even for just a few months, led me to see that there were indeed monsters lurking below the surface, that the undercurrent of public opinion did not hold singlehood in the highest regard. Single men are sometimes stigmatized as immature, narcissistic, commitment-phobic players. Single women, especially childless ones who live with cats (as I did), are sometimes seen as crazy old maids, spinsters, and man-haters living like nuns. *So they say.*

History treats marriage (and having children) as the sole definition of what a successful adult looks like. It screams to the outside world, "You're desirable! You're loved! You're happy!" regardless of whether the people in the relationship feel that way.

In fact, it wasn't until 1974, one year before I was born, that a woman could own her own credit card and house without her husband's permission. Even single women could be denied a credit card or a home loan without a male co-signer. Happiness be damned. Being coupled was a necessity for women to navigate societal expectations.

As I grew up, women's opportunities expanded with easier access to higher education, the passing of legislation like Title IX, and increased visibility for strong female role models who, in some cases, put their own lives on the line to buck societal norms to achieve remarkable feats. Today, women can, thankfully, earn their own money, put it in their own bank account, spend it on their own house, and decorate that house to their heart's content with their own credit card without being married.

Still, it seemed that no matter your gender or sexual preferences, if you weren't dating or partnered with someone, society deemed you undesirable, lonely, and clearly unhappy. An outcast who needed rescuing. Coupledom is salvation. Even my friends treated my possible singlehood as a contagious condition to be cured. They tried to comfort me with sentiments like "Don't worry. If your marriage falls apart, you'll find someone else someday." *So they say.*

These stereotypes seemed harsh—and not just because I was on the verge of becoming one of them. Fortunately, I found plenty of articles on The Almighty Library of Life Wisdom—the internet—that challenged these notions and suggested that single people lived at least as happy, if not happier, lives than married ones—albeit at a higher price. Singletons shoulder the entire burden of living expenses and household chores. They pay more in income taxes than their married counterparts. And if they don't want to participate in synchronized snoring with a stranger in the same hotel room, they must cough up pricey single supplements when traveling in groups.

Was that happiness?

The more I read and the more I heard, I didn't know who—or what—to believe.

Especially when standup paddleboarding was one of the few outdoor activities I felt comfortable doing on my own. I didn't have to wait for anyone to go. I didn't have to depend on anyone to help me transport my board or my gear. It wasn't expensive. I wasn't going to get chased by a grizzly bear—or by society's judgments—on the water. I simply threw the rolled, deflated board in the backseat of my truck, found a waterway, inflated my board, and floated whenever I wanted for however long I wanted.

On numerous hot summer mornings, I did just that. I tested my new board on reservoirs like Saguaro and Canyon lakes—both bloats of the Salt River, a tributary within the Colorado River watershed—to the northwest of the Phoenix metro area. My frequent daylong paddles not only provided cheap therapy from Mother Nature, but it also helped to prove, if to no one other than me, that I could do things on my own now, that I could exist on my own, without Craig or anyone else by my side. And perhaps even enjoy it. Paddling for hours filled the hollowness of heartbreak. Calling these excursions "training runs for my epic paddle on Lake Powell this November" made me sound way more badass, though.

On one hot and steamy morning in early August, I stood in knee-deep water at the Butcher Jones launch area on Saguaro Lake and held a private naming ceremony for my SUP. Three dots of clouds gathered overhead and a hillside of stately saguaro cacti along the shore acted as my witnesses. "I now proclaim you 'Liridon.'" It meant "free-willed" in Albanian.

I raised my paddle to the sun and lowered it on the board's surface like a queen tapping the shoulders of a new knight. "I shall call you 'Lir' for short," which was Celtic for "god of the sea." I took a swig out of my water bottle then poured a splash over Lir's nose to christen him.

I pushed off into the glassy green water, repeating the name. *Lir*. The sound reminded me of William Shakespeare's tragedy, *King Lear*, which reminded me of his quote, "Nothing comes from nothing" (which the Greek philosopher Parmenides first expressed). That

Mom and I on a training run at Saguaro Lake in the summer of 2015. Mom is in a different inflatable kayak than the one she paddled on Lake Powell. I was on my newly christened standup paddleboard, Lir.

implied something came from something. Or if quantum physicists were to be believed, something could come from nothing.

"I know paddling alone wasn't your plan," I told myself while admiring the craggy mountains called Four Peaks rising above the desert on the distant horizon. "But you have more than nothing. You have at least three things now: a paddleboard, a new plan, and naïve enthusiasm. Plus, family and friends who support you."

If playwrights and scientists were right, then something had to come from my trip on Lake Powell, even my separation. I just could not say—or know—what right now.

Besides, if the Colorado River ever had her own plan, becoming a reservoir wasn't a part of it.

~ ~ ~

The Colorado River, the nation's sixth-longest waterway, once flowed unimpeded for 1,450 miles to the Gulf of California (also known as the Sea of Cortés) in Mexico. She did what a river should do: tumble, rumble, and ramble. Until she stumbled into a series of manmade impediments. In 1905, she stopped freely flowing when the United States Bureau of Reclamation built the first of many dams—the Laguna Diversion Dam—near Yuma, Arizona.

Seventeen years later, on November 24, 1922, seven Western states signed the Colorado River Compact. This agreement split the Colorado River Basin in two. Upper Basin states included Wyoming, Colorado, Utah, and New Mexico. Lower Basin states included Arizona, Nevada, and California. The two basins defined who would get how much water from the Colorado River. Though the river meanders almost a hundred miles through Mexico, they didn't see a formal water allocation until 1944. Officials apportioned precisely zero water for the river herself.

Compacts, federal laws, court decrees, and regulatory guidelines adjusting distribution levels have since followed. These handshakes are now collectively known as "The Law of the River." The Colorado is one of the most managed and litigated rivers in the world. Every drop of her water is now controlled and allocated for use.

To ensure the Upper Basin could provide the required water to the Lower Basin, Congress enacted the Colorado River Storage Act in 1956. Immediately thereafter, the Bureau of Reclamation began erecting the Glen Canyon Dam in a narrow sandstone chasm near what would become Page, Arizona. Upon completion of the 710-foot-tall structure in 1963, the river stopped up into Glen Canyon like a backed-up toilet and swelled into the second-largest reservoir in America (the first being its neighbor to the west, Lake Mead, the result of the construction of the Hoover Dam downstream on the Arizona-Nevada border in 1936).

Officials named the resulting pool "Lake Powell." The first half of the name is misleading. Lake Powell is not a true lake. River water blocked behind a dam is not natural. Reservoir Powell or Powell Reservoir are more accurate labels.

The second half of the name celebrates the famed explorer Major John Wesley Powell. The one-armed Civil War veteran led an expedition in 1869 wherein he and nine men rowed the Green and Colorado rivers in four wooden boats. History books recognize their daring journey as the first known navigation of the Colorado River through the Grand Canyon by Anglo-Americans.

It's hard to say how Powell would have felt about his name being used, especially considering he and his boatman had named this area "Glen Canyon" in August 1869 after marveling over its many glens and alcoves. In 1893, as westward expansion continued, Powell warned the authorities "…there is not enough water to supply the land…" His nephew, Arthur Powell Davis, eventually led the Reclamation Service agency (which later became the Bureau of Reclamation) and was a hydroelectric power proponent.

So some people believe Powell might have praised the West's attempts at conservation. The Bureau of Reclamation touted the lake as "The Jewel of the Colorado River" in a 1965 pamphlet. In this same publication, Stuart Udall, the then-Secretary of the Department of Interior, said the reservoir was "…an exciting new concept of conservation" through the "creation of new beauty to amplify existing beauty which is our heritage…" The government believed it had done the right thing by "taming the wild river and making it a servant to man's will." (Udall later confided to friends that supporting the construction of the Glen Canyon Dam was his one great regret.)

Others think Powell started puking in his coffin the instant the dammed wild and free waters he had explored took his name. Those in this faction often refer to the pool as "Lake Foul." Or a big mistake. Famous outspoken opponents like author Edward Abbey argued that the Bureau of "Wrecklamation"—a name Abbey gave to the responsible party in his book *The Monkey Wrench Gang*—had destroyed a desert paradise.

Author and singer-songwriter Katie Lee described what was lost in her 1997 letter to the National Geographic Society, the very organization Powell helped to establish:

> There was hardly a single bend in the 180 miles of the Glen that did not contain banks, bars, and Islands (sic) of vegetation—single leaf ash, boxelder, willow, live and scrub oak, cottonwood, redbud, vines, rabbitbrush grasses and chives, even the exotic trash-tree, the tamarisk; plus what the 125 or so clearwater side streams contributed in fern, flowers, cattails, bullrushes, natural lakes and more trees—all supplying nutrients to the downstream system.

Sierra Club Executive Director David Brower also led intense environmentalist outrage against the dam. Brower featured the work of acclaimed nature photographers like Philip Hyde and Eliot Porter in his "battle books." One of these books, *The Place No One Knew* by Porter, celebrated Glen Canyon. The title was a misnomer. Although it hadn't risen to the status or popularity to gain a national park designation, plenty of people knew about this place. The riches of this arid topography had allured Native Americans, gold seekers, uranium miners, explorers like Powell, and outdoor enthusiasts alike to the river's edge for centuries. That said, many of the politicians sitting in high-backed leather chairs in Washington D.C. had never set foot in the landscape they altered before, during, or after the dam's construction. In fact, when Brower brokered the deal to build Glen Canyon Dam in exchange for not building one upstream at Echo Park in Dinosaur National Monument on the Colorado-Utah border, *he* had never seen Glen Canyon with his own eyes. He first floated the channel in 1962—as the dam was being built. The book he commissioned, as inspirational as it was, was a funeral program.

Growing up east of the Mississippi River, I didn't know the Colorado River existed until I saw it glistening at the bottom of the Grand Canyon during my move to Phoenix in my early twenties. Similarly, I had no first-hand knowledge of the damage done to Glen Canyon. Yet I knew of Lake Powell's appeal. Craig and I first visited the reservoir in 2006. We piled in a small powerboat with a few of my photographer friends and explored the southwestern part during one of our work sabbaticals. We motored around the lake every couple of summers thereafter with Craig's family, once in a houseboat and a few times in his dad's C-Dory.

Today, more than four million visitors vacation at the manmade lake in the Glen Canyon National Recreation Area. As the idiom goes, "There must be something in the water." *So they say.*

Because of the Glen Canyon Dam, there really *is* something in the water in Lake Powell. Drowned ancient Native American sites, historical towns, natural foliage, and Glen Canyon for starters.

But now the reservoir is drying up. Despite a series of overly ambitious political promises made decades ago unwittingly based upon data from one of the wettest-known periods in the West, Lake Powell has reached "full pool"—or 3,700 feet above sea level—only three times: in 1980, 1983, and 1984. Water levels in the lake fluctuate from year-to-year, month-to-month, day-to-day even. The unpredictable supply from seasonal snowfall upriver hasn't kept up with ever-increasing demand from thirsty downriver mega-metropolises like Southern California; Las Vegas, Nevada; and the Arizona Sun Corridor, which includes Phoenix, Tucson, and the surrounding areas. Residential sprawl, industrial development, and agriculture slurp water through their long straws faster than Mother Nature can replace it upstream in Lake Powell. If you add in the evaporation, seepage into the porous sandstone surrounding the desert lake, and a persistent 20-plus-year drought in a warming, drying climate, the chances of the reservoir filling again or staying full for any length of time are slimmer than a slot canyon.

Lake Powell currently faces the threat of "dead pool," the point at which the dam can no longer generate hydroelectric power, should water levels in the holding tank drop to 3,370 feet above sea level. As the ongoing drought worsens—and society demands more, more, always more from the thinning Colorado River—talks about the dam's ability to support life in a parched Southwest continue to intensify. Some speculate about its possible decommissioning either through human choice or by nature's hand. Despite man's best laid plans over the last hundred years, opposing currents still create friction.

Harnessing a free-willed river was one of modern civilization's answers to a long line of questions about how to sustain unrestrained and sprawling human settlement in a stark landscape with severely limited resources. In humanity's quest to provide drinking water, agriculture, electricity, and flood control in the arid West, the river has become an innocent victim of overly ambitious expectations.

Would the river dry up under excessive societal burdens? Could modern civilization in the West continue to exist if the reservoir drained and the river returned to her true self? Or would her flow stay impeded by a dam forever?

Sitting around and contemplating the Colorado River's fate wasn't going to make rain fall out of the sky any more than questioning mine was going make Craig come home. It wasn't solving anything. It only caused heated debate, and I was tired of fighting. Instead, I needed to get flowing—because my window of opportunity to do so on Lake Powell was shrinking with every passing hot, dry day.

~ ~ ~

After slogging through another night of thickening rejection and loneliness, I decided one morning over tea that it was time to introduce Lir to Lake Powell. On August 29, 2015, I threw my board and gear in my truck and drove five hours to the far southwestern end of the lake straddling the Arizona-Utah border near the town of Page.

It was a sweaty ninety-degrees Fahrenheit when I arrived late in the afternoon at the mile-long beach called the Lone Rock Beach Campground. The sandstone butte, from which the dispersed camping area gets its name, towered 300 feet out of the water to the northwest in Lone Rock Bay. The blocky monolith with a stocky base looked like a hand forming a fist or the cross-section of a small church depending on the angle of your view.

The bay surrounding Lone Rock didn't exist before Lake Powell. Wahweap Creek used to amble through gravel, sand deposits, and the yellowish-grey rolling hills of Entrada Sandstone—and past Lone Rock—before it joined with the Colorado River near the present-day Wahweap Marina. The water from the creek and the river pool here,

Lir gliding through the blue-green waters of Lake Powell in Lone Rock Bay on August 29, 2015.

sitting still and unsure, waiting for their release from the Glen Canyon Dam, which resides around the corner to the southeast, about eight miles away as the striped bass swims.

The waterfront campground was packed with RVs, ATVs, white pop-up tents, pirate flags, and plastic flamingos. Radios thumped out of sync. The place reeked of sunscreen and gasoline, of barbecue, warm beer, and freedom. I nestled my truck in an empty spot between two white trailers on the soft sand, as far away as I could get from the party scene—and steps away from where I could launch my SUP on the lake.

The next morning, as the pre-dawn sky yawned from black velvet into a steely cobalt sheet, I surveyed Lake Powell's shoreline and the stair-stepped cliffs of the Grand Staircase-Escalante National Monument in the distance through my Alaskan Camper's windows. I rubbed my eyes. I checked the day's weather forecast on my iPhone: a moderate chance of an afternoon monsoon storm, an expected prediction for Arizona this time of year. I looked at the cloudless sky again. An afternoon storm here seemed as unlikely as mathematicians finding the end of pi.

I intended to do an easy fifteen-mile solo paddle around Lone Rock, into the heart of Wahweap Bay, and then back to my campsite. At my lackadaisical pace, averaging two to three miles per hour, I estimated I would be off the water no later than one or two in the afternoon. Even if this was just the proverbial calm before the storm, I would no doubt finish my short tour well before the weather turned ugly—if I didn't dilly-dally. I put on my two-piece swimsuit and started packing a single dry bag for the day.

I slid Lir into the calm, tepid green waters in the bay and glided away from the summer circus at the campground and into nature's soothing serenity. I took my time circumnavigating Lone Rock, taking sips of coffee in between paddle strokes. I passed rounded sandstone mounds, chiseled white cliffs, and airy tamarisk waving in the gentle breeze against an otherwise treeless horizon. The rising sun bathed the stark landscape in its rich auburn rays. I eventually made my way east into the stomach of Wahweap Bay.

More and more of my lethargic brain cells began responding to my gradual intake of caffeine. Questions about my November expedition started to swirl in my head like the kettle of turkey vultures circling in the sky above.

Would Mom and I survive paddling in forty- to fifty-degree air temperatures? Yes, but I should buy neoprene boots and remind Mom to do so as well.

Were three days of rest among the fourteen-day plan going to be enough? Or too much? Who knows, but we should still plan to rest when we feel like it.

Would Mom and I be capable of paddling like this, non-stop, for two weeks? In pristine, glorious conditions like this? Heck yeah!

Of all the solvable logistical challenges, one concern remained: how would the fourteen days I planned ever be enough time? With all the side canyons and inlets and hidden coves to explore, I wasn't sure I'd be able to stay focused long enough in the main channel of the Colorado River to make it to Wahweap Marina. Maybe I'd stay out there forever.

Growing cumulonimbus clouds to the southwest snapped me out of my ruminations. A sizeable squall was moving in early. And fast.

I started paddling toward land. About a half-hour later, I landed on a sandy, crescent-shaped beach on the north side of the bay near Castle Butte. The silver-bottomed storm clouds had not yet obscured the bright summer sun overhead. I couldn't see lightning from the isolated cell, but thunder rumbled. A curtain of rain started crossing the reddened backside of the Vermilion Cliffs in the distance to the southwest. I reminded myself, "Don't dilly-dally."

I devoured an energy bar and then hopped on my paddleboard to head back to the safety of my camp. Within 20 minutes of paddling, dark clouds consumed the sun. A soft drizzle fluttered on top of the water. I was at least two to three miles away—and on the opposite side of the lake—from my camp. I pulled onto a rocky ledge at the base of a sandy dune on the north side of the channel to wait out the shower. I dragged Lir out of the unsettled water and chewed on my fingernails.

Now what?

The winds swirled and the angry sky started unleashing its fury. I crouched underneath my beached board. Heavy raindrops pelted my exposed skin as if the sky had begun to play the opening movement of

Lightning from a passing monsoon storm strikes over the cliffs in the Grand-Staircase Escalante National Monument as viewed from Lone Rock Beach in Glen Canyon National Recreation Area, Arizona, on August 29, 2015.

a piano concerto on my head and back. Nature's orchestra came to a crescendo, and I winced each time a cold bead of water oozed down the curve of my tailbone and dripped onto the gravel. I cursed my decision to leave my rain jacket and pants behind at my camp, believing it was too warm and too clear to need such practical protective equipment for my short jaunt on the lake.

Lightning flashed over the top of Lone Rock.

One Mississippi. Two Mississippi…Twelve Mississippi.

The sky grumbled. Sound travels approximately one mile every five seconds, so the storm was a little more than two miles away. Two miles too close.

I stood up to move my belongings to the lowest protected spot I could find, below scrubby bushes at the top of the rock spit about ten feet above the lake. I tucked my paddle under Lir to protect it from the wind. I tried to remember how to assume the lightning position from an article I had read just a month earlier. For the next forty-five minutes, I balanced on the balls of my feet while squatting on top of my life vest next to my board.

The storm eventually passed. In its wake, it left a dash of sunshine, a strong headwind stirring up one- to two-foot white-capped swells, and two cramped quadriceps muscles. I shook the stiffness out of my legs and quickly gathered my gear. A line of isolated storms extended as far as I could see on the horizon. They were moving toward me.

"You should have prepared better for this," I said, shaking my head. I needed to make the crossing to the other shore and the last couple of miles back to camp right away, or I was going to end up sleeping overnight in a puddle on this shore in nothing but my swimsuit.

I pushed off the submerged sandstone shelf. Instead of standing up, which made me a human sail, I sat down on the inflatable chair attached to the center of my board (which I call my "loveseat"). I paddled only on the left to keep me on course toward my camp. With each stroke, I kept repeating, "What doesn't kill you makes you stronger." *So they say.*

My feet touched sand about an hour later. Muscles I did not even know I had in my arms, shoulders, and fingers throbbed. Even the webbing between my fingers ached. Aliveness pulsed through my veins.

I cleaned, dried, and packed Lir in haste as darkening clouds approached from the southwest. Twenty minutes later, the next thunderstorm shelled me with hail. From the time I landed at about 1:30 until dark, eight squalls had passed. The seventh flattened my neighbor's three-person tent.

That evening, while the winds whistled, I lounged in my fluffy bathrobe and sipped wine from the posh comforts of my camper (which I named "Juno" after the "queen of gods" in Roman mythology). I wondered what I had gotten Mom and myself into. Was paddling across this lake a smart idea?

I considered the same question I had pondered earlier in the day but added an important caveat: were Mom and I capable of paddling like this, non-stop, for two weeks...if conditions like *this* prevailed?

LAKE POWELL: WAHWEAP AND WARM CREEK BAYS

Artistic rendering only. Map not to scale and should not be used for navigational purposes.

Lunch stop:
October 28, 2015
GLEN CANYON NATIONAL
RECREATION AREA
WARM CREEK BAY
Camp 2:
October 28, 2015
Camp 1:
October 27, 2015
Castle
Rock
"The Cut"
UTAH
ARIZONA
To Bullfrog/Halls Crossing
NAVAJO
NATION
ANTELOPE
ISLAND
N

6
TESTING THE WATERS

"We'll send you a text as soon as we are headed back across the bay," I said as Mom and I waved to my dad. "See you in a few days."

On the afternoon of October 27, 2015—which happened to be Glen Canyon National Recreation Area's 43rd birthday—Mom and I pushed away from a small graveled patch of land next to the concrete boat ramp at the Wahweap Marina. She sat in our cleaned-up two-person touring kayak for the first time. I sat on Lir. Two months had passed since my stormy maiden voyage on Lake Powell. Since then, Mom and I had continued to practice paddling across Saguaro Lake closer to home. Still, I wondered if paddling across a big reservoir was a smart idea. I figured the best way to get answers was to do a test run, a two-night shakedown, together on Lake Powell.

We weren't planning on going far—only about six to eight miles—across Wahweap Bay and into Warm Creek Bay, its neighbor to the east. Weather forecasts suggested a cold front would make its way to the area in the next two or three days. Should the storm arrive early, we figured we could dash back to Wahweap Marina in the wind and rain without too much pain and suffering. Although almost two months had passed, the memory of Lake Powell's placid waters seducing me ahead of monsoon storms remained fresh in my mind. At least on this trip, I could tuck experience into my life jacket next to my map.

At the same time, we hoped to get far enough out to get comfortable with being uncomfortable, settle into our new equipment, finalize our gear list, and estimate how much food we would eat. We also wanted to test our communications process with my dad, who had declined the invitation to join us on this and our November adventure. I had a new Garmin InReach, a satellite communications device that allowed us to text each other while out of cell phone range. It would summon the authorities by pressing the SOS button should a life-threatening emergency occur—a feature I hoped we would never use.

Under a mostly cloudy sky, Mom and I glided side-by-side through silk for about three miles to reach the Castle Rock Cut. "The Cut" is a mile-long, hundred-foot-wide canal that was chiseled through the rock at the southern base of Castle Rock in 1972. It's a shortcut, as the name implies, that trims off about twelve miles when traveling up the lake from Wahweap Bay but only when the water elevation exceeds 3,580 feet. Our water level was at 3,606 feet.

Circling south around Antelope Island, an isle that exists only because of the dredged passage, was an alternative. Even though it follows the natural course of the Colorado River, I opted to skip this route. What takes a motorboat an hour or two to travel would take us a day or more moving under our own power. Plus, I knew from my past boating trips that ample sandy beaches—and thus, excellent camping locations—existed along the northeastern side of Antelope Island. I didn't know anything about the rest of the landmass. I didn't want to risk our trip going south.

As we entered the mouth of The Cut, chiseled sandstone walls at eye-level on both sides grew taller and taller into the sky, perfectly and unnaturally vertical, until they towered over our heads. A light breeze pushed us from behind as we moved from west to east through the straight channel. We exchanged pleasantries with a friendly couple in a passing open-cockpit fishing boat. The manufactured cliffs soon melted back into sandy beaches as we entered the open waters of Warm Creek Bay.

We turned south, still hugging Antelope Island, to start looking for a spit of sand to sleep on overnight. When we rounded the corner, the

Mom and I ready to launch at the Wahweap Marina boat ramp on Lake Powell on October 27, 2015. Photo by Bob Miniuk.

playful waft shifted into a mean fifteen-mile-per-hour, cheek-slapping crosswind.

"Let's land over there," I shouted. I pointed toward a small crescent-shaped beach inside a U-shaped cove on Antelope Island. It was no more than a half-mile away. I'd camped there before with Craig and his family a few years earlier.

Two strokes later, Lir started spinning. Cool, translucent waves hurled over my board and drenched my bare feet. My legs wobbled from side to side. I dropped to my knees and fell back into my loveseat to avoid falling in. I glanced over my right shoulder. Mom struggled to tame her long kayak in the one- to two-foot whitecaps. Her head tucked to her chest, shoulders hunched, teeth clenched. Each wave soaked her.

I shook my head. This was absurd. We didn't have to work so hard to get to an arbitrary spot.

I spotted a sprawling west-facing beach on the horizon on my left. It seemed about double the distance from the one on Antelope Island. Sand Hills, I remembered reading on the map before we left. With a name like that, there had to be sand. And where there's sand, there are campsites. I couldn't be sure of it, but I knew getting to Antelope Island would force us to battle against Mother Nature. And Mother Nature always wins.

"Hey, Ma, don't fight the wind," I called back to her while pointing to the mostly flat stretch of land to the east. "Let it take you across the bay. We'll camp over there instead."

She nodded, dropped her shoulders, and rested her paddle on top of her deck. I set my paddle across my knees and let the wind take us wherever it wanted to. After about ten minutes, with only a few strokes to steer, we coasted onto a long sandy beach. Right where I had not planned to be.

I tugged my paddleboard out of the water. Mom pulled in behind me. She stepped out, one foot at a time. The splashing waves rocked her kayak sideways and knocked her off balance. Her arms spun like a windmill. She stumbled backward then regained her footing and stumbled onto dry land.

"Whew. That was tough," Mom said, as she dropped her paddle on the beach.

"The crossing or the landing?" I asked with a smirk. "I'm sure glad we changed directions. Much easier to paddle with the wind than against it."

I surveyed the beach with my hands on my hips. "Plus, this doesn't look too shabby for a camp, does it?"

"It's perfect," she said.

"It's every bit as good as the ones on Antelope Island, if not better," I said, nodding my head. "Yet, I didn't even know it existed before we left."

Mom began unloading her gear from her kayak with as much focus, diligence, and speed as an assembly line worker. Even at sixty-four-years young, she lived up to her nickname, "The Energizer Bunny." As she shuttled gear to and fro, I ignored my pile. Instead, I opted to soak in the view of the majestic, flat-topped Romana Mesa at the northern end of the shoreline.

I extended my arms and held my thumbs and forefingers in a box to visualize possible photographs. Waves crashed against a cluster of sandstone in the foreground. A shaft of sunlight broke through the leaden clouds, highlighting the rocks in the distance. These were perfect conditions for a photograph. I pulled my camera from my dry bags and began setting up my tripod.

"Funny, I wouldn't have been able to make these images from Antelope Island," I mumbled. "Thank you, wind!"

I made a few snaps. Out of the corner of my eye, I noticed Mom bending over and circling my board while squeezing an eyedropper. I watched her for a few seconds, then tilted my head sideways in bewilderment. "Ma, what are you doing?"

"I'm surrounding the area with peppermint oil," she responded without looking up.

"What?" I snickered. "Ummm, why?"

"Keep the rats away from the boats and our stuff," she replied. "So they don't bite through your inflatable board."

"For real?"

Windy conditions kicking up waves on Lake Powell. This was our view looking west-southwest from our first camp on an unnamed beach near the Sand Hills on October 27, 2015. Castle Rock, where we camped on the second day of our trial run, is the largest rock formation visible on the left side of the horizon.

I knew of the damage woodrats could cause. On a backpacking trip with Craig and two friends on the Grand Canyon's north rim in 2009, I had forgotten to stash my dried strawberries in our rodent-resistant food bag overnight. With my pack resting against a rock, vermin chewed through its mesh pockets and helped themselves to a fruity feast. Since that Grand Canyon backpacking trip, I had become more conscientious about keeping my food, and other odorous objects, out of animals' reach. Mom and I secured anything smelly—food, deodorant, toothpaste, sunscreen—in our Ratsack, a book-bag-sized pouch made with stainless steel mesh. As extra protection, we'd hang it from my extended tripod overnight.

I hadn't thought about animals taking a bite out of Lir. When I did, a rather ridiculous vision popped into my head. I imagined a long-eared, black-eyed cartoon rodent, no bigger than a grapefruit, carrying off my SUP on its back and then sitting down to gnaw on it as if it were eating an ear of corn. Even when I considered more realistic ramifications, I still had a hard time believing I'd wake up to see teeth marks on a deflated board. But what if? I had packed a repair kit, suitable for small punctures, but I had nothing to fix a gaping rathole.

Mom squeezed a few more drops of peppermint around our scattered gear. "You can learn so much from reading about what people on the internet have gone through."

She admitted to spending hours browsing hikers' blogs (especially those on the Pacific Crest Trail) and watching survival TV shows, collecting handy outdoorsy tips, like this tried-and-true method for deterring rodents. I would never hear her name announced after "And the Lightest Packer Award goes to…" But rest assured, she always had the most random piece of equipment right when you needed it. Peppermint oil. Bouillon cubes. Small hotel sewing kit. You name it, she'd pull it out of her pack. After amassing a wealth of experience—both on her own hikes and from living vicariously through others—she had turned into a dutiful Girl Scout demonstrating the motto "Be Prepared."

"It's a full moon tonight," I said. "We should sleep outside."

"You mean, like, without a tent?" she asked. "Like cowboy camp?"

"Is that another term you got off the internet?" I laughed.

"I've never done it. But the cowboys in the movies do it all the time," she said, stuffing the peppermint oil back into her dry bag.

I shook my head. I pictured her sitting in front of the television with a bag of popcorn and a notebook in her lap, binge-watching movies like *Stagecoach*, *Unforgiven*, and *Three Amigos* not for the plots—assuming they had one—but rather to learn how to survive in the great outdoors. Who better than John Wayne, Clint Eastwood, and Chevy Chase to teach women the ways of the wild?

"What about snakes and scorpions?" She looked around our camp. "And rats?"

"I'm sure they're out here somewhere. It might be a little cold for snakes and scorpions, though." I scanned the beach for footprints. "I don't see any tracks from woodrats. Besides, didn't you just dowse our camp with peppermint oil? This place smells like a box of Thin Mints."

Mom pursed her lips and threw her hands up in the air. "Oh, all right. What the hell? If cowboys can sleep outside with only a blanket, then I can sleep out here with my warm sleeping bag, sleeping pad, and pillow."

"That's the spirit, Ma!"

I poked at her, but I understood her concern. After all, I had not slept in a tent in the wild until November 1997. Craig and my friend Jen (who was my freshman-year roommate at Stanford) dragged me to Joshua Tree National Park in southern California for my first backcountry overnight camping trip. The possibility of a Charles Manson-like, grim reaper-esque psycho hiding in the shadows of jumbo rocks and waiting to bludgeon us to death with a sledgehammer in our sleep made me edgy before and during the trip. We were three miles from the closest trailhead and many more miles from the closest semblance of civilization, mind you. This was obviously where all the scary monsters lived.

Once Craig and I crawled into our tent, I felt blind and vulnerable beneath the thin yellow curtain of tent fabric. My eyes darted from side to side trying to make sense of the nothingness of night. With each little unfamiliar rustle, I tried to crawl under Craig. I whispered, "What was that? What was that?" All. Night. Long. Craig pulled me close to him and kept repeating, "It's just the wind." The tiny imprints we saw in the sand the next morning made it clear that only small desert animals—and not Freddie Krueger from *A Nightmare on Elm Street*—had scurried around us that night.

I first "cowboy camped" in the Valley of the Gods in Utah in April 2008. Although I didn't call it that. And it wasn't intentional. I had forgotten to pack my tent poles. My friend Scott offered me his tent while he slept on a tarp outside. I turned him down. Thoughts of snakes cuddling up to me in my sleeping bag, packrats scampering across my stomach, and coyotes sniffing my feet in the middle of the night terrified me. Even so, I put on my big girl panties—and every article of clothing I had packed, including a down coat, fleece jacket, fleece pants, long johns, hat, and gloves—and crawled into my zero-degree bag. I tightened the cord taut around my cheeks such that only my mouth stuck out like a blowhole. I slept so soundly that the snakes, packrats, and coyotes could have held a dance party on my face, and I would have missed it. Since then, I had slept under the stars countless times—and with far fewer clothes on. I now felt more comfortable sleeping outside without a tent in the presence of animals than walking to my own mailbox in the presence of humans.

Mom and I unrolled our sleeping pads and bags next to each other on a flat sandstone ledge about fifteen feet away from the water. We also set up the tent nearby just in case Mom decided in the middle of the night that she no longer wanted to play Ringo Kid.

The wind settled as the sun made its final plea with the skyline. Clouds scattered and gathered along the edges of the horizon. A blank sky remained overhead. One by one, freckles of stars appeared against the smooth jet-black canvas. An almost full moon peaked over the eastern ridge, wrapping a silver cape of light around our shoulders and our sandstone surroundings. The lake sparkled with celestial reflections. I had to make a photograph of it.

I started creating images of the moonlit landscape with my cable release in one hand and a glass of white wine in the other. Mom and I huddled around my camera after each thirty-second exposure. We squealed and giggled and jumped up and down like schoolgirls on a playground every time the photograph flashed on the screen. The lake's scenery appeared as bright as daylight in my images. Pencil-thin star trails swirled across the sky and revealed otherwise imperceptible evidence of the Earth's constant rotation. Because of digital sensor technology, at night, the camera tends to "see" more than the human eye.

"It's so pretty out here," Mom said, looking at one of my frames.

What struck me more was that *she* was so pretty out here. Her shoulder-length grey hair fluttered in the warm breeze as she stood next to me. Her inquisitive brown eyes, rounded cheeks, and thin, bony 5'9" profile glowed like a Leonardo da Vinci chiaroscuro-style painting. I hoped I was as beautiful as she was when I was sixty-four years old—and I hoped I had half of her energy then too.

But yes, she was right. It was so pretty out here. So much so, I

The moonlit landscape beneath the night sky from our first overnight camp near the Sand Hills on Lake Powell on October 27, 2015. Romana Mesa is the shadowed plateau extending out of the right side of the frame. While made in the dark, the photo appears to depict daylight because of the camera's sensitivity to moonlight.

wondered between shutter clicks, why I had always associated dark with despair and light with hope when endless possibilities, beauty, and magic surrounded me here and in the obscure cosmos overhead. I started questioning what now seemed like misguided assumptions I'd carried with me since childhood.

Like so many kids, the dark had terrified me. I had slept with my closet light on, door wide open, every night growing up. I thought the boogeyman lived under my bed and waited for me to fall asleep so he could eat me. I'd often sneak out of bed, grab a book, and sit in my brightly lit closet guarded by piles of my stuffed animals and dolls. My eyes flitted from book to dark, book to dark, book to dark until the lurking Sandman lulled me to sleep.

(At what point should I start to wonder if watching horror movies in my youth was bad for my developing psyche?)

I grew out of this irrational behavior by junior high school. But

I stared my fear in the face once again when I started spending more time outdoors as a photographer. Then grew out of it after cooking meals in the dark after long hikes, getting up to pee in the middle of the night, and rising at "0-dark-thirty" to catch a sunrise in some scenic locale. Then stared it in the face again when I started sleeping in my own home by myself.

I knew the boogeyman had moved on long ago to terrorize other kids. Yet the darkness and accompanying uncertainty that filled my empty master bedroom with its empty king-sized bed had all but consumed me every night after Craig left. When anxiety rolled over and pulled the covers away from me, usually around two or three in the morning, I'd turn on my bedside lamp hoping the evils of insecurity would disappear. They didn't. Light had always provided me clarity and comfort. Now, no matter how bright, it wasn't enough to illuminate the depth and unruliness of my own shadows.

Since my separation, I had been fighting to stay in the light, to stay safe in what I thought I knew about myself and understood about the world around me. So far, it had kept me standing motionless in the middle of rough waters, paralyzed by self-doubt. My fear of the unknowable, the unobservable, and the uncontrollable, combined with my overactive imagination, had convinced me that only the worst, not the best, was waiting for me in the muddy waters, the darkness of night, and in the haze of my heartache.

Negativity bias stalks perfectionists. So does Murphy's Law.

On the shores of Lake Powell now, I stood face-to-face with the dark—with reality—and it was hauntingly beautiful. So much so that I made photographs of it, so I'd never forget it. I wondered if I could revere the darkness I encountered in my life in the same way that I admired the darkness of the night. Besides, a new star was born only after a cloud of gas collapsed. I had collapsed on my kitchen floor plenty over the last seven months. Could I find a way to shine through the obscurities of my situation?

Maybe life wasn't about shining at all. Maybe it was about letting our eyes adjust and appreciating what lies within the darkness. Maybe it was about recognizing the dark exists because of the light, the light because of the dark. Maybe it was about giving each part equal value. Maybe it was about tossing out judgments and labels like "good" and "bad," "best" and "worst," and embracing what is, exactly as it is, instead of welcoming the "positive" ones with open arms and trying like hell to avoid the "negative" ones. After all, we can't see stars when the sun shines. We see stars because of the dark. And there were no good stars or bad stars, best stars or worst stars. Just stars. If not for humans, they wouldn't be called anything. They'd just exist. Yet, they'd still sparkle in the atmospheric wind.

I curled my bare toes into the sand. I didn't know what scared me more, staying stuck in the past—what felt like light—or facing my uncertain future—what felt like dark. I raised my chin to the sky above for guidance. The night stared back in silence. It wasn't giving away any of its secrets.

Our energy finally waned after an hour or two. Mom slid into her sleeping bag. I climbed into mine and pulled the covers over my head. Calmed by the artificial blackness and the soothing sound of waves lapping against sandstone, I woke the next morning not remembering falling asleep.

I rolled over to face Mom, who was already sitting up and rubbing her eyes. "Way to go, Ma. You survived," I said while propping myself up on my elbows. "How was your first cowboy camp?"

"Didn't feel any different than sleeping in a tent," she said as she stuffed her sleeping bag into its stuff sack. "I was warm, almost hot, all night. Were you warm?"

"Definitely on the warm side of cozy," I said. Temperatures had dropped no lower than the mid-forties. I looked up at the spotty ashen clouds that had rolled in overnight. "If it doesn't rain, we can do it again tonight if you'd like."

"Sounds good to me."

The Energizer Bunny had packed all her gear before I even thought of getting out of my sleeping bag. The rising sun turned the distant clouds over Romana Mesa into the pink hue of cherry blossoms, a spectacle that encouraged me to get up and grab my camera. I didn't go far. I photographed a composition two feet from my bed. Mom

Paddling in Warm Creek Bay on Lake Powell on October 28, 2015.

brought me hot tea. Between exposures, I gathered my belongings and loaded my board.

We launched into the heart of Warm Creek Bay with a less vigorous breeze than the night before. The winds seemed to calm, save for an occasional patch of cat's paws skimming across the surface. Mom stayed ahead of me. My one hasty paddle stroke was no match for her two nonchalant ones.

We meandered into a wide thumb extending to the northeast of the bay, and everything stilled. A mirror image of the commanding flat-topped plateaus near Romana Mesa reflected into the water. The reflection looked like a Rorschach inkblot design turned on its side. Abstract, chunky, symmetrical. It stretched from shore to shore and grew larger as we neared it.

A large cul-de-sac of windswept sandy beaches came into view on the west side. The pristine shoreline curled around the base of yellow-grey Entrada Sandstone cliffs. Scraggy tamarisks dotted the shoreline.

Jagged buttes and mesas, stained black, orange, and beige, lingered on the distant horizon ahead of us to the northeast.

A little before noon—and after paddling for about five miles—we picked out a spot at the head of a small cove on the west side to rest and eat lunch. I hadn't been to this part of the lake before. Still, I recognized the distance plateau as the Nipple Bench in the Grand Staircase-Escalante National Monument. I spotted a small dirt road I thought could be Crosby Canyon Road. Several years ago, Mom and I had tried to explore this rocky and rough track from Smoky Mountain Road. A washout in the dry creek bed had prevented us from reaching this point on the lake. But now, here we were.

I stopped paddling about thirty feet from the shore. When Lir's glide slowed, I stepped off my board into knee-deep water and pulled it onto the beach. Soft grains of sand oozed through my toes. Beads of sweat dripped from my forehead. I wore a lightweight long-sleeved shirt and pants, which I had rolled up below my knees, but I was cooking. The air temperature couldn't have been any warmer than sixty-five degrees. "I'm hot," I whined as the sun peaked out from behind a cloud. "I wish it were about ten to twenty degrees cooler."

"Me too," Mom said, pulling her kayak next to my board. "It should feel perfect in late November for our trip."

I tossed the dry bag with my lunch in it onto the beach. I straightened up and said with a sly grin, "We should go for a swim, Ma."

"Sure, go ahead," she said without looking up from her gear. Her tone made it clear that she had no intentions of partaking in such shenanigans.

I turned to the lake, then closed my eyes. I recalled a sepia-toned photograph Martin Koehler made in 1957 of Katie Lee in Cattails Canyon, a small, now-submerged finger on the northern side of Glen Canyon somewhere around present-day Friendship Cove. I had a poster of it hanging in my office. In it, Katie is standing naked with her backside to the camera and on top of a boulder that's wedged into the mouth of a narrow, fluted canyon. She's looking up at the swirling cross-bedded pattern on the walls above her head—not down at the shadowy crevasse below her feet. Her curves mirror the hourglass shape of the walls framing her. Her freckled and tanned skin matches the tone of the sandstone. If not for her unkempt short blonde hair, she would blend into the rock. Even still, she was the rock. She was the sculpted, curvaceous canyon. Many still called her "The Goddess of Glen Canyon." Or, as the title of Koehler's photograph indicates, "The Nymph of Glen Canyon." Katie called this same photograph "The Pagan" in her book *All My Rivers are Gone*.

Once an actress and folk singer in Hollywood, Katie first rafted the Colorado River though Glen Canyon in 1953. It only took one run to turn her into the canyon's biggest fan, supporter, protector, and lover. She took many trips down the "Colly Raddy" (her nickname for the Colorado River), where she gathered fodder for her music and writings—and fire for her fight against the misguided water management policies of the West. The only thing Katie hated more than the Glen Canyon Dam was the people who built it. "When they drowned that place, they drowned my whole guts," she said in a 2010 interview. "And I will never forgive the bastards. May they rot in hell."

When Koehler made his photograph in 1957, Katie had to have known that the construction of the Glen Canyon Dam had begun a year earlier. She had to have known the canyon she stood in—and all the other ones like it she had come to cherish—would disappear beneath Lake Powell. Yet, in Koehler's image, she stands resolute, with a touch of, dare I say, cheekiness, in defiance of the inevitable fate of her beloved Glen Canyon.

I had no idea if my separation would lead to reconciliation or divorce. Like it or not, the walls of the dam Craig had started to build when we separated were rising. I couldn't stop it. My whole guts were drowning in the swelling waters. As it happened, I wanted to stand on that rock like Katie. I wanted to feel strong, fearless, and feisty as I stared down my loss. I wanted to shed my pain and identity as a failed wife. I wanted to expose myself, bare it all to these waters, and let this river, this lake, and my separation polish me into something new.

I opened my eyes and saw a blank slate of glistening blue-green water in front of me. What was I waiting for? I could be anything I

Time for lunch! Landing on an unnamed beach in Warm Creek Bay in Lake Powell on the afternoon of October 28, 2015. Photo by Jacque Miniuk.

wanted to be here. The ravens and the cliffs and the water couldn't care less who I was or what I'd become.

I took off my clothes and piled them on top of my food bag. I'll start by being naked. Just like Katie.

"The water is cold," I said as a statement of fact, not a complaint.

"No, it's not," Mom stood up. "The water is nice and warm, and it's hot out.

I huffed.

"Go for it," Mom continued in a singsong voice and clapped her hands. "On your mark. Get set. Gooooooooo!"

On her cue, I ran into Warm Creek Bay. Here's to you, Katie Lee!

"Whip it, baby!" Mom yelled.

I splashed at first, my arms thrashing from side to side, throwing water into the air. I fell forward into the chilly waters, then rolled onto my back. I couldn't stop laughing.

Mom kayaking in Warm Creek Bay toward Castle Rock on October 28, 2015.

"Yahoo!" Mom started cackling. "Take a bath!"

I caught my footing on the soft floor of the lake and waddled back to the beach like a penguin. My wet feet slapped against the sand. My arms coddled my body for warmth and discretion. Deciding I didn't need either, I raised my arms above my head and yelled, "Woohoo!"

I fell back into the sand next to my clothes, not caring about getting dirty after my so-called bath. "That was cold!" I said.

"Yeah, but I bet it felt good," Mom said.

It did. My cold skin tingled as it warmed in the sun. Beads of water dribbled off my skin. Liberation felt invigorating and cozy.

I redressed and grabbed my lunch bag. I laid out a buffet of pita chips, almond butter, banana chips, and energy bars. Between bites, we mulled over our plans for the afternoon. This flat, sandy beach offered an inviting camp, but we had five hours of daylight left. These calm conditions were ideal for paddling.

"I vote to keep going and find a camp closer to Wahweap, in case the storm arrives early," I said, packing my food wrappers back in my dry bag. "Besides, what else do we have to do today?"

"Agreed," Mom said.

We also agreed that, whenever conditions were good during our November trip, we would paddle as far and as long as we could, day or night, even if it meant traveling farther and longer than we had scheduled. When conditions were too dangerous, we would rest. That sounded like a good plan, but I wondered how well it would sit with she who couldn't sit still.

After an hour-long break, we pushed away from the beach and pointed our vessels south toward Wahweap Bay. We followed the curvaceous western-most edge of Warm Creek Bay paralleling each other. A few boats motored around Antelope Island in the distance. A colony of gulls squawked overhead. Patches of blue appeared between the thinning marshmallow clouds. We reached The Cut a couple hours—and six miles—later.

"Let's pull into the beach around the bend once we get out of The Cut," I said, pointing my paddle to the right. "I haven't stayed there before, but I bet it's a great camp. We'll have a bird's-eye view of the Wahweap Marina from there. We could watch the weather and decide when to cross the bay tomorrow. It should only be about two miles to the boat ramp from there."

Minutes later, a rambling, arced beach appeared to the west of Castle Rock. It was empty. We glided into the sandiest part of the beach and set up our camp.

Eventually the sun disappeared into its slumber. We disappeared into ours. A transcendent serenade of coyotes yipping and howling on the ridgeline behind us put us to sleep.

Steely blue twilight greeted us as we woke before sunrise. I moved like a slug, even slower than my normal sluggish morning pace. I wanted to stay on the lake forever where I could press my footprints into the sand and sing with the singing coyotes and paddle in winds that didn't care if I was married or separated, if I was happy or sad, if I was a success or a failure. Where I could be me. The exposed, broken, stubborn-as-hell me.

I hadn't cried a drop about Craig, my separation, or my miserable existence in the past two days. It was the longest I had gone without a meltdown since April. I smiled. I'd celebrate as if it were my birthday. I'd have some pie when I got home.

To the west, ominous clouds with dark gray underbellies urged us to get a move on. We packed our belongings while boiling water for our routine oatmeal and tea breakfast. I stuffed one piece of gear after another into its designated dry bag. As I did so, I decided whether it would remain on the packing list for our November trip. Had I used it? Would it provide us support on the journey ahead?

Ahead of our test run, I had visualized using each item in various practical situations we could encounter. So I wasn't surprised when I deemed everything should stay, including my solar charging panel and accompanying battery pack, the only things in my bag that I hadn't used. I had packed both to keep my Garmin InReach, iPhone, and camera batteries powered. None of those electronics needed recharging on this short trip. They certainly would on a longer one. The panel and battery pack remained on the list.

"Expert planner I am," I said in my best Yoda voice—which may have sounded more like Kermit the Frog.

Before pushing offshore, I sent Dad a text on the Garmin InReach, "Arriving in 1 hr." We were at least three to four hours earlier than we had planned.

Dad responded a few minutes later, "Already here."

"I guess our communications setup works," I said and winked at Mom.

We spotted his white 4Runner at the bottom of the boat ramp. It was just like him to be early. I wasn't sure he could see us, but we waved to him anyhow.

A soft drizzle began tapping on our shoulders. I glanced up at the somber sky overhead and opened my mouth to try to catch the drops, to drink in every last bit. Rain or shine, November 24 could not come a day too soon.

Ready to "cowboy camp" on an unnamed beach near Castle Rock in Wahweap Bay on Lake Powell on October 28, 2015.

7
PLANNING FOR SUCCESS

"What if there's a storm?" Dad asked, stroking his steaming coffee mug.

It was customary for me to meet up with my folks for breakfast at a local restaurant at least once a month. We'd normally talk about how work was going, how Craig was doing, and other chit-chats. In the weeks leading up to our trip, our conversations focused less on daily details and more on over-analyzing countless rational—and irrational—what-if scenarios about our paddle. Mom and I had sorted out many issues on our trial run, but Dad still had questions. Over eggs and toast, we chewed on his concerns.

"If we see lightning, which is not likely in November, we'll take cover," I said. I ate another bite of scrambled eggs. "I'm bringing a weather radio, so we will assess things as we go. We'll stop and rest if conditions get too awful."

"What if you or Mom get hurt?" he asked.

"I have basic first aid and CPR certifications. Plus, we are both bringing first aid kits. We'll try to not get hurt, but if we do, we'll take care of ourselves. If one of us gets injured, we'll text you to figure out what to do next. If it's life-threatening, we'll press the SOS button on our InReach. The authorities will land a rescue helicopter on top of us."

"What if you puncture your board?"

"I'm bringing a repair kit. If it is not repairable, we will text you. Mom is paddling a two-person kayak. I can always jump in with her."

"What if the water level around Hite isn't high enough to paddle and you have to portage 150 pounds of gear?"

I paused mid-chew and looked at my dad with wide eyes that said, "Are you kidding me?" He took a sip of coffee. Our eyes connected. He wasn't kidding. He was waiting for an answer. I pulled my phone out of my purse and started sifting through my photos.

"Guy sent me a picture yesterday from the Hite Overlook. Here. See?" I flashed my screen at him. "Plenty of water. It's a flowing river, for crap's sake. We won't have to portage."

"What if your food gets wet?"

"Then we'll have to eat all the potato chips right away!" I joked. "Mom will carry half the food. I'll carry the rest. At any time, one of us has about ten-days' worth of food."

"What if an animal eats your food?"

"Mom has peppermint oil for the packrats. I'm sure a bobcat or coyote has tastier things to eat than our freeze-dried lasagna. Like rats."

"What if you get cold?"

"Based on our trial run, I bet we're going to feel warm most of the time, especially while paddling. I'm sure there will be times when we will be cold, though. I'm bringing the same clothes I wear in Acadia National Park [in Maine] in the dead of winter. My sleeping bag is rated to zero degrees, Mom's is a minus thirty. Plus, we'll have plenty of hand warmers."

"What if you fall in?"

"We'll get back in the kayak or on the board." I rolled my eyes. "Or swim to shore. If we're cold, we'll take off our clothes, change into dry clothes, make tea, and start a fire if we have to. We can cuddle in a sleeping bag if it gets bad. The water temperature should be in the high fifties. We'd have about an hour or two before hypothermia sets in."

"What if you get separated?"

"At no time will one of us be out of sight of the other. Not for scouting purposes. Not because of our physical capabilities. Not for any reason within our control."

"What if I don't hear from you in four days?"

"We will be at Halls Crossing in four or five days, so we will find a way to check in there even if we've lost communications with the Garmin InReach. Don't worry until you hear something from us."

"What if the InReach stops tracking you, and I can't see you online anymore?"

"Don't worry until you hear something from us."

"What if I get a cryptic message from you?"

"Don't worry until you hear something *sane* from us."

We reviewed what would trigger the need for Dad to contact the authorities on our behalf. He had already called the Glen Canyon National Recreation Area ranger station to inquire whether the National Park Service (NPS) patrolled the lake on a regular basis. They did. Dad had also talked with Tony at the Halls Crossing Marina to see if they accepted overnight deliveries. They did. Dad confirmed he could order us anything we needed, if needed, and we could pick it up at the marina's office as we passed by.

"All I ask is that you bring Mom home alive," Dad said at our final breakfast get-together.

I thought, "Hey, what about me?" But didn't say it.

"We will make the best decisions we can with the information available at the time," I said, pushing my hash browns away from my scrambled eggs. "We will not push things. We will not make stupid choices to beat an arbitrary clock. We just need to be back before our food supplies run out. Which, based on my calculation, will happen sometime in 2050."

"But if Mom decides to do something stupid," I said, pointing my fork at Mom, "like she gets too close to the edge of the cliff as she tends to do, and falls off, that's her decision. I can do nothing about that. You know as well as I do, I cannot stop her."

"I'm not going to go near any edge of a cliff," Mom chimed in. "I will be safe, I promise."

"I'm assuming you won't be on any cliffs," Dad said.

"We should be on the water or a sandy beach. That's it," I said.

I knew, no matter what responses we gave or how many times we told him he shouldn't be concerned, Dad would feel edgy until our trip ended and we were home safe. Worrying was a full-time gig for him. My dad's concerns concerned me, which, of course, only made him—and me—more concerned. Maybe Dad was onto something. Maybe we were in over our heads.

Let's face it, it's not like Mom and I were experts in paddling. Less than six months ago, I hadn't even owned a paddleboard. Mom hadn't steered the ocean-going kayak until thirty days ago. We were borrowing dry bags. Neither Mom nor I had camped out of our water vessels overnight until a month earlier, and we only had done so for two nights during our trial run. Even on previous backpacking trips, neither of us had slept outside for more than four consecutive nights. We had signed up ourselves for at least thirteen.

My emotions oscillated like a hormonal teenager. I mean, we were *only* paddling across a lake. How hard could this be? The next minute I teetered into, "What in the hell are we thinking?"

I compensated for my anxiety by overanalyzing, well, everything. Churning in a constant state of scrutinizing, calculating, and preparing is how I had always believed I controlled my success. I was my father's daughter after all.

In high school, I watched tapes of my opponents' volleyball games. I tracked each player's every move and outcome on a homemade spreadsheet on graph paper. Who served the ball to which position? Who passed it where? Who hit it across the net and against how many blockers? I outlined how I would respond, so that the next time we played their team, I could anticipate their actions. We'd win, of course, which I attributed to my perfect execution of my perfect little plan.

At Intel, I plotted to a nauseating level. I scheduled everything but bathroom breaks and breathing on a Gantt chart. After my teams delivered projects ahead of schedule or under budget, management promoted me for my "attention to detail," "flawless execution," and "achieving the highest standard of excellence"—all Intel's core values listed on my badge. One of my annual performance reviews highlighted that "Colleen is a recognized project management role model." *So they say.*

I also planned my wedding in April 2001 on a Gantt chart. Of course, it, too, was delivered impeccably on time and under budget. Bias be damned, the event was the very definition of perfection. So was the Gantt chart.

Micromanaging every logistical detail strengthened my confidence in our abilities to paddle 141 miles into the unknown. I spent hours studying maps, guidebooks, and Google Earth to determine our possible camps. I calculated and recalculated our anticipated daily paddling mileage on a spreadsheet. But had I planned enough to guarantee our success? I studied the maps a little longer.

As the trip neared, our intentions started dribbling into conversations with friends and strangers. The more people I told, the more we talked about it, the more real the imminent adventure felt. Besides, if "everyone" knew about the trip, how could I escape from beneath the heavy foot of societal pressure and wimp out?

(This was the same reason I *avoided* telling people about my split from Craig. I didn't want it to be real.)

While I received ample encouragement and support, I also endured plenty of odd looks and raised eyebrows. Some brave souls came straight out and asked, "Are you crazy?" I once responded to this with "Not clinically. But I recently bought a selfie-stick to use with my new GoPro video camera while on the lake, so that may affect my status."

The comical comments from doubting Thomases and nervous Nellies made me laugh and then check my head for loose screws. In the end, I shrugged off those who said I couldn't or shouldn't do it—just as I'd done with teachers, classmates, coaches, managers, and strangers. They, whoever "they" were, just gave me sizeable doses of motivation to proceed. I wanted to prove the naysayers wrong, to prove that I could and should do this—and to prove that I was, in fact, finally good enough.

In the final days leading up to the trip, I scurried through my final to-do lists. Answer emails and clean up my inbox. Update my voicemail greeting. Call close friends to say adios. Let important clients know I'd be out of town. Review my packing list for the 222nd time. Set up my Garmin InReach tracking device to share messages with my family and

One last gear check in my parents' garage on November 22, 2015 before departing for Lake Powell. Photo by Jacque Miniuk.

friends so people could track us. Answer more of Dad's questions. And finally, meet with Craig for dinner. We didn't reconcile, as I had hoped, as I always hoped. At least he wished us luck on our trip and offered his help if we needed it.

My parents and I spent a sunny and warm Sunday afternoon packing their 4Runner at their house, which was a quick twenty-minute drive east from mine. We stacked dry bag after dry bag into the backend, then tied the kayak down on top of the SUV. I admired our packing job. How little we could boil life down to for fourteen days.

We left for Blanding, Utah, a small and sleepy Mormon farming community, before Monday morning's rush hour. On Tuesday morning, I opened my eyes and stared at the hotel room's white popcorn ceiling. A blank slate. A new day. A new beginning. Under my own power for the next fourteen days with my sixty-four-year-old mother. For 141 miles.

"Happy unbirthday," I whispered, tossing the covers aside. "Let's do this."

"Only dead fish go with the flow."
~Old saying

PART II:
IN THE FLOW

LAKE POWELL:
FROM NORTH WASH TO HALLS CROSSING

Artistic rendering only. Map not to scale and should not be used for navigational purposes.

8
CHARGING AHEAD

Day 1: November 24, 2015
Miles 141 to 131, from the North Wash/Dirty Devil Takeout to Fourmile Canyon

Dad looked at the temperature gauge on the 4Runner's dashboard. Thirty degrees Fahrenheit. A few minutes later, he checked again, this time by wiping his thumb across the display as if freeing it of dust would reveal a different answer. It did. Thirty-one degrees.

"We'll be fine. Please don't worry," I said, turning to him from the front passenger's seat. Mom patted Dad's shoulder from the back seat.

She and I repeated this and other similar sentiments on our drive from Blanding to our launch site in the early hours of November 24, 2015. An open road can aggravate the open space of a restless mind. We had eighty-five miles to cover.

State Road 95 traveled into the heart of the Colorado Plateau, connecting the lush farm fields south of Blanding with the "blink-and-you'll-miss-it" blip on the map called Hanksville. The road is also known as the Bicentennial Highway. Calling it a "highway" is a misnomer. The two thin lanes snaked through the desolate pinyon-juniper woodland hills of Cedar Mesa and Bears Ears National Monument. As we passed the turnoff for Natural Bridges National Monument, the thick forest of trees dissolved into naked undulating hills of white sandstone, which grew into a fantastical theater of red rock cliffs, buttes, and spires as we neared Glen Canyon National Recreation Area. Tufts of browned desert grasses rimmed the one-inch shoulder. Not a single hotel, gas station, or restaurant exists along its 121-mile stretch. No rest areas either. It's where the wild things live, where coyotes and bats and bighorn sheep outnumber people. Not a single vehicle passed us in either direction during our two-hour drive. The road was so devoid of human presence, we could have easily been the lone survivors of the apocalypse.

The road eventually curved around, over, and past the Dirty Devil River, then between a forty-foot-tall tower of sandstone (informally known in the river community as Boat Ramp Butte) and its flat-topped mother plateau. This cut in the rock was our cue. I sat up taller in my seat to spot the unmarked turnoff on the left just beyond the passageway. I pointed to ensure Dad saw it too.

"We're here," I said.

A few minutes before nine, Dad turned into the small and otherwise unremarkable gravel parking lot known as the North Wash/ Dirty Devil Takeout, or the "Rafter's Takeout." It was empty save for two vault toilets both adorned with a "Closed for the Season" sign on the door. Had it been spring or summer, the lot would have been filled with four-wheel-drive trucks with winches and boat trailers waiting to pick up river rafters who had completed their multi-day run through Cataract Canyon. This place marked the end of their river journey. For us, it was just the start.

Under a vibrant cyan sky, I stepped out of the 4Runner and walked to the graveled shore of the rustling Colorado River. Four-foot-tall silt terraces capped with swaying tamarisks lined the narrow channel. Her caramel waters were laden with sediments from iron-oxide-rich rocks in the Glen Canyon Group and mud from the trickle of the Dirty Devil River upriver. Millions of years of history—burdens of the past—moved downstream quietly and effortlessly. The water gathered and curled around an elbow bend, then disappeared into the base of reddened rock towers and cliffs.

Any nerves I had were calmed the second I saw the Colly Raddy again. I had waited eight months for this, for the winter sun to spotlight a new path for me, for the river to hold the weight of my past and sculpt me like the landscape around her. Did the river have enough persistence and patience to make me as beautiful as the cliffs surrounding me now? I watched bubbles bob in the current. We were about to find out.

I walked back to the car while stripping off my jacket. "Let's get a quick photo of us with the kayak on top of the car before we unpack."

Mom, Dad, and I posed for the requisite "We Were Here" photo, then I repositioned my camera and tripod near the water to record a time-lapse video of us loading the boats. I hadn't finished dialing in my settings before I heard a vehicle speeding into the parking area. I grinned and waved. I had invited one other person, one who would understand and appreciate the significance of this moment—and one who lived only about two hours away from the ramp—to see me off on my fresh start.

Guy and his persimmon-colored Australian cattle dog, Millie, spilled out of his truck. Millie trotted over to me and buried her nose between my legs. "Hi, Miss Silly Millie!" I said, bending over to scratch her belly.

Guy followed close behind. "Mom. Dad. This is Guy and Millie. Guy and Millie, this is Jacque and Bob."

"We've heard so much about you," Mom said as she hugged him. "Thank you for helping Colleen through these last several months."

"She's helped me too," Guy said, shaking my dad's hand.

"Hey, that's what friends are for, right?" I hugged Guy.

After a few more pleasantries, Mom clapped her hands and chirped, "Okay! Let's get moving." She popped the tailgate open and started pulling dry bag after dry bag out and into a pile on the rocks.

I loaded my paddle, an extra paddle, and three of my bags filled with clothes and other personal belongings on the front of my board. On top, I carefully tied down one of our most critical supplies: a hearty supply of cabernet sauvignon by Black Box Wines, which, true to its name, came in a convenient black box for easy packing. Mom tucked the rest of my gear and hers into the small compartments in her kayak like a squirrel storing nuts in a midden for the winter.

As Guy (far right) and Dad look on, Mom and I pack our gear before launching at the North Wash/Dirty Devil Takeout along the Colorado River in Utah on November 24, 2015. Guy's dog, Millie, is in the water next to Mom.

Minutes after Mom and I launched from the North Wash/Dirty Devil Takeout along the Colorado River. We are floating backwards here. (I realized quickly after this photograph was made that, in the excitement of our departure, I had forgotten to put my life vest on. I remedied the situation immediately.) Photo by Guy Tal.

"I guess that's everything?" I said, looking around the ramp.

"Wait, one more thing," Guy said. He walked to his truck, grabbed a stuffed reusable grocery bag, and handed it to me. "Don't look now, but it's for your trip."

"How exciting!" I squealed. "It's like it's my birthday! Thank you!"

I strapped in Guy's gift on top of the boxed wine. We snapped several more celebratory photos along the water's edge. We hugged and shared well wishes for the days ahead, then hugged again and shared more well wishes.

I turned to face the muddied Colorado River. One stroke of a paddle was all that separated months of planning the adventure and turning it into reality. It was time.

Dad helped Mom push her loaded kayak partly into the river. Guy helped me do the same with Lir. I waded into the shin-deep water, then sat down on my loveseat. I jabbed my paddle hard against the gravel to shove away from land. The plastic-coated needle nose barely moved. I leaned back to release any extra pressure on the front of my board, then pushed again. Lir grated and scraped against the rock. Then we suddenly let go. The shore released me from my past and into my future. Backwards.

Mom followed, backwards too. A few seconds later, the fast-moving current turned our bows forward almost simultaneously to face the wild unknown as if to say, "This way, please."

"Holy shit, this is really happening!" I shouted. "Mom, we're doing this. Can you believe it? Whoohoo!"

We were free. I was free. I was *finally* free. I wanted to cry.

I turned to face Dad and Guy one last time and cupped my hand to wave like the Queen of England. "I love you!"

Oh, no, no, no! What I meant was…

I panicked. I wanted my dad to know that I loved him should anything happen to us, but I could not bear to qualify the statement with "Dad" while my best friend Guy stood there next to him. Did Guy understand the context of my comment?

I *did* love him, as one of my best friends, for the support and advice he had provided me since April. The fireside chats about "the big Life" in beautiful places. The philosophical debates about the meaning of freedom over email. Encouraging "Way to go!" texts from him when my biggest accomplishment for the day was getting out of bed. Guy had become my BFF, my spiritual guide, my divine intervention. With a declared "spit and shake" promise to look out for one another in Moab, we had helped save each other—and ourselves—from falling into our wells of despair time and time again.

Of course, I loved him. But not like *that.* The river pulled me away. I left the ambiguity lingering in the air.

Mom and I paddled in tandem at the base of 500-foot-tall tawny cliffs topped with bare rounded and folded sandstone and jagged overhanging blocks of rock. We followed the curve to the south, then straightened our course, passing Hite Marina's now-defunct boat ramp to the east. The long concrete slab fell short of touching the water's edge by about one hundred feet. It looked like an abandoned airplane landing strip isolated among overgrown tumbleweed and tamarisk.

Minutes later, we reached the mouth of North Wash, a dry drainage joining the river from the west and the site of the drowned historical miner's camp of Crescent City. I looked over my right shoulder and up to the top of the surrounding precipice, shielding my eyes with my hand. I saw a silhouette of a person barely poking out of the bluff, as obvious as a lone tree in a treeless desert landscape. I knew it was Guy.

The Hite Overlook was located only a couple miles to the west of where we launched—and on top of the sandstone towers we were now sailing by. Guy said he would stop at the scenic viewpoint on his way out and snap a few photos of us from the aerial vantage point. (After the trip, I learned that Dad had joined Guy at the overlook, although we had not spotted Dad there from the river.) I wondered how big—and by that, I meant small—we looked in the sprawl of river and rock below.

"Guy!" I waved, hoping he'd catch my movements with his observant eye. "Hey, Guy!"

I suddenly felt disoriented and started falling forward. "Oh! Oh no!" I yelled. I dropped to my hands and knees on top of my bags.

"Colleen!" Mom called out.

View of Mom and I—the two blips on the bottom right on the Colorado River—from the Hite Overlook, looking upstream. The North Wash/Dirty Devil takeout, where we launched, appears near the top left by the cream-colored rocks along the channel. Photo by Guy Tal.

"Pay attention, or you're going to fall in." I steadied myself, then stood back up, brushing off a few splashes of water from my pants. "That's not how you want to start off, is it?"

I glanced over my shoulder. I whispered a simple, "See ya in a bit." Whether Guy saw me would have to wait two weeks. It too would linger in the air.

Just as I caught my breath, Mom started patting her life vest. "Where's my camera?"

She wriggled from side to side in her kayak. "I hope I didn't leave it on the beach."

She opened one bag, then another, then another. "I just need to get settled in here," she said. "It's so stressful just getting ready, getting everything packed up, and all."

"Do you know the best place to leave all that stress, Ma?" I asked.

"Where?" She didn't look up.

"On that shoreline back there. Leave all of it—stress, worries, everything—back there," I said, pointing the tip of my paddle toward our launch site. "This is our time now. Our time to have fun. Besides, we don't have any more room in your kayak or on my board for that kind of baggage."

"I'll find it here somewhere," she said, stuffing loose gear back into her bags. "Or I'll just use my iPod Touch."

"I have my two cameras and a GoPro," I said as I kicked my pile of dry bags. "You can borrow any of them anytime you want to."

"I'll figure it out," she said, picking up her paddle.

I rested my paddle against my shoulder and then reached into the right pocket of my jacket. I pulled out a folded piece of paper. "Hold up, Ma. Guy wrote a meditation for me. I've only read it once before when he sent it to me last week. I'm going to read this to us."

I looked ahead to be sure I would not run into the muddy bank if I stopped paddling for a few minutes. "Are you ready?"

"Yeah, let's hear it," Mom said.

"A meditation for your time on the river," I started.

> Hold nothing back. Put it all on the line. Rethink everything without preconceived answers or expectations. Ask and let the answers come to you, in their own time, in their own way and in whatever form. Question the things you never dared to question before, then keep your mind and your heart open, and let the answers be what they will be. Don't look for the obvious, don't look for omens, don't look for revelations or strokes of insight, don't look for anything, just be. Expect nothing. You may receive answers to questions you did not even know to ask.
>
> Don't allow small discomforts and frustrations to distract you from the magic. The magic will be all around you, all the time. When you realize you can't see it, realize also that the barriers are within you. Let them go. Tear them down. Push them out of your mind. Every so often during the day, close your eyes and turn your face to

the sun and smile, even if you can't think of a reason. At night, set aside time for silence and look deeply into the stars, and remind yourself of the immensity of it all. You are not here to change the world. You are here to be changed by it. Let it change you. Allow yourself to change, but don't force it. Trust that you will. You may not always know when it happens. The seeds of change might take time to germinate and blossom, and you may not realize they are even planted until much later. Offer fertile soil for them, and see what takes root. In time, you will know.

Experience first, be present, savor and admire and indulge in whatever feeds your soul and gives you joy, and don't overthink anything as it happens; there will be time for that later. Do not consume experiences; allow yourself to be consumed by them.

Protect your solitude, if only within. As much as you can, keep your thoughts elevated and pure and free of anger and sadness and anxiety. Let your thoughts flow out of, and into, every part of you. Write down the ones worth keeping. Should you find yourself in the throes of darkness and despair—take charge, hold the demons at arm's length, and study them closely and objectively for anything of value, then toss them in the river.

Be yourself, even if your self turns out to not be the same self you always were or thought you were. Then lose yourself again in thought and wonder until it comes back to you in whatever form. Repeat as necessary. Allow yourself to break down into tiny pieces, then put together the ones that are worth keeping. Mark the graves of those that are not. Thank them for their part in getting you to where you are, and say goodbye.

Marvel at everything. Seek beauty and joy and magic in everything. Don't be afraid to cry.

Mom kayaks along the striated red cliffs called The Palisades.

I refolded the paper and put it back in my pocket.

"That was amazing," Mom said. "He wrote that?"

"Yep. It's brilliant." I took a stroke, then waved my paddle-free hand across the sky. "Here we are, Ma. This is the big Life with a capital L. This is our life for the next fourteen days. Enjoy the hell out of it."

The river bowed again, this time a sharp ninety-degrees to the west. I looked back. What seemed so big and overwhelming when we launched now looked so small, even trivial. Individual fragments of rocks we first saw as pleated, dimpled, and pocked melded into an almost featureless ridgeline of bald plateaus stretching across the horizon. The sinews of the desert transmuted into a wholeness like the details of the last forty years of my individual experiences had faded into a singular memory called "my past." The little voice in my head reminded me never to forget where I came from. After all, the successes and the pain had led me here, trying to make sense of my new reality. Trying to belong to the Colorado River. Trying to belong to myself.

Before the trip, I wondered if we would feel the river's current in the lake. I checked my Garmin InReach to see it had clocked our speed at an impressive 5.7 miles per hour without us paddling much. It made sense. Lake Powell's water level was around 3,605 feet elevation, about one hundred feet shy of full pool. Less lake meant more river.

We coasted past dried mud flats to the north and "The Palisades," a corridor of rust-colored sandstone cliffs, to the south and settled into a hypnotic tempo. Stroke. Stroke. Stroke.

About an hour after our launch, Mom spouted, "You know? This was a good idea."

"Some people think this is a really stupid idea, Ma," I said with a laugh. "I'm glad you don't. Especially since turning around is no longer an option."

"You're afraid to get here," she said without breaking her rhythm. "Then you get out here, and it's ten times better than you thought it would be."

"Only ten times better? More like a million times better. We get to see wonders and places few people have ever seen." I looked over at Mom. "How lucky are we?"

She rested her paddle on top of her kayak and looked up at the cliff walls, now hugging both sides of the river. "If everyone knew just how beautiful it all is when you are out here, everyone would be here."

"And not wasting away in a job they hated, doing things they don't want to do only to make money for things they don't have time to do," I said. "I'd take these wild red walls over those confining grey cube walls any day."

The river broadened, reshaping into the curvatures in the widening and receding canyon walls. The mouth of a bay came into view. Farley Canyon, I believed. I was just about to make a proclamation when Mom said, "You know, I've been afraid my whole life. Growing up especially."

"What were you afraid of?" I said with a grin. Nature was stripping us to our core a mere hour and a half into the trip. Mission accomplished.

"I don't know. I just was," she continued. "When I had you, when you were born, I knew I had to be strong for you. I knew I had to stand up for you and fight for you, so you would have the best life possible."

"Ya done good, Ma. I mean, look at where we are at right now." I circled my paddle in the air in an arc. "This is a pretty great life."

I studied the sixty-four-year-old history written in her youthful gaze. I tried to recall a time when I thought Mom was frightened. I remember her clutching onto me and sobbing after a man tried to pull me into his car while I stood, waiting for the bus, in front of our house in 4th grade. I would never forget the terror in her voice when I was eleven years old and had accidentally hit my head doing a double flyaway dismount at gymnastics practice—even if my eyes were bloodied and swollen shut, and I couldn't see it in her face. Or the panic that ensued after my parents received a random phone call from an unknown man telling them he had kidnapped me when I was seventeen. (He hadn't. I was sitting in my business law class pretending to be a prosecutor in a mock trial when he called.) There was no question Mom's biggest fear was losing her two children and husband. As far as I could tell, though, it was her only fear.

My parents seemed to race into the handful of scary incidents I could recall like Batman and Robin. They cleared the way for me in almost every situation, especially when I needed help or an extra boost.

They may have stepped in a few times when I didn't need the help too, as devoted parents sometimes lovingly do. I attributed many of the opportunities I had—and the achievements that often resulted—to their unwavering dedication to my and my brother's well-being.

Mom paddled her kayak on the river with ease. The memory of her childhood in Coral Gables, Florida, where visits to the ocean and splashing in the surf were as common as going to the grocery store, propelled her. Her arm muscles flexed. Her strength as a dedicated and protective mother left a seam in the river. Even without Dad by her side now, she didn't look scared.

She turned her inquisitive brown eyes to me. "Aren't you afraid?"

I pulled my paddle out of the water and rested it on my board. Stillness helped me digest her question. What *was* I afraid of?

I did not worry, like far too many do, about fulfilling my basic needs. I had no trouble finding my next meal, accessing clean drinking water, or knowing where I would sleep. Privilege had provided me safety and security.

But participating in activities that threatened to kill me or could cause severe bodily harm, like skydiving, BASE jumping, and swimming in shark-infested ocean waters? Those things terrified me. Fear served as a motivator to my ongoing survival. I saw no need to tempt the greedy Grim Reaper.

"I don't know," I said. A knot swelled in my throat. "Craig was my everything. Losing him was one of my biggest fears."

"You lost not only your husband but also your best friend," she said. "That's losing a lot."

"My best friend of twenty-two years and my husband of fourteen." I took a restless stroke. I had been making memories with Craig for over half my life.

As my relationship deepened with him over the years, I had started obsessing about him dying and leaving me to fend for myself. I worried his burdened heart would fail as his mother's did at fifty-six years old. When his work schedule intensified to span twenty-four hours a day, seven days a week—as he moved up the corporate ladder and likely as his dissatisfaction with me increased—I badgered him about how

My view from Lir looking downstream at Mom and The Palisades.
Our conversation about our fears started right about here.

the demands of sitting in an office left him little time to take care of himself and any stress-related health issues. Then in April, Craig was gone. Not from a heart attack but rather by his own decision. Just as I feared, I was on my own.

I had tried to pretend otherwise—and I certainly wasn't going to admit it to my own mother, who had put everything she had into molding me into a confident, independent woman—but now that she asked and I had nothing to do other than paddle and think about it, I feared much more than being a burden on others, being taken advantage of, losing my keys in pit toilets, and murky water. I feared everything.

I had tried to convince her (and so many others) otherwise through the poised, put-together front I showed to the world. Socially prescribed perfectionists like me act not out of trying to be the best but rather out of anxiety of being seen by others as the worst. I feared failing. I feared losing control. I feared saying the wrong thing. I feared not being loved. I feared being exposed as a fraud, that someone would pull back the curtain I hid behind and see how unsuccessful, unlovable, and unworthy I was. Craig hadn't just peaked behind the façade. He had ripped it down, validating my incessant internal narrative that I was inadequate.

I wiped my cheeks dry and drifted back into the cadence of paddling. Ever since Craig and I separated in April, many of my fears had materialized, maybe even through my own doing, by feeding energy into my own insecurities for so long. I had failed. I had lost control over my life. I had said so many wrong things. I had lost love. I wasn't perfect despite trying my damnedest to be. And if the divorce were to happen, it would cement all this into the fibers of my being for the world to see.

"If he leaves me for good, what else is there to fear?" I asked, not expecting Mom to answer. She didn't.

What was fear anyhow? Most of these thoughts were nothing more than figments of my imagination, manifested in a vain attempt to live up to made-up personal expectations and overzealous societal standards. I had let these irrational bullies follow me around in my shadow. Why? Allowing fear to control my actions and decisions was like constructing a big concrete dam in the middle of my flow. How much time and energy had I wasted fighting against the unnecessary pain from something I should have never built in the first place? Fear wasn't going to ever go away on its own. Nothing prevented me from plowing through the dams I had built for myself or even the one Craig was building in our marriage. Except me.

"Yeah, well, I still fear water," I said, bursting out in a giggle. I hoped humor would redirect the conversation away from a difficult topic. I did not want to sink on our first day.

"And here we are, on one of the largest bodies of water in the country." She smiled. "How ironic, huh?"

"That's right." I grinned. "Here we are. Plowing through the fear."

"Let me ask you this," she said a few minutes later. "If you were still with Craig, would you be out here now doing this trip?"

"No. No separation means I would have enjoyed a 40th birthday trip in some exotic locale, which means no Moab, which means no standup paddleboarding on the Colorado River, which means no birthday pie or delicious revelations, which means no idea to paddle Lake Powell, which means no adventure on Lake Powell with you now."

"Sometimes things happen for a reason," she said and smiled.

I laughed. I shouldn't be here. Lake Powell shouldn't be here. Both of us stripped of our identities against our wills, both outcasts in the lives we thought we would have; I couldn't imagine any more apropos place to be than on the Colorado River. Especially given that today, November 24, was the anniversary of the 1922 signing of the Colorado River Compact, when humans separated one river into two parts—the Upper and Lower basins—and determined which states got how much water. Some forty years later, out of fear that the Upper Basin states might not be able to fulfill their water obligations to the Lower Basin states, the Bureau of Reclamation built the Glen Canyon Dam.

No compact would have meant no separation for the river, which would have meant no dam, which would have meant no adventure on Lake Powell for us now. I looked down into her unruffled waters.

I doubted the Colorado River cared whether things happened for a reason, let alone at all.

I then realized I had no idea where we were.

"I haven't seen a milepost marker yet," I said, turning to Mom who was behind me. "Let's pull up at this spit of land on the right to get our bearings."

I knew from my previous trips from Wahweap to the Escalante Arm on southern Lake Powell that navigational markers lined the main channel. A red or green buoy displayed on their sides the approximate distance from the Glen Canyon Dam. Arguably, it would have taken effort to get lost on the narrow river we had been traveling on for the last two hours. At its widest, the canyon walls were no more than a half mile across. But as they flared, and the lake swelled, these critical mile markers would help guide us and keep us on track with our plans. Even as we celebrated our relatively anti-climactic start, released our worries, and swirled in life philosophies, there was no way we could have overlooked them.

"I'll follow you," Mom said as she angled toward the beach.

A few strokes later, I spotted something curious ahead in the water. A clouded contour, where the color of the water abruptly changed from a murky brown into a translucent green, appeared fifteen feet in front of my board, then ten, then five, then two, then one. It spanned across the bay for as far as I could see in either direction. I creased my eyebrows behind my sunglasses. I lifted them and stopped paddling.

"Holy shit! Ma, you have to see this." I turned back to her and pointed to the water with my paddle. "The river. She gives up right here! Oh my god, the river runs out of steam right here!"

I dug my paddle hard in the water to stop on top of the line where the Colorado River conceded its inevitable fate and melted into Lake Powell. No sound. No struggle. Her color just disappeared.

I dipped my left foot into the chocolate milk in a curtsy to thank the river for carrying us thus far. I dropped my right foot into the glistening green water to introduce myself to the lake.

I stared at nature's handshake and shook my head in disbelief.

The confluence of the Colorado River and Lake Powell near Farley and White canyons as viewed from our lunch stop on an unnamed beach.

How could a river as mighty as the Colorado just vanish? How could she just disappear after gathering strength and power along her long journey from her headwaters in Rocky Mountain National Park in Colorado? How could she seem to waste away after the Gunnison, Green, Dolores, and Dirty Devil rivers come together to feed her? For hundreds of miles, she rages full speed ahead into a situation she did not ask for or expect—the Glen Canyon Dam. Faced with a sudden new reality, when the river met the reservoir right where I stood, I wondered, did the river give up or give in? Is she a drowned river? Or an overflowing one?

The Colorado River doesn't care. About anything. The river does not care how she got to this point nor whether she gets anywhere at all for that matter. The river adapts to her new condition. In her altered state, she goes with the flow through Lake Powell until she reaches the dam. There, she waits and waits and waits until she's spewed out of her confinement and into what many believe is the grandest, the most breathtaking scenery on Earth, through the last stretch of Glen Canyon, then on to Marble and Grand canyons. She keeps flowing, dam or no dam, politics or no politics, people or no people.

I circled around the line to float over the top of the transition once more. For my entire life, I had raged full steam ahead through mountains of achievement. Now I stood in the canyon of despair, at the head of a situation I did not ask for or expect—my separation. Dissolving into my shocking and sudden new reality as of April, I wondered, was I a drowned woman or an overflowing one? Would I give up or give in? Would the very thing disrupting the path I had planned set me free and trigger the grandest of journeys of my life?

I heard the river say, "Be the water. Keep evolving as your surroundings change. Do not fear what lies around the bend. Find your flow and see what is waiting for you on the other side of your own dam."

I inhaled the river's musky wisdom in one deep breath.

I surrender. Colorado, please teach me how to be a river.

We pulled into a small cove on the right, just to the north and east of the transition line, finding a wide, clear spot to land among the mix of burnt orange sand, hand-sized chips of broken sandstone, and debris. Stripped tree trunks from previous floods, some as long as a house is tall, were bunched together in almost perfectly arranged stripes from the shoreline to midway up the rocky beach. Each horizontal row of skeletal, intertwined branches laid in repose six to eight feet above the next one. I stepped over a stack of logs to revisit where the river became a reservoir. I stared at the water. My transition from wife to whatever I was now hadn't been as clean or as conciliatory. If only human emotions worked like the river.

I made a few images and then returned to our landing. We pulled out a smorgasbord of snacks from our dry bags for lunch. I licked my fingers free of sticky almond butter to grab the map strapped to the top of my largest dry bag. Mom and I hovered over it and fit the topography around us to the lines on the paper.

"That's gotta be Farley Canyon on the left, White Canyon on the right." Mom tapped the blue veins on the map while surveying our 270-degree view from left to right. To the east, red-stained, rolling hills embraced the wide mouths of both canyons, which were hardly distinguishable at this water level. The Henry Mountains peeked over the plateau to the west. "I think we're here, at the head of Trachyte Canyon."

I nodded in agreement. In less than two hours, we had traveled seven miles, thanks to the river's flow and our own adrenaline.

"I think this is where Fort Moqui and the old town of Hite City used to be," I said, staring into the water.

Despite its name, Fort Moqui, also spelled Moki, was not a fort. It was an ancient stone dwelling constructed by the Ancestral Puebloans sometime before 1300 AD. The twelve-foot walls stood prominently on a sandstone rim near the mouth of White Canyon. Why these Native Americans built this type of structure in this location remains a mystery. It wouldn't be too big of a stretch to believe the wide-open space and life-giving water—as well as the promise of valuable resources—drew them here, the same things that later attracted gold seekers like Cass Hite.

Thanks to the help of a Navajo Indian chief named Hoskininni, Hite found gold here in 1883. Hite then founded Hite City as other prospectors arrived. He also found what he thought was an easy place to cross the river and called it "Dandy Crossing." Travelers who had to ford—and sometimes swim—in the deep river with their wagons, supplies, and animals (and without the assistance of a boat) didn't always agree with that name. In 1946, Hite City resident and gold prospector Arthur Chaffin established a more formal—and certainly a more "dandy"—ferry service for automobiles and passengers alike using a pontoon boat. It was all for naught. By 1969, Fort Moqui, Hite City, Dandy Crossing, and Chaffin Crossing disappeared as the Colorado River expanded into Lake Powell.

I wasn't sure of their exact locations, now that they lived underwater 250 feet below me along the old riverbed. I imagined what life here would have looked like without the reservoir. Was I looking for a piece of the past? Or just peace from the past?

A sudden and dry southwesterly breeze stirred loose grains of sand across the gravel shore. Waves slapped the beach. We had the rest of the afternoon to finish the last three miles of our ten-mile goal, but we wasted no time getting back on the water. In the fresh six- to eight-mile-per-hour headwind, we paddled backward, which gave us both more power to escape our windy cove. We turned around with a couple of energetic strokes once we reached a slightly calmer area in the shadows of cliffs.

With a mild headwind—and now without a current—we slogged past Trachyte Canyon and the thin mouth of Twomile Canyon at a meager two miles an hour. Even though our progress slowed, I felt a sense of pride that we were now moving under our own power. Our unhurried pace allowed us to study our ever-changing surroundings. Truck-sized boulders rested along the shoreline. I imagined the sound they made after they tumbled off the cliffs ages ago, sloughed off by relentless forces of wind, water, and gravity, and shattered into a million pieces—albeit large ones. Methane bubbles rose to the water's surface. I wondered if they came from historical relics gasping for air from the bottom of the drowned canyon. A siege of great blue herons silently intermingled overhead, flapping their wings, attacking only the wind. They seemed to ignore our presence, which suited me just fine.

"I think that's Fourmile Canyon up ahead," I said, pointing my paddle toward a sunlit butte in the distance on the right. "That's where we're supposed to camp tonight. But, from here, those walls at the bottom of the canyon look too high to get in there."

The map had promised great camps in this finger. What it didn't suggest—and I hadn't previously considered—is that the canyon's entrance could be blocked by rocks at this lower water level.

The walls surrounding us soared forty to fifty feet into the sky. I scanned the whitewashed cliffs, their rock bases scarred by the "Bathtub Ring," a calcium carbonate residue left behind by higher waters after the dam's construction. The top horizontal line indicated the high-water mark when the reservoir filled in 1980. Receding waters had left behind a white paint wainscoting around the lake's periphery, an unintended scar from humans trying to tame a wild river.

From our distant vantage point, accessing the canyon did not look promising. I couldn't pick out an obvious break, a mouth, along the walls. We kept paddling toward it anyhow. On the way, Mom spotted the first red buoy on our trip, one marked with a white "132" on its side. She also noticed a sliver of light illuminating a small rock where the mouth of Fourmile Canyon should have started.

"Can we get in right there, by the light? Do you see?" Mom asked.

"It's worth a try," I said.

The chances of us finding a nice sandy beach or a shallow sandstone shelf to camp on in the main channel among the cliff walls and rock falls were as likely as us finding a Ritz-Carlton resort around the bend. "We don't have much choice out here."

I took a deep breath. I hoped I had not screwed this up for us so early in our trip. I consoled myself with the same words I had offered my dad earlier in the day, "We'll be fine. Please don't worry."

As we approached the small inlet of water, another red buoy appeared, this one marked "130." I was glad to see a steady stream of navigational markers along the lake now, but we knew we had not traveled two miles since the last one marked "132" we had passed no more than five minutes ago. Mom and I shrugged at each other.

We paddled toward the pointy sandstone formations and crumbling rock walls near the mouth of Fourmile Canyon. The landscape gradually gave way to more inviting rock ledges that pointed into the narrow channel. Undulating waves slackened. The wind calmed. I felt relieved but not settled. I wouldn't feel truly relaxed until we were in a camp, heating water for dinner, and resting comfortably in our down booties.

Within a half-mile of entering the side canyon, multiple campsites appeared before the water petered out at the base of a ring of serrated sandstone monoliths. Minutes ago, I had been worried we would not find a single camp. Now we were staring at enough options where we could be picky. One previously used site looked too muddy. Another too rocky. The next, too steep to make an easy landing. We spotted a relatively level, wide sandy beach nestled in between two clusters of white boulders near the head of the canyon that could do.

Mind you, this was no tropical beach. First, the sand wasn't white. It was a mixture of beige and burgundy, as rich in color as in a glass of merlot in some spots. The unusual hue came from the Chinle Formation eroding and blending with remnants from its younger top rock neighbors, the sheer Wingate Sandstone cliffs and sloping Kayenta Formation ledges rising above the older slopes. Second, there were no palm trees here. Stringy thigh-high tamarisk and tumbleweed, both thirsty, water-loving invasive species from Eurasia, grew out of cracks in the rock-strewn landscape instead.

"I don't see a tiki bar serving Mai Tais with umbrellas in them," I said, hugging my paddle. "But how does this beach look for tonight?"

"Looks good enough to me," she said from behind.

I had more control landing on shore than Mom did in her larger kayak, so like I had done before on our trial run, I dropped to my knees and paddled onto the barren spit first. I set my right foot into the shallow waters and smiled. We had made it to our first camp.

"PLUNK!"

That wasn't a sound a SUP makes when it lands on a beach. I looked down. My iPhone was sinking to the bottom of the lake. My solar panel battery connected to it was floating on top of the water's surface.

"Oh noooooo!" I pulled the electronics out of the water and threw the tangle of gear onto the sand as if it were on fire. "No! No! No!"

I coddled the individual pieces of gear in my shirt, hoping to dry them before the water seeped into the electronics. My iPhone remained on and functional, but the supposedly waterproof battery lost power immediately. I turned them both off in hopes they would recover.

How could you be so stupid?

At lunch, in order to charge my iPhone as we paddled, I had left the battery and the solar charging panel sitting loosely on top of my board. When the winds hit, I had wrapped the cords around my right leg so the electronics would not get blown into the water. A few minutes thereafter, I forgot about doing so. Until now.

Of all the equipment I brought, the only piece of gear I should have brought a backup for, but did not, was the solar battery. I should have, at least, protected it with my life since we had brought it to help protect ours.

No, really, how could you be so stupid? This could end our trip.

I slumped my neck over my tired shoulders toward my chest, staring dejectedly at the pile. Be nice to yourself. Being mean is not going to solve this. A plan will. Get it together. Pronto. Like, do it before Mom lands on this shore so she doesn't find out.

I peeked over my shoulder to see where she was. Mom, still in her

Our first sunset as viewed from our camp in Fourmile Canyon.

Celebrating the end of the first day in our camp in Fourmile Canyon. Photo by Jacque Miniuk.

kayak, was investigating the scenery as if she were exploring a new house room by room. She seemed oblivious to the disaster that had just occurred. I pretended to busy myself by sorting through the pile and started formulating my next steps.

If the charger does not turn on by tomorrow afternoon, I'll text Dad on the InReach. I'll ask him to order a new battery and deliver it to Tony—the gentleman at Halls Crossing my dad spoke with prior to our trip, who suggested he could get anything to us on the lake overnight. We could pick up the new system at the marina as we passed through that way on Friday or Saturday. Considering Thursday was Thanksgiving, shipping packages might take a little longer, especially to such a remote location. We could afford to stay at the marina an extra day or two through Monday if we needed to. I would start limiting how much I used my camera, GoPro, and iPhone since I no longer had the ability to charge the batteries I brought. No problem, those were luxuries on the lake anyhow. Perfect. Good plan.

I only had to make sure my InReach had enough juice and that it, too, did not fall in the water, at least until we reached Halls Crossing. Then I realized I had also not brought a backup for the tracking device.

UGH! How could you be so stupid?

Based on my usage thus far, I estimated we had three solid days of power left. If I shut down the tracking capabilities, I might get an extra day out of it. We planned to arrive at Halls Crossing in three more days. Assuming my math added up, we could make it. Math had never been my strong suit. In this case, I couldn't afford to be wrong.

We'll be fine. Please don't worry.

"Alright, your turn." I turned around to Mom, faking a smile. "Bring it on home."

"Don't you dare tell your mother about any of this," I said through my gritted teeth.

She slid onto the sand. I bent down to pull the kayak tight to the soft shore. "High five, Ma, we did great today."

She exited her cockpit and went in for a motherly hug instead. "Good job, Colleen, way to go."

In the late afternoon shadows, we unloaded our dry bags and sorted them into piles on the beach. Tent-related gear, clothes, and toiletries ended up in a single stack about fifty yards up the beach. The cooking supplies, propane, and food stayed closer to the shoreline and on our small blue tarp. Camera equipment, electronics, and the remaining miscellaneous gear landed in their own designated place in between the two. By the time we unpacked, it looked like a yard sale. A well-organized one, though.

We slipped into our warmer evening attire—I into my down booties, more for comfort than for warmth. We set up the tent together, carefully positioning it so that both doors (and thus both of us) had equally impressive views of the lake. Mom found her camera right where she had put it—in her fleece jacket pocket—and celebrated the small win by snapping a few frames of our newly established camp. She baptized our belongings with peppermint oil. I started boiling water to hydrate our freeze-dried dinners.

While dining on cheesy rehydrated lasagna and sipping on boxed red wine, we watched the sun slowly release its hold on the summit of the pyramid-shaped mountain across the small channel. A nearly full moon rose in the lavender backdrop of the Earth's shadow on the opposite horizon. It took over where the day's glowing orb had left off and kept a keen watch on the tips of the monoliths until slow-moving, thin cirrus clouds dimmed the silvery spotlight. Darkness crept in.

Fish splashed in the calm waters in front of our camp. At first, we heard a couple of jumps next to our beached vessels, then farther away from the shore. Carp trying to find their own dinner, I presumed. I tried to distinguish a pattern from the sounds, trying to make order out of the seemingly random chaos like I tried to pick up the rhythm and beat of a song I had never heard before. I took another sip of wine and grinned at nature providing harmonious disharmony. Or was it disharmonious harmony?

I yawned, then crawled into my warm sleeping bag a little before seven o'clock. At least it felt like seven. It could have been 6:23. Or maybe 8:14. I had no idea and didn't want to attempt to turn my phone on to find out. Out here, seconds, minutes, hours, days, weeks, months, and years were nothing more than human constructs trying to tame and mark the universe's movement in ways we've defined—and haven't defined—by science. They had no relevance.

Over the past week, given the blend of excitement and jitters surrounding the start of our trip, I had not slept more than four hours a night. Even so, once in bed, I stared at the top of our tent. Mom settled in her sleeping bag and fell asleep immediately.

I adjusted my tired body on my cozy sleeping pad only to notice a blue light emitting halfway down and inside my sleeping bag. As I often do when I camp, I had tucked my phone inside my sleeping bag earlier to keep the battery warm, to prevent it from draining in cold temperatures overnight. I thought I had inadvertently activated my iPhone when I rolled over to get comfortable, but a blank black screen stared back at me when I reached down to it. I turned it on successfully. The blue glow, however, remained unchanged. My heart raced. My battery!

When I had moved my belongings into our tent, I had also slipped the battery inside with my iPhone to see if it, too, would warm up, dry out from its earlier accidental swim, and return to life. I tapped the device to see if I could get the display to come up. No response.

I tried again. Nothing. My heart sank. The blank LCD stayed blue. I clung to hope that the device would somehow charge.

I considered sacrificing one of our freeze-dried chicken and rice meals. Putting wet electronics in uncooked rice is a popular method for drying them out. It works much like the "Do Not Eat" desiccant bag one might find in beef jerky packages, vitamin bottles, and strangely, shoe boxes. I decided using up one night of food for a solution that might not work wasn't sensible, especially since we were likely to lose at least a day or two at Halls Crossing waiting for the new solar charging equipment. We might also face other unknown challenges that could delay us in the days ahead. Besides, it didn't make sense to try to solve a problem I was not yet sure I had.

I returned the charger next to my side then slathered hand salve on my dried and stiff hands. I leaned back into my pillow and fell asleep whispering, "We'll be fine. Please don't worry. We'll be fine. Please don't worry. We'll be..."

9
MORE RIFFLES

Day 2: November 25, 2015
Miles 131 to 129, from Fourmile Canyon to The Horn

Mom and I unzipped our doors simultaneously. Dim blue pre-dawn light filled the inside of the tent. A chill washed over the warm, breathy air that had collected inside overnight. I shivered, then rubbed my eyes.

Angry clouds hovered in the north and east. White cottonballs peppered the sky overhead and then thinned into wispy mares' tails on the distant horizon to the south and west. Cirrus floccus and cirrus uncinus. The two together indicated a warm front, then rain, was on the way. Or so folklore says.

That's not what the forecast predicted yesterday. A cold front, ushering in winds over thirty miles per hour, was supposed to arrive sometime this afternoon. I looked up again. Were we out of the storm? Or heading into it? Who—and what—should I believe?

I turned on my weather radio but only heard static. No signal meant no report meant no answers. I tossed it back in my dry bag. It was dead weight now.

I reached down to test the solar battery. The blue light radiated, indicating a pulse of life. But the screen wouldn't turn on. No solar battery. No weather radio. Was this turning into a National Lampoon's trip in less than twenty-four hours?

"We should take this lake by storm before a storm takes us first." I turned to Mom, hiding my nervousness with a few mock sleepy eye rubs. She had already packed her sleeping gear. I hadn't gotten out of mine. I hurried to gather my belongings to heed my own advice.

Mom wiggled her kayak off the muddy bank. I fell in line behind her. We were on the move again, headed toward Good Hope Bay.

I took a couple of strokes, then caught a whiff of something more pungent than the dank aroma of wet mud. I turned my head into my armpit, then cringed. In my rush to pack up, I had forgotten to comb my hair, brush my teeth, and put deodorant on.

"Oh well! I ain't competing for the Miss America Pageant out here," I mumbled to myself.

Only one person would likely come within sniffing range of me today. I doubted evaluating my personal hygiene was high on Mom's list of things to do while we were out here. Besides, she had seen me in far uglier and far smellier conditions throughout the course of my life. Poop. Piss. Blood. Snot. I didn't have any of those four things smeared on my body at the moment. I laughed. That made me the best smelling thing out here.

"Wouldn't it be great if we had these conditions all day?" she said as I pulled up next to her.

"Gahhhhh. Don't jinx us in the first five minutes of the day." I eyed the dark clouds starting to collect in the southeast. "Besides, I'm not sure we'll be so lucky."

Water lapped against the smooth pale white boulders jutting out of the water at the mouth of Fourmile Canyon. An occasional light breeze teased us as we re-entered the open main channel. Five minutes later, as we veered east, waves splashed over the top of my gear. A hurling crosswind nearly pushed me off my board.

"Don't fight the wind. Let it take you," I yelled, even though Mom was no more than twenty-five feet away.

"Go toward that point." I pointed toward a knob on a distant plateau called The Horn.

I sat down on my inflatable chair. "I'll meet you there."

I glanced over my shoulder. Mom bobbed her way over the two-foot whitecaps toward the southwestern shoreline. I wanted to follow her lead, to go forward and to the right. The winds wanted me to go backward and to the left.

I took twenty hard strokes on the left side. One stroke on the right. Twenty more on the left. One stroke on the right. Counting strokes made me feel like I was making progress even if I wasn't. It took another right pull, then twenty more lefts, before I met up with Mom on the southern edge of the lake.

We continued together along the bases of a hundred-foot-tall cliff walls dwarfed by thousand-foot-tall cliff walls until we came upon a protected cove on the right. We landed on a rocky, steep beach beneath a flat-topped butte rising 250 feet out of the water. It wasn't an ideal spot to stop—it looked like a moonscape—but it offered enough protection from the wind that we could have a conversation without shouting.

"Whew, I'm tired. Tough conditions out there," Mom said, anchoring her kayak to the thin base of a tamarisk at the top of the rock mound. "I almost rolled."

I nodded, feeling too drained to put together a verbal response. I tied my rope to hers, then untied my day bag from my stack of gear. Before unpacking anything, I sat down and leaned back into a loose pile of white-stained cobble to catch my breath.

I pulled the solar panel from my bag and plugged it into the battery charger. I prayed the circuit board had dried out and regained life over the course of the morning. It hadn't. The blue light had remained on, but it was brain damaged.

I rolled onto my side to discreetly text Dad on the InReach. Just as I had outlined yesterday, I asked him to buy a new PowerMonkey Extreme solar battery charging system with the Aquastrap and send it to his Halls Crossing contact. "Pick up on Fri., Sat., Sun., or Mon., OK," I wrote, not knowing if or when he could get the new panel to Halls Crossing—or even when we would arrive to pick it up.

I received an immediate text back from him acknowledging my

Pumping water at our first stop in a semi-protected cove on Day 2. Photo by Jacque Miniuk.

request. Fifteen minutes later, another message came through to confirm he had ordered and shipped the package to Halls Crossing overnight.

That seemed too easy. I imagined Dad sitting at home watching our progress from the InReach tracking on the computer screen when he received my message. I smiled knowing he was an even greater part of our journey now. Superman to the rescue! I set the battery on the rocks, rocked onto my feet, and joined Mom—Superwoman—to help pump water.

"Were you able to get your iPhone and all your other electronics charging?" she asked.

I looked down at the water. How did she know? Did she know? Do all mothers have Spidey sense?

"Well...we had a little hiccup with the solar battery yesterday, but I have it all worked out now." I paused to gauge her reaction. Nothing. She kept pumping water.

"I've been trying to get it to work, but I haven't been successful. The blue light turns on, but I can't charge anything."

Pause. Still no reaction.

"I texted Dad," I said. "He's already shipped a new one to us. We can pick it up in Halls Crossing in a few days."

"That's good," Mom said, finally looking up and closing the lid on the now-full water bottle.

"Based on our current power consumption, we'll lose tracking abilities on the Garmin in the next one to two days," I said, trading her the full water bottle with an empty one. "I'm going to turn it off when the battery gets around the twenty-five-percent level so that we can make an emergency call if needed."

"Sounds good," she said, still pumping, still nonchalant. If my battery blunder fazed her, she wasn't showing it. She maintained a firm poker face.

"Yeah, let's just hope it all works out," I mumbled under my breath.

In the time it took to fill four water bottles, the winds seemed to settle down enough for us to try paddling again. We tucked our gear back into our dry bags, eager to make more miles than the two we had. "Each stroke we take gets us one step closer to our goal," I said to Mom but intended to give myself the same pep talk. I slapped the tip of her paddle blade with mine. "We can do this!"

We launched and paddled uncontested for a few hundred yards down the lake, tracing the shoreline of a thin peninsula comprised of alluvium—a mix of loose gravel, silt, sand, and other sediments. When we started to round the lowlands at the base of The Horn, a fierce headwind moaned against the sandstone walls and brought our vessels to a halt. Tumbleweeds bounced off the shore and skipped across the water's surface. Foam and spray drifted in the air, a foggy mist spinning and floating like ghostly apparitions in front of the flat-topped plateaus. The wind whistled through the skeletons of dead tamarisk trees in the shallows, making them bend from side to side.

Tears from the piercing wind streamed from my eyes. I looked to the rocky shoreline on the left, then the right. I couldn't see any place

Cirrus floccus clouds formed as we unloaded some of our gear on an unnamed island, one we called Gilligan's Island, near The Horn.

Mom repairing a hatch strap on her kayak with Leukotape on Gilligan's Island.

to take refuge within the next mile or two. Didn't matter if I could. We couldn't get anywhere in these conditions.

I waved my paddle in the air. "Back to the shore!"

The headwind blew us backward and into a mucky, but flat, landing only a few hundred yards around the corner from where we'd last stopped. Mom heaved her kayak onto the cobble beach. I did not trust our anchor holding in these waves, so I dragged my board out of the water and onto the smooth rocks. I stood up and put my hands on my hips. As long as these winds were here to stay, so were we. For how long, I had no idea. An hour? Two days? Regardless, we would be warm and dry, even if sand pelted our bare skin in a salvo of tiny bullets.

We didn't bother to unload everything in case we decided to make a quick departure. I grabbed my notebook, a pen, an assortment of snacks, and Guy's gift bag—which I hadn't opened yet—then ventured up ten or fifteen yards to a thick patch of dried-out tumbleweed resting on top of the high point on the ridge. At its base, I found a long piece of driftwood with smooth ivory-colored arms extending to the sky, a throne of sorts, where I could lean back and take notes in my journal.

I started scribbling in my notebook, holding the paper flat against the breeze.

"Oh! Oh! Oh, crap!" Mom cried out suddenly.

I looked up. Mom reached out for her sand-colored hat as it bounced across the beach. It flew into the air and dive-bombed into a flotilla of tumbleweeds floating on top of whitecaps about fifty yards offshore.

Before I could yell, "Grab my paddle," which rested right next to her feet, I jumped up, tossed my notebook aside, and hobbled down the beach barefoot. I grabbed my paddle and pushed Lir into the water.

This was not just any hat. It was Mom's favorite hat. Losing it would have been as tragic as leaving a child's security blanket behind at a hotel on a family vacation. Besides, doctors had removed skin cancer under her left eye a few years ago. Ever since, she was diligent about covering up when she went outside. The clamshell brim and neck cape protected her from the sun. As if those weren't reasons alone to save it, we embraced the "Leave No Trace" principle. I wasn't going to leave anything but footprints behind if I could help it. Certainly not Mom's favorite hat.

I pulled against the water as hard as I could while sitting down on my loveseat. The wind pushed waves upstream, in the opposite direction of the river's natural flow. Once I navigated close enough to Mom's hat, I pinned it with my paddle, ushered it toward my board, and lifted it out of the water. After a couple of hard tugs on the left, I faced Mom. I swung her dripping hat over my head like a cowboy spinning a lasso and hollered, "Yeehaw! I got it."

"Whoohoo!" Mom called back. She pumped her arms above her head, then dropped them to her knees as she bent over in relief.

Back on shore, I spun the hat one more time over my head before offering it to Mom with two hands and a regal bow. She attached it to her kayak with a hiking carabiner and several slip knots. Even still, the neck flap thrashed in the wind like one of those spastic inflatable air dancers in front of a car dealership.

Mom recounted "The Great Hat Escape" and patted me on the back as we walked up the beach. I sat and wiggled my butt into the gravel at the base of my makeshift wood recliner. She wandered around until she found a similar roost against a different wooden statue a few yards away and settled in on her back.

I decided to peek into Guy's surprise gift bag. I pulled out a bottle of tequila, one I had won from him in an earlier poker bet, studied the label, then set it aside for later consumption. The next treat was his out-of-print book of essays and photographs *Exposures: Views from Both Sides of the Camera*. I wedged my thumb into the middle of his book and opened it to a white title page. "The Decisive Experience" displayed across it in bold blue letters. I snorted. "The decisive experience? Yeah, I'd say so. And we're only midway through Day 2."

Mom lifted her head. I flashed the page to her. She snickered. "Isn't that the truth?"

I snapped a photo of my finger pointing at the page to show Guy later. "He'll die laughing when I show him this," I said.

Waiting for the winds to stop felt more brutal than the winds themselves. I read pages from Guy's book. I snacked on pita chips. I

How we passed the time on Gilligan's Island: I read Guy's book, and Mom napped. She's somewhere under all those clothes.

tapped my notebook with my fingers. I checked the power consumption level on my InReach. I chewed on my pen. I ate more pita chips.

My muscles, though taxed from the past two challenging hours, did not need a day of rest. We had traveled only twelve miles in our first twenty hours. I huffed. We were already behind in our paddling plan. I wanted to continue downstream. The wind blew upstream. The dichotomy between reality and my expectations—however unreasonable and unnecessary—made me uncomfortable. So did sitting still.

I turned to Mom. "Want to go for a walk?"

"I thought you'd never ask," said Mom, who had been pretending to nap, as she sprung to her feet.

I placed rocks on top of my belongings. "Let's follow the shoreline."

The abrupt edge between gravel and sand along the shoreline guided our path. In less than three minutes, we were back to where we had started. We laughed and slapped high fives. We had unknowingly landed on a 300-foot-diameter island.

We circled the isle again, but counterclockwise and more slowly this time, now that we knew our boundaries. We became "Thing Finders" like my childhood hero, Pippi Longstocking. We stumbled upon a wheel-shaped slice of petrified wood, its smooth face as colorful as a swirling nebula. We studied bizarre etched driftwood patterns resembling the night sky in Vincent van Gogh's painting *Starry Night*. We marveled at how and why mineralization by natural elements caused "this" rock to appear a rich mauve with small white polka dots and "that" rock a pure, but faded, olive green. I picked up five or six pebbles one at a time, studying each of them with as much rigor as a scientist might study cells under a microscope. "Each one is so different but still so beautiful in its own way," I said while petting the top of a polished, red-striped rock.

After rounding the island at least four more times—we had nothing else to do—we stopped to admire our million-dollar, 360-degree view of our sandstone wonderland. The burgundy and golden layers in the rock resembled tiramisu. Or maybe I just craved tiramisu. In any case, having a prolonged layover on a small hill of rock wasn't in our plans, but there were worse places in the world to get marooned.

I turned to Mom and said, as one of my friends likes to say, "This does not suck."

As the afternoon ripened, the winds intensified. Deteriorating conditions made our decision to sleep overnight on what we called "Gilligan's Island" a simple one.

"We'll stay here until the water stills," I said, staring at the waves in the channel. "If the lake settles down and the clouds clear during the night, we can paddle under a full moon."

Mom nodded her head in agreement. Neither of us had paddled during the night before. November's Frosty Moon would rise 20 minutes after sunset, giving us ample light to do so if conditions cooperated.

"If the waters don't calm until the morning, we'll just carry on then," I continued.

"And if that happens three days from now, I'm going to chew off my right arm," Mom said with a laugh.

"And your left one too." I playfully yanked on her left arm. "You're going to need both of your arms to finish this paddle, so find some chips or nuts or something else to eat."

Grim storm clouds gathered overhead. The callous breath of the cold front panted against the back of my neck. A hesitant drizzle dribbled on the water. Tonight wasn't the night to play John Wayne and sleep under the stars. We searched for a place to pitch a tent.

It wasn't easy finding a flat spot on an island shaped like a conical rice hat. We ruled out the top layer which was covered in dead tumbleweed. The steep middle ground was of no use to us either. We headed to the shoreline and zigzagged through the dead tamarisk sticks poking out of the cobble and mud. We tested a few spots by laying the tent's footprint on the ground and eyeballing the angle.

We finally settled on smoothing out a set of small undulating cobble ridges about 20 feet from the water. It was the Motel 6 of tent sites. Clean, simple, just enough room. But there would be no chocolate mints or rose petals atop our pillows.

The skies dimmed. The winds hissed. Mom held the frame of the tent in place while I threw bag after bag inside to help weigh it down. It still bucked with each gust. I climbed into the tent and sat in the middle, pushing our gear to the edges to distribute the weight. Mom darted from corner to corner, staking each one down.

The soft rain stopped, so we decided to skip attaching the rainfly. Mom crawled into her side of the tent. I moved over onto mine and snuggled into my sleeping bag, not because I was tired but because I had nowhere else to go. Through the mesh, I watched the rising full moon illuminate the backsides of darkening clouds, ones I wanted to ignore. Mom saw them too. She turned her head toward me and asked, "What if it rains during the night?"

I scrunched my nose. The loose fabric of the tent slapped my face with each gust. Suffocating was a bigger concern for me at this point. "Then we'll get up and put the rainfly on."

Mom eats dinner on Gilligan's Island.

Mom contemplated for a few seconds. "We could pull the tarp on top of us."

"Yeah, great idea," I said, closing my eyes. The notion that we could keep dry by draping a tarp over us inside—not outside—the tent was absurd. We both knew it too. We were just too comfortable to move.

"We should put the rainfly on now," she said a few minutes later.

"If you want to put the rainfly on, we can put the rainfly on," I said. "One person needs to sit in the tent to ensure it doesn't fly away to Kansas in the next wind gust while the other attaches the rainfly. Which person would you like to be?"

"I'll put up the rainfly," Mom said. She unzipped the tent and was outside before I answered.

"Great, I'll sit here and look pretty." I sat up.

She stepped on one corner of the cover then tossed the loose fabric to me on the opposite side of the tent. I blindly groped for the right hook out my door. "Got it," I said.

"Alright, I'm ready for the stakes," she said.

"I don't have them."

"What? I don't either."

"Last I saw them, they were on the rocks while we were putting up the tent," I said. "Do you see them there?"

"No, I just looked there."

I clung tightly to the flapping rainfly outside while I patted around the inside of the tent with my other hand.

"Found them," I said and handed them to her from my side of the tent. "Under my sleeping pad, right where I do not remember putting them. Here you go."

As soon as Mom finished staking all four corners, the tent stopped shaking. I expected the rainfly to keep us warm and dry. On the other hand, I thought it would act as a sail, and thus, would be more susceptible to the impacts of the wind. I had no idea adding the rainfly would make our home more resilient. You should get out more often, the voice in my head joked.

Mom clambered back into her sleeping bag. I stared at the top of the tent, listening to the wind ride through the darkness. Twenty or thirty minutes passed. The pitter-patter of raindrops started to dance on the tent, the sweet sound of nourishment for a parched desert.

I closed my eyes and said out of the corner of my mouth, "Good call, Ma. Good call."

10
REAL WORLD PERFECTION

Day 3: November 26, 2015
Miles 129 to 113, from The Horn to an unnamed beach across from Sevenmile Canyon

The silence startled me. I sat up in my sleeping bag, turned my ear to the sky, and froze in one sharp motion. No wind. No rain. No waves slapping against the rocks on the shore. I heard nothing. I looked at my phone. 3:32.

I quietly unzipped the tent, so as not to wake Mom, and stuck my head outside. I scanned the landscape. No light. No shadow. It was still. I looked up. A thick coat of clouds had settled in all directions overhead, obscuring the moon. Paddling in the middle of the night without the moonlight would be too dangerous.

I zipped the tent and reset my alarm to 5:30.

My alarm rang. I sat up. No rain. No clouds. Waves sloshed against the graveled beach, stirred by a steady breeze. A moonlit paddle in the wind would also be too dangerous.

I curled back into my sleeping bag and rolled my eyes. Seriously, how hard could it be to get all the variables to behave simultaneously?

I leaned back into my pillow. A half hour later, I poked my head out of the tent and held my palm up to the sky.

Mom rolled toward me in her sleeping bag and asked, "How does it look?"

"No rain. Cloudy overhead, but the clouds taper off to the south. It looks clear where we're headed."

The ghostly moon started fading behind silver-lined clouds rimming the distant red cliffs above Fourmile Canyon. Waves laved against the cobble. A manageable breeze nipped at the tent. I turned to Mom and said, "Looks good enough. Let's do this."

Instead of waiting for water to boil for tea and oatmeal, we ate our lunch—protein bars—for breakfast while packing our belongings. Multi-tasking seemed like a brilliant idea until neither of us could breathe through our full mouths. Mom grumbled, "Oh my, iss sicking to da toff of my mouff." Hard to say, but I believe this translated into "Oh my, this is the best breakfast I've ever had in my life. This tastes just like bacon!"

In the soft blue glow of civil twilight (the time about thirty minutes before the sun rises), we said goodbye to Gilligan's Island—our beloved pile of rocks—at the tip of The Horn. "Boy, am I glad to be off that island," Mom said as we pushed off. "It just made me so claustrophobic."

"I don't know, I think I could have stayed there longer if we needed to," I said. The spot had grown on me. Even though we had spent less than twenty-four hours there, I felt a tinge of nostalgia about our little island. It had taken us in when we needed it and offered us a safe haven, comfort, and intrigue. It was a place just to be. And I could imagine far worse places to be.

"I'm excited we get to see new things today, though," I added. We would soon find out if there were, in fact, better places to be on this lake.

Yesterday's frothy whitecaps had mellowed into undulating rolling waves in the four- to six-mile-per-hour headwind. My sluggish leg muscles ached as my board rocked from side to side. "Come on, now," the voice in my head quipped, "if you were able to stay on a four-inch-wide balance beam doing backflips, you can stay on this thing."

Lir's platform was over two feet wider than a gymnastics beam. My legs perked up, remembering the act of pushing down with my feet and up with my shoulders simultaneously from my youth. My toes curled in my neoprene boots to grip the padded surface. I raised my arms, spreading each to the side to create wings to gain my balance.

"Very good," I said with a laugh as Lir stabilized. "But I am *not* doing a backflip."

The spreadsheet in my pocket suggested we were a manageable twelve miles away from our next planned camp at Good Hope Bay. Manageable, that is, assuming accommodating weather. We were twenty-four miles from our designated Day 3 stopping point in Forgotten Canyon. I had no idea how far we would get considering the conditions, and despite the plan I had carefully constructed while sitting at home on my couch eating Cheetos, I no longer cared. Save for reaching Halls Crossing to pick up a functioning solar battery before I lost power, getting off the reservoir fast was not one of my goals. It's not like anyone, other than my cat, Nolan, missed me. And cats being cats, even that was questionable.

A band of what looked to be calmer water on the opposite side of the channel called to us, so we traversed the open water to the southeastern shoreline to tuck ourselves beneath the sandstone walls. As we closed in on those distant waves, we realized the trickster, Mother Nature, had fooled our sleepy morning eyes with an optical illusion. The bluffs blocked, at least in part, the southerly breeze, yet the waters bobbed just the same on the south side. I wondered if we had made too rash of a decision to leave this morning. I hoped we hadn't been duped by what sailors call a "sucker hole."

In less than a mile, the rigid sandstone blocks surrounding The Horn eventually melded into an orgy of folds, chasms, and mounds near the mouth of the barely noticeable Scorup Canyon. My two guidebooks suggested "no camps" existed along this stretch, but alternating fingers and coves skirted in sand seemed to invite refuge. The fluctuating water level obviously changed the position of the beaches, which made it all but impossible to predict and communicate accurately in a static book or map. What was accessible at our low water level disappeared at higher ones and vice versa depending on the time of year. Low water revealed the past. High water swallowed it.

Three miles later, we latched onto an overhanging rock wall along a skirt of striated ledges beneath the aptly named Castle Butte. We rested for a few minutes, sipped water, and chewed on another protein bar. Feeling spry, we rounded the buff, orange, and pink sandstone hills and paddled into a sprawling unnamed bay where Blue Notch and Red canyons converged.

Everything changed.

The winds suddenly died. The water turned into a sheet of glass. It was as if someone had flipped a switch.

We entered a euphoric dream. It felt like we had jumped aboard a Walt Disney World theme ride, passed through invisible whimsically decorated shutter doors, and plunged into a new fantastical world. It was so surreal, I started singing the Peter Pan song "You Can Fly."

I glanced over my left shoulder toward Blue Notch Canyon to see a storybook scene of light, shadow, and a palette of pastel colors dancing an elegant tango from mesa to mesa, bluff to bluff. The sun peeked out from clearing clouds, spotlighting individual alcoves and arches otherwise hidden among the jigsaw-puzzle patterns on stoic rock faces. It was as if the famed Western painter Thomas Moran was brushing the landscape to life right before our eyes.

I looked down into the perfect mirror reflection beneath my board. I floated on clouds. Spellbinding skypools frolicked on the lake's surface. Water dripped from my paddle, splashing into concentric circles on top of the water's surface. I was an intrusion in this masterpiece, a mere visitor passing through this coliseum of rock. Nothing here was mine to own, yet all this delicious experience was mine to have and to hold if for no longer than for just this moment in time. I tried to paddle gently, quietly. A conspiracy of cawing ravens flapping their wings overhead added their own beat. *Whoosh whoosh whoosh.* Then they disappeared over the cliffs.

"How nice is this?" Mom whispered. "It's like paddling through silk. I feel like I'm hardly moving."

We had measured our speed thus far based on how fast the rocks streamed by us when we hugged the shoreline. In the bay of open water, the only way I could tell I was still moving was by staring at the mesmerizing ribbons of waves streaming from the bow of my board and by watching the clouds scrolling behind the buttes in the opposite direction of our travels.

I tried to count the number of different shades of blue in the sky overhead through my polarized sunglasses. Navy, indigo, turquoise. Azure, sapphire, aqua. Cobalt, cerulean, cyan.

Everywhere I looked, beauty appeared. I held my hand against my face not only to feel the warmth of the sun on my chilled cheek but also to be sure I was still alive. Ecstasy radiated throughout my body. This, *this*, is what perfection should feel like.

In three days, I had surrendered to nature. My soul was melting in her warm hands like chocolate. Right on time too. Scientists call this the "three-day effect." David Strayer, a cognitive psychologist from the University of Utah, and other researchers believe it takes a three-day stay in nature to cleanse one's soul of emails, phone calls, Facebook posts, traffic woes, and the other unfulfilling crap most of us fill our precious daily lives with. During one of his research trips in the wild, Strayer explained, "On the third day, my senses recalibrate—I smell things and hear things I didn't before."

In their research paper on a similar topic, Stephen and Rachel Kaplan, psychology professors at the University of Michigan, suggested spending time outdoors was "...a therapy that had no known side effects, was readily available, and could improve your cognitive functioning at zero cost." I was certainly getting more than my money's worth of therapy out here.

I rested my paddle against my shoulder and squatted down to find my camera to get some quick "happy snaps" and "I-was-here" photos. I sighed. In the morning's mad dash, I had stashed my camera at the bottom of the dry bag now sitting at the nose of my board—unfortunately, and unquestionably, out of my reach. I had put it there in case we encountered more wind and waves later. What seemed like a smart move then now seemed like a poor packing decision. I tried to brush it off. It didn't matter. No photograph could have ever done this scene or sensation justice anyhow. I took as many mental snapshots as possible of what was one of the most idyllic scenes I had ever witnessed.

So idyllic, in fact, I started to wonder what Glen Canyon must have looked like if Lake Powell looked this beautiful. I looked down at the water sparkling in the sun, hoping to catch a glimpse of the rock piles, hanging gardens, and natural bridges entombed in its green translucent coffin. I saw nothing but visions of my own creation.

Stop! Stop wanting more, more, always more. Don't ruin this moment. I could long for the past, even fight for a future, but I had to learn how to appreciate the present moment exactly as it had transpired.

A different, gentler voice in my head chimed in, "Remember your birthday? Be nice to yourself. It can't get any more glorious than right here, right now. Just enjoy this. This is enough."

I glided effortlessly with a dopey grin on my face for who knows how long. The channel narrowed and then expanded into Good Hope Bay as we passed Ticaboo Canyon on our right. Mom, who was wearing her own equally dopey grin, eventually said, "Look, Colleen. There's buoy 125."

"Can you take a picture of me next to it?" I pulled harder on my paddle to propel myself toward the green buoy. "My camera is buried."

I grabbed onto the mile marker, grinned for the picture, and broke the serenity with the most rambunctious "Whoohoo!" I could muster.

"Do you want a picture next to it?" I asked, paddling toward her.

"Nah. I'll get one later."

"Well, if someone remembered to place them all, there are 124 more opportunities ahead." I laughed. "Can you see the next one?"

My mind started comparing our travels from buoy to buoy to running around a 400-meter track. I imagined unfurling one lap around the track into a straight line and then piecing four of them together to comprehend the one-mile distance in between the navigational beacons. I scanned the horizon to see if I could not only spot the next buoy but also to gauge how accurate my track association was. It was like playing "Where's Waldo."

"There it is, eleven o'clock," Mom said.

I could barely see it, the sliver of red blended into the surrounding orange rock. "Good eye, Ma."

Assuming it was buoy 124, we had a long way to go to paddle a single mile. No wonder we got a little jolt each time we saw one. With

Making progress! Photo by Jacque Miniuk.

each one we passed, we were a step—or more appropriately, a stroke—closer to finishing. I did a quick calculation. I *only* had 496 laps around the track left. I grimaced. I didn't want this to end.

Before we reached the buoy, which was indeed labeled 124, we waved to a couple on a small fishing boat across the channel. I did so with more enthusiasm than the chance encounter with strangers a half-mile away likely warranted. "They think they are just waving to a couple of paddlers," I said. "To us, they are the first people we've seen in two days. This is so exciting."

Our lunch stop at Good Hope Bay on Thanksgiving Day. Bottom photo by Jacque Miniuk.

Although we shared this space with herons, seagulls, and fish, the lake had been our private playground. When two humans appeared, I wanted to go give them a high-five. They, too, obviously understood this place and this connection with nature that yielded insatiable freedom.

I tilted my head into my armpit. I hadn't put deodorant on again this morning. Thank goodness for the still air. As much as I wanted to make new friends, I hoped they didn't come any closer to us. I was in no shape for a social engagement.

We lost sight of the fishing boat before we reached mile 122. Near mile 119, we pulled onto a sandy beach on the right on the northwestern edge of Good Hope Bay. Red and white sand from Kayenta, Wingate, and Navajo sandstone rock formations behind us softened beneath our feet. Still no palm trees or tiki bar, though. In four hours, at a lackadaisical pace, we had paddled a few hundred yards shy of eleven miles.

Under an almost cloudless blue sky, we filtered water to fill our water bottles and the kettle for our hot tea and oatmeal. We sat on a patio of gravel at the base of the four-story-tall Good Hope Mesa with an incredible 180-degree panoramic view. An amphitheater of towering pale orange and reddened stone cathedrals hugged the glistening blue-green waters. The lake looked so much bigger in person than it did as a small blue string across the map.

I suddenly remembered what day it was. "Happy Thanksgiving, Ma." I raised my empty travel mug to hers. "What a way to celebrate!"

"Sure is." She put her arm around me. "Happy Thanksgiving!"

"I know we need to conserve batteries, but we should send Dad and the rest of the crew a quick text to let them know we are still alive," I said.

"Good idea," she said.

I moseyed down to my SUP and sorted through my dry bag, pulling out the InReach. I also dug out my camera. Midday didn't always offer optimal lighting for a photograph. Still, I wanted to make some images of this remarkable place and to commemorate the occasion.

I sat cross-legged on the beach, typing out an "All OK" message to my dad, Craig, Guy, and a few close friends watching our progress. (I later learned this same message also posted to my Facebook page accidentally.) "Happy Thanksgiving. All great but will lose track/power tonight. Picking up new solar battery Sat. Stay tuned."

My friend Terry Gunn responded, "Smooth sailing ahead!" I couldn't decipher if his comment was well wishes for the future or a weather forecast. I hoped for both.

Shortly thereafter, Craig chimed in, "Happy Thanksgiving!"

True to his worrying nature, Dad sent a terse, "Turn off tracking to save power" and then a more relaxed second message: "Happy Thanksgiving."

Based on battery consumption, I could track through the evening and still have about twenty percent of power left. I assumed that would be more than enough for me to send an emergency message if we needed. I wasn't worried.

Guy wrote, "Can I help?"

"All good," I responded and set the tracking device aside.

"So, according to my spreadsheet, this was supposed to be our camp last night," I said to Mom while stretching my legs out in front of me. "It can be our camp tonight if we'd like it to be. But it's only a little after noon right now. Should we stay here or keep going?"

Before Mom answered, I had already formed my opinion. I wanted more.

Although we had met our paddle distance goal for the day, it seemed a shame to waste these perfect conditions sitting on a beach, watching a bluebird day and glass-like waters pass us by. Especially after the winds had halted our course so suddenly the day before. That said, the map suggested we were about to enter a twelve-mile stretch of the lake where precipitous cliffs would dominate the shoreline and make it difficult—if not impossible—to find an ad-hoc camp.

"The question is, could you repeat this morning's run? Could you go twelve more miles to Forgotten Canyon if we had to?" I stood up and started walking toward Lir and her kayak. I had no idea where the next suitable plot of land would be ahead—or what we'd find in

Forgotten when we got there. I knew we had about five more hours of daylight left to figure it out.

"I feel great right now," she said, standing up and arching her back to stretch.

"Me too. We said during our trial run in October that if conditions were bad, we'd stop. If conditions were good, we'd keep going," I said. "It's gorgeous out here right now. I'd vote to continue."

"Yeah, we can just stop whenever we find a camp, whether that's in three miles or six or twelve or whenever," she said.

"Exactly." I nodded my head in agreement. "Let's go."

A slight headwind kicked up, but not a strong enough one to deter us, as we pushed away from the sandy shore heading into the unknown. When we rounded a tall spire to the west of Good Hope Bay, the wind paused. I glanced over my shoulder, leaving my paddle dragging in the water.

"Hey Ma, quick. Look back when you get a chance. As soon as we go around this corner, we will no longer be able to see where we came from today."

It felt appropriate to recognize the significance of our decision to leave the safety, comfort, and ease of the known behind in this way. The Horn loomed on the far distant horizon, but Gilligan's Island, Red Canyon, Blue Notch Canyon, Good Hope Bay, and all the thrills we had experienced earlier in the day blended into the obscurity of overlapping mesas, overhanging cliff walls, and rounded sandstone hills. Our past was literally set in stone.

I couldn't help but notice how the shoreline of the lake converged and disappeared into the rock but not before the water thinned into a line and took on the contour of a river. Maybe it was another illusion, or me just projecting my wistful desires upon reality. It pleased me nonetheless. I couldn't distinguish the river from the reservoir beneath my feet, but I could feel the river's presence—her strength, persistence, and the beauty of her handiwork—everywhere around me.

When I started soaking in the immensity of our progress thus far, I realized just how silly this all was. Here I was on a SUP, Mom in her kayak, paddling the length of Lake Powell in the middle of a part of

Glen Canyon few have, or will, ever see. I never dreamed during my childhood, or even a year ago, that *this* is where I'd be at forty years old, that *this* is where the flow of the river would bring me—to water, my biggest fear and now my biggest joy. I turned to face the narrowing channel downstream ahead of us and started deliriously cackling like Uncle Albert in the movie *Mary Poppins*. I had either lost my mind or finally regained it.

Mom pulled ahead of me as the canyon made almost a ninety-degree turn to the northwest about a half mile later. We followed the curvaceous shoreline on the right, drifting together on a conveyor belt past countless nooks and crannies carved into the near-vertical cliffs. I paddled close enough to one wall to run my hand across the warm sandpaper of sandstone as we floated by. A plate-sized slab of calcium deposits from the Bathtub Ring sloughed off and crumbled between my fingers. I cringed at first, knowing I should leave no trace, but then marveled at how easy it was to put a part of Lake Powell's history in the palm of my hand. I called the shedding "an accidental exfoliation of animosities."

In another mile, the channel made another ninety-degree bend, this time to the south. We crossed to the western side to take a more direct route. We hugged the rocky shoreline, where towers capped with bulbous and embroidered sandstone looked on. The grandeur, the barrenness, the variations, it all started to feel like sensory overload. Going a relaxed two-to-three-mile-an-hour pace through Glen Canyon was much too fast. The ageless rocks hid their tumultuous history in every grain, line, crack, and fold. And each house-sized boulder, box-sized slab, and marble-sized gravel carried its own story of how it came to be in this rugged topography.

I wanted to pull up a chair and listen to each of their tales one-by-one. When did *this* happen? What caused *that* scar? What did it sound like when your neighbors sloughed off the cliffs? What did the crash sound like when they met the shore? Did John Wesley Powell gaze upon you in his travels through here? In what kind of light did Philip Hyde photograph you? Did Katie Lee sing about you when she saw you?

The ever-changing views of rocks along Lake Powell's shoreline from Good Hope Bay (mile 119) to mile 114. The Bathtub Ring is visible at the bottom of the cliffs in both photos. Top photo by Jacque Miniuk.

Mom paddling out of Good Hope Bay and into her own contemplations.

How significant something as seemingly insignificant as a single pebble in this eternal canyon became to me. Given the vastness of it all, I wondered how a single rock stood out enough to grab my attention. Whether I noticed it, whether the sun illuminated it for a fleeting moment, or whether a passing storm cried on its shoulder, each rock remained steadfast to its exquisite form, polished over time by wind and water, its beauty embedded in its simple, strong, yet ever-changing existence.

I had never been confident enough in myself to blend in like a rock. I had spent a lifetime trying to stand out, siphoning attention from others to fuel my burning desire to achieve and fan the flames of approval. Even when someone offered an ember of praise, I rarely believed it. When Craig told me how beautiful I was—and he told me often—I brushed him off every time. The negative narrative playing in my head was too different for me to accept his—or anyone else's—compliments. I had puffy cheeks. I had two bucked front teeth and three chin hairs. I had plump hips that no Victoria Secret model would ever envy. I used to think Craig obviously doesn't see what I see.

Not a soul, save for my mother, could see my performance in the spotlight here. My armpits smelled like onions; I had bits of apple cinnamon oatmeal stuck between my teeth; my greying and thinning hair had started to mat beneath my winter cap; and my pants, stained with dirt, had a flapping sand-dollar-sized hole in them. Yet, without notice, in both the light and shadow, I finally felt beautiful in my simple, strong, and ever-changing existence on this lake.

That boulder? Once a cliff. This reservoir? Once a river. This woman? Once a wife. I tightened my knees and straightened my back, then spread my arms out to the side, inviting the wind and water to continue polishing me.

The subtle tint from a tiring sun wrapped a gentle warmth across the front of my fleece jacket. Shadows waltzed from rock to cliff, cliff to canyon, softening and lengthening across the channel. Although it was only two in the afternoon, it felt more like five. By the time we approached mile 114, my feet had turned to lead.

Worse yet, I needed to pee. I wished I had a penis, where I could just whip out the hose and piss off the side of my board with little fanfare. Before the trip, while shopping at my local REI, I had seen those female funnel contraptions that enabled a woman to relieve herself while standing up without having a sex-change operation. I never thought I would need such a device. I had never had an issue digging a cat hole and squatting over it behind a bush. Seeing how I could not perform such an uncomplicated task from my board, I scanned the perpendicular cliffs, undulating slick rock, and jumbo boulders, looking for a crack in the landscape, a beach or rock or shallow ledge—anything to land on.

I was about to give up and hang my lower half off the side of Lir out of desperation when Mom spotted a dimple in the wall ahead and to our left. A tiny, but suitable, sandy beach tucked into a cove at the head of a wash appeared between rounded mounds of Navajo sandstone on the southern shore. After winding through just shy of six additional miles from Good Hope Bay, we had found not only a bathroom with a spectacular view of the mouth of Sevenmile Canyon and a green buoy marked "113" in the distance but also our home for the night.

Mom pulled her kayak onto the flat landing first so that she'd be out of the water while I peed. The water in the small cove was shallow enough such that I dismounted my board into knee-high waters about ten feet from shore and walked Lir in before relieving myself.

Overlapping knolls of sandstone slanted directly out of the lake and rose 400 feet above us on the right. Weathering had created a swiss-cheese-like pattern of small holes, called tafoni, in the surrounding sandstone walls, which looked like two long arms hugging the beach, gradually descended and disappeared into the lake. The sandy spit between them was just large enough to fit a three-person tent and tarp with some wiggle room. Behind us, a steep wash wound its way up a dry waterfall of stones and sparse foliage. I surveyed the solid blue sky overhead. Had rain or clouds—and thus the possibility of a flash flood—threatened, I would have never chosen to camp in such a precarious spot. As the saying goes, though, the coast was clear.

On shore, we started with our camp chores. Set up the tent. Stuff sleeping gear inside. Pump drinking water. Spread out the blue tarp. What was novel and messy two nights ago was now routine and organized.

We finished quickly, allowing us some free time before the sun's pointy rays curled around the distant horizon. We rewarded ourselves with a holiday bath. I tiptoed into our swimming pool-sized inlet up to my knees and bowed my upper body to let my stiff oily hair kiss the cold water. Even in the warmth of the afternoon sun, I shuddered and decided to clean the rest of my body with bath wipes instead.

After wearing my sports bra for three straight days, I declared "the girls" needed to breathe for a little while. As in for the rest of the trip. I was not trying to impress anyone out here, and I no longer cared if society thought my breasts sagged. Besides, my life vest squeezed them into place already. Baring them to the breeze felt as refreshing as drinking a tall, chilled glass of lemonade on a humid summer day. I would never call myself a nudist, but there was something freeing about baring skin in the wild.

We brushed our teeth and put on fresh clothes as if we were preparing to join the family for a holiday dinner. I indulged in one of my seven "Beef Stroganoff" meals while Mom selected a spicy "Mexican Rice Burrito Bowl with Chicken" for her turkey dinner substitute.

While the water heated, I pulled my notebook closer to me. My

Our overnight camp on Day 3 near mile 113. Photo by Jacque Miniuk.

topographical map dropped out of the front pocket. "Look, Ma. We've made it so far." I pointed to the blue sinuous path cutting through the torn tanned paper. "We're on the next fold of the map."

We toasted our cups of celebratory wine, then inhaled our dinners like star-nosed moles. The quantity of food we consumed in such a short amount of time should have put us to sleep in a hurry. For Mom, it did. We hugged, then she crawled into bed. I poured another cup of wine and sat on our tarp. Stars erupting one by one onto the black velour sky seduced me into not giving up on this glorious day so soon.

The full moon rose behind our camp but out of view. It announced its presence by coloring the distant cliffs near Cedar Canyon with orange light. A few minutes later, Luna peered over my shoulder and drenched the rest of the landscape with such luminous intensity it looked like dimmed daylight. The waves gently lapping against the sandstone slowed into silence as if mesmerized by the dancing universe overhead.

Peace and stillness, two things I hadn't felt in months, years even, cozied up next to me. I typed a note to Guy on the InReach. "This is a million times better than expected." That was a gross understatement.

I believed I was coming down with something. To be sure, I walked over to Lir and dug out Katie Lee's book *All My Rivers are Gone* from one of my dry bags. Guy had gifted me a signed copy ahead of my trial run in October. I had already read it twice. I flipped through the many dog-eared pages of my favorite quotes to check on my symptoms. Page 40 read:

> Now another facet of Explorer's Syndrome takes hold. No one can follow you. No one's in front of you. And maybe—just maybe—no one's been before you. *You are alone.* Something clicks inside. Your heart rate quickens. All senses sharpen. You are out of earshot. The only sounds are those of the canyon, the essence of it, pure, distilled.

That settled it. Sure enough, I had contracted what Katie referred to as "canyonitis." I had it bad too. I hoped no cure existed.

I turned to another marked page and whispered another quote from Katie's book, one she had written while in Glen Canyon, into the ear of the land: "How can *anything*, any reality, be this perfect? What have we done to ourselves that we can only find it in rare moments and in rare places? Why can't the *real* world speak to us like this one does to me tonight?"

I gazed at moonlight sparkling on the water. What was the "real" world anyway? The one I was living in now or the one I left behind? Sitting out here by myself felt more real than anything else I'd ever done. I downed the last sip of my Thanksgiving wine, then declared: *this* is the real world. Everything outside of nature, the world where most humans lived, I deemed the manufactured world.

How I wished Katie was sitting next to me to philosophize about this place. I had so many questions for her. Once the rising waters behind the dam filled the bottom of Glen Canyon, she never returned. She sang about it. She wrote about it. She even fought politicians

Moonrise and a starry night from our camp on Day 3.

with fiery expletives about it. But she couldn't bear to even look at the reservoir.

Why didn't she come back to see her old love in its new state? Why did she leave Glen Canyon and the Colorado River behind? Is there a point where the pain of change and loss is too much, too unbearable, that it forces you to give up on the very thing you love?

I wanted to yell into the night, "But Katie! It's not the river's fault she became a reservoir. The Colly Raddy doesn't want to be Lake Foul. She wants to be a river! These are still her waters. The river still exists here. She's not gone."

I closed her book. I wondered if my sentiments were for her…or for Craig. I didn't want to be a reservoir either. I wanted to be a river.

Water, no matter the form it took, had started to pulse through my veins. I might not be the person I thought I'd be at this point in my life, but I still existed. I wasn't gone yet.

11

WHERE THE WIND BLOWS

Day 4: November 27, 2015
Miles 113 to 95, from an unnamed beach across from Sevenmile Canyon to Halls Crossing

Overnight, the winds tickled our rain fly. Our "welcome mats," the plastic garbage bags we each placed outside our tent's doors to keep dirt and sand from coming inside, rustled. I tossed and turned in my sleeping bag. With each gust, each crinkle, I imagined an animal, like a woodrat, gnawing a hole in our tent even though Mom had sprinkled her peppermint oil magic around it before we went to bed.

Just as the morning's sun started giving shape to the top of the cliffs across the channel through the purple haze of dawn, I poked my head out of the mesh door. Juvenile waves splashed onto our little stretch of paradise. A cool breeze out of the northeast grazed my tousled hair and warm cheeks.

"Finally! A tailwind!" I celebrated with a little dance, a wiggle of my upper body and head, before springing out of my sleeping bag.

Making it to Halls Crossing eighteen miles downstream felt like a stretch, especially after our long day yesterday. But no doubt, we could make it to Forgotten Canyon—our next intended camp only seven miles away—in no time in these favorable conditions.

We packed up quickly. Still full from the previous night's freeze-dried feast, Mom and I grazed on protein bars while we gathered our belongings. We agreed to stop for tea and oatmeal for lunch at a convenient spot like we had done yesterday.

Once we loaded all our gear, Mom and I searched for a smidgen of privacy behind a pile of tumbleweeds to take care of our, well, personal business. She took one side. I took the other. Still, we crouched down in clear view of each other. Thank goodness we were related.

I unfolded the contents of my WAG bag next to me and squatted. WAG stands for "waste-alleviation-and-gelling"—although "weird-ass goo" *had* to have come up in their branding brainstorming sessions. This handy package was a sanitary garbage bag filled with a granular substance resembling cat litter that enabled humans to contain their feces while recreating outside in places where modern bathrooms didn't exist. The Glen Canyon National Recreation Area's long-standing regulations demanded that "...every party camping within one-quarter mile of the lakeshore have a portable toilet system for containing solid human waste." Piles of people's fecal matter strewn across beaches would cause serious health concerns in this sensitive place. With its fluctuating water levels, without such guidelines, Lake Powell could be full of crap.

The breeze inflated my bag. I grabbed it with both hands and wrapped it around my butt cheeks, tucking the ends in the squeeze between my thighs and calves as I squatted. "See? It won't blow away if you do this," I said to Mom but looked away, up the wash, to lessen the intrusion.

A few seconds later, Mom yelped and began mumbling incoherent words. I looked through the wiry branches to see her sitting down in her bag on the pinkish sand. She stood up, turned her bare butt to me, and asked while laughing, "Do I have any on me?"

"Um, yeah, right cheek." I tried to respond with aloofness in hopes of affording her some semblance of dignity.

"Shit," she said, rolling her eyes.

"Yes. Yes, that's exactly what that is," I said with a smirk.

She waddled to her kayak with her long johns wrapped around her ankles. "This requires a Wet One."

"I had no idea I needed to be so explicit with my instructions. Like, 'Hey, don't sit in your own shit.'" I giggled. "I thought that part would have been pretty obvious."

While the WAG bag itself was a clever invention, the paltry tissues provided in the package were not. They were smaller than a Kleenex cut in half and then cut in half again. Which meant they were barely big enough for dabbing a drippy nose but certainly not for wiping a dirty booty. On top of that, eating freeze-dried food for multiple days in a row had made our excrement, well, sticky. The square tissue paper clung to my skin like Velcro as I wiped, which only caused an even bigger mess.

"Let me have one of those Wet Ones too," I said. "You know, since you're already up."

Once we finished cleaning ourselves, we each wrapped our personal litter boxes in their accompanying plastic containers and dropped them in our growing garbage. We intended to make our first trash deposit in the receptacle at the floating toilet in Forgotten Canyon when we arrived there later.

We bid adieu to our small Thanksgiving beach just as the morning sun illuminated our spit of sand. The brisk tailwind zipped us past the rocky nose overlooking the mouth of Sevenmile Canyon on our right and the navigational buoy 113 bobbing in the center of the channel. The one-foot swells were just rough enough to prevent me from standing with confidence, so I sat in my loveseat. Except for an occasional stroke to steer straight in the main channel, the wind and waves pushed us almost three miles in less than forty-five minutes.

When we approached the shadowed opening of Cedar Canyon on the left, the wind pushed us across the main channel to the sunlit entrance of Warm Springs Canyon on the right. A glowing 700-foot-tall, mile-long, curved, precipitous bluff—the formidable and imposing Tapestry Wall—came into view ahead on the western horizon. Dark desert varnish dripped down its veneer like paint running down the side of a paint can, its orange coat mixing with the minerals embedded

Mom fighting to keep control over her kayak near mile 110 before we reached the Tapestry Wall.

in the sandstone and weaving a classic plaid pattern of blacks, browns, whites, and auburns—the Glen Canyon Group tartan of the Colorado Plateau. On any other day, in any other conditions, I would have marveled over its magnificence for hours. I snapped only a few photographs of it before a wave crashed into the side of my board and jostled me.

As we neared the head of Tapestry Wall, the lake made a sharp bend to the south. Our welcomed tailwind suddenly turned into an intimidating crosswind. Lir contorted over the growing waves, bending through the troughs and flexing over the crests. I dragged my paddle in the water to serve as a stabilizing brace. Mom's rigid, long kayak took on a mind of its own. The erratic rollers rocked her left, right, left, and backward, then right, left, right, left, and backward again.

Two-foot whitecaps splashed over Lir's nose. I shoved my camera inside the nearest dry bag to protect it from the blowing spray and slid my foot under the tangle of bungee cords holding my gear to the deck. I tugged at my leg strap. If I flipped—and it felt like I might—at least I would stay connected with my board as I had when I fell in the Colorado River in Moab last April.

"Do you know how to undo your spray skirt with one hand?" I yelled over my shoulder to Mom.

"Yes." She demonstrated a flawless one-handed release. Her hands tightened around her paddle. She clenched her teeth.

"Good. Look for a place to pull off. Sand, a low ledge, anything. We need to get off this lake. Fast. Before this gets worse."

The Tapestry Wall now commanded over the waterway. At the head of the tall bluff, bullying waves and huffing winds pushed us toward the cliff's whitewashed base. I stroked hard to the right over and over just to stay straight. Once the ridgeline tapered from a monolithic plateau into a heap of a hundred-foot-tall rolling mounds of petrified sand dunes, we decided to stop fighting. We let the crosswind push us into the open waters and across the channel again, this time to equally steep, but shaded, walls in front of us on the southern side of the canyon. We thought we could find protection by tucking ourselves under the wind. We thought wrong. We had started the day on a moving sidewalk. We were now riding on a roller coaster without a lap bar.

After we passed Knowles Canyon on the east side of the channel, as the lake curved almost ninety degrees to the west, the reservoir transformed into a raging river. The crest of one wave grabbed the nose of my board and hurled me into another. And another. And another. The next wave bounced me off my loveseat and brought me to my knees on the floor of my board. I clawed at my bungee cords with one hand. I clung to the side of my board with the other. Before I could find my seat, the next wave pitched me into the next. And the next. And the next.

Mom drifted twenty yards ahead. "Stay right!" I yelled into the bellowing winds. She was too far away to hear me. The current pulled me further away from her and into the middle of the narrow lake.

Waves exploded like fireworks against the southern wall. One moment Mom appeared on top of a wave. Then she disappeared behind another one.

Then reappeared.

Then disappeared.

Then reappeared.

Then disappeared.

I waited and waited and wondered if this would be the last time I saw her.

A wave shattered off Lir's nose. I wiped my face. Another one slapped me in the face.

She reappeared.

What do I do? I don't know what to do.

My mind squirmed in a straitjacket. We couldn't paddle upstream against the wind or waves. Letting the current take us wherever it wanted to was suicidal. But we had no place to take refuge. Towering cliffs loomed on both sides of the canyon. We had to keep paddling, pushing as hard and as fast as we could, through the turmoil.

I considered paddling next to her and throwing her a rope to pull her away from the cliffs. Brushing against the textured wall could punctured my inflatable board. I could sink.

I couldn't let that happen. I *had* to stay on my board. If I fell off, not only would I likely die, but leaving her alone out here would likely kill her too. Our only ability to communicate with the outside world—my Garmin InReach—dangled from the top of one of my dry bags. If I flipped, it would go down with me. If I drowned, Mom wouldn't know where to look for it. Even if she could find it, she wouldn't know how to activate the SOS button. We hadn't reviewed that procedure in our preparations.

God, how could you be so stupid? I scorned myself for yet another massive oversight.

I knew if anything happened to me, Mom would take desperate measures to save me, her only daughter, one of two children who were her reason for being. In no more than an hour or two in the fifty-five-degree water, she would become fatigued and hypothermic. If she somehow made it to shore, she would be alone in the backcountry with limited food, with little protection from the elements, and have no way to get help. She would die. And it would be a slow, torturous, inhumane way to die. She had demonstrated solid outdoor skills and resourcefulness in other outings. But no extreme situation like this had ever tested her by herself. I had to do whatever I could to stay on my board and stay alive. For both of us.

A reverberating wave pulled Mom's kayak toward the canyon's white-washed wall.

"Mom!" I screamed. I recoiled, curling my shoulders into my chest, wanting to absorb and lessen her pain.

Is this the end? Is this how we're going to die?

I watched in horror as the receding waters revealed a small alcove hiding beneath the water's surface. An incoming wave tried to suck her into the gaping maw. Had her kayak been any shorter, an incoming surge would have crushed her between the wave and the pitiless rock.

She knew it, too. She raised her paddle above her head, forced it against the rock, and shoved herself away from the wall. She let out a terrifying primal scream. Her rage ricocheted throughout the canyon. Wincing in agony, she then paddled as hard and as fast as she could against the waves. It was no use. The next swell pitched her into the cliffs like a rag doll.

"Oh my god! Mom! Don't give up!" I wailed into the spray. "Please, please, please make this stop!"

Before the trip, I had promised Dad that I would bring Mom home. I did not know if I could fulfill what seemed like a straightforward commitment. My stomach churned. Remnants of my morning's protein bar rose into my mouth. I spewed vomit back at the swells.

We had no choice but to go with this terrifying flow. No number of expletives, prayers, begging, or bargaining could change our situation. I could not paddle for her. I could not make the waves, or the wind, die down. I could not make a sandy beach appear among the endless precipices. I could only hope with every part of my existence that she was strong enough to survive.

A small strip of light filtered through an opening in the cliff walls on the left about 200 yards ahead. It looked like a mirage, but I paddled toward it anyhow with all the strength I had. I turned into the slot canyon first. Mom followed several minutes later. The waters were calm in the shallow but deep V-shaped chasm comprised of tall and polished orange and buff Navajo slickrock. It was no place to land a boat. But it was a place to find refuge.

"Are you okay?" I asked Mom, resting my paddle across my lap.

A blank "Oh my god" dribbled from her chapped lips.

"Drink some water," I said while grabbing the side of her kayak and pulling it toward me. "Are you okay?"

She sat still and stared vacantly at the rock. I swirled a drink of water around my mouth, not only to model the behavior I wanted her to take but also to clean the vile taste of puke out of my mouth. After a few minutes, Mom came out of her daze, took a gulp of water from her bottle, and slammed it down onto her kayak's deck. "Oh my god. That was fucking crazy," she huffed with her eyes closed.

My eyes widened. Mom hardly ever swore, so when she dropped the f-bomb, I knew she had been pushed to her extreme. "It definitely was," I said as calmly as I could. "But you made it through. You did awesome."

I glanced over my shoulder at the main channel, still fuming, then looked at the polished near-vertical, white-washed arena of sandstone encircling us. My chin dropped to my chest. I shook my head. We would have to return to the madness. I didn't know if we could physically or mentally handle such a task after what we had just endured. We had no choice, though. We couldn't stay here.

Right before we had turned into this small chasm, I had noticed another strip of light glistening on the water just past the sandstone mound at the mouth of our canyon. "I think there's another canyon around the bend," I said. "Let's make a quick push around this small headland to see if we'll have better luck there. Yes?"

Mom took another swig of water and nodded. I patted her on the back. "We can do this," I said, not certain we could.

We stroked in unison, pushing ourselves into the roaring winds. We bounced from wave to wave, paddling as hard and as fast as we could, straining from crest to trough to crest for at least a quarter mile. On our left, an opening between rounded sandstone hills and pocked palisades lengthened into what looked more like an expansive bay than a canyon. We turned into its wide mouth. The waves lost their whitecaps in the large bay but still stirred and splashed. I had no idea where we were but hoped we could at least find a place to rest, if not a safe overnight camp, somewhere in here.

After taking a few strokes, a snow-colored buoy, bobbing up and down, came into view in front of our vessels. We hadn't seen a white mile marker yet, only red and green ones. As we closed in on it, the words "Forgotten Canyon" came into view across its face.

My shoulders dropped. We had made it to our intended destination in three hours. After two hours of struggling to stay on top of my board. After an hour of wondering if Mom was going to die while I watched without recourse. The biggest wave we had seen all day washed over me: relief.

Forgotten Canyon received its name in the 1920s after river explorers discovered a large canyon along Glen Canyon had been accidentally omitted from the United States Geological Survey map. The guidebooks had indicated "good" camps existed here.

"Forget good. We just need to find 'good enough,' a beach or ledge to land on and recover for a while," I muttered to myself.

Under the protection of the 200-foot-tall grey canyon walls, the winds had calmed but still whipped and whistled loud enough such that we shouted at each other despite paddling only a few yards apart. We first passed by a house-sized alcove in the Navajo Sandstone at the mouth of the canyon to the west, then ventured into another bay to the south. To our left, shadowless cliff walls striated with white and pale pink ribbons hovered over us. To our right, a rocky talus slope stretched from the base of a giant clam-shell amphitheater. Rocking side to side in the center of the cove behind a yellowed lone rock was one of Lake Powell's eight floating toilets. It looked like a swimming platform with a square white deck and a ladder on one side, but two or three times larger, and housing a tan rectangular building advertising "Restroom." We had planned to drop our trash here. As I scanned our surroundings, it seemed to offer the only viable place to land.

We paddled beyond it, though, and into a narrowing channel. When we arrived at a fork in the canyon, I yelled, "Stay here! I'll look to the right."

Mom stopped and waited for word as I paddled around the corner. I passed overhanging sandstone rock faces. No camp. I paddled by slopes littered with bus-sized boulders. No camp. I searched deeper and deeper into the narrowing channel until the nose of the canyon tapered into a dead end. No camp. No camp. No camp.

"What the hell?" I shook my head. "Where are all these 'good' campsites?"

I retraced my path to rejoin Mom and to relay the unfortunate news.

"We're too far away from the main channel here to see what's going on there," Mom said. "We need to go back."

I agreed. Not because I thought being close to the main channel would buy us much of anything but because I was too frustrated and exhausted to decide anything else. We returned the same way we came in, leaving the two other canyon fingers on the left unexplored.

Instead of continuing to paddle into unknown territory, I advised we pull up to what seemed like our only choice. "Let's head back to that floating toilet and rest for a minute."

"I'm not sleeping on the toilet," Mom snapped.

"You are if it's the only place we can find in these shitty conditions," I said over my shoulder with more attitude than I should have and turned around to paddle toward it.

Mom didn't follow. She paddled toward a shallow, but not shallow enough, sandstone ledge rolling into the water on the north end of the main canyon. I had passed it by just minutes before, deeming it tempting, but too dangerous, to land on. Bad decisions made in desperation rarely turn out well.

"There's a small spit of sand over here we can land on instead." I pointed to the talus slope we had bypassed on the way in to try to convince her to abandon her plan. "Come over here. That's not safe."

The wind pushed me toward the toilet and away from her. I waved at her to encourage her to follow, watching as she eyed the rock ledge. She looked possessed. When she started lifting herself out of her rocking kayak next to a rounded sandstone hill, I shook my head. "No, Ma! That's not safe."

From fifty yards away, I screamed with all the power of the beasts that lived inside me, "LISTEN TO ME, GODDAMMIT!" I slapped the water's surface with my paddle as hard as I could, smacking the edge of a temper tantrum.

She fell out of her trance. She conceded furiously but began paddling toward me. I had no idea why, but we *had* to be near that toilet.

I beached on what was about four feet of sand in front of a shaded, boulder-strewn, 200-foot-high, sloping pitch of white Navajo Sandstone. I guided the nose of Mom's kayak onto the sliver of land next to me. With my frozen, numb feet on solid ground, my body started shaking. I offered my trembling hand to Mom to help her out of the kayak and guided her onto a flat white-washed, table-sized boulder.

On shore, she put both hands to her face and started sobbing. "I'm done," she said.

"Well, I'm not," I said.

"Are you crazy?" She dropped her arms, glared at me, and pointed at the water. "I could have died out there."

"Yes, I know. I'm sorry," I said with surprising composure.

I had no idea how I could have avoided what we had just endured, and I regretted getting us into this situation. But we had not eaten lunch. We had no place to sleep. We didn't know when these winds would calm enough for us to progress down the lake. We were stuck in a remote canyon thirteen miles away from Halls Crossing. Done was not an option.

"Hurry and get out of your wet clothes," I said.

She hugged herself with her eyes closed, shivered, and kept repeating, "I'm so cold. I'm so cold."

She made no effort to move.

"Do something about it! Put your warm clothes on."

Mom was not one to complain. When something went wrong, she fixed it and moved on. I expected her to kick into her Energizer Bunny mode at any second. Not this time. I realized she was likely in the early stages of hypothermia and shock. I changed my tune.

"Sit for a minute," I said. "I'll help you."

I peeled off my cold neoprene boots and slid my stiff feet into my down booties before reaching into Mom's wardrobe of warm clothes. I handed her hat, gloves, down jacket, long underwear, and socks to her, one piece at a time.

As she sat on a boulder and slowly redressed her shaking stiff body, I pulled out the stove and fuel canister to heat water. It was after noon, and we had not eaten anything more than a protein bar hours ago. My stomach muscles cramped. Even so, I could not bear the thought of eating bland oatmeal. I lit the stove anyhow and put my hands behind my head.

We're okay, I kept telling myself, not sure it was true.

I had no idea what we would do next or where we would go. We could not stay here overnight. I couldn't find a flat ledge big enough to set up a tent anywhere on the rocky and steep cliff. However, we could rest here, consult the guidebook buried in my dry bag, and regroup long enough to regain a touch of sanity. Plus, from here, I could see the floating toilet—currently our best option for our evening camp despite Mom's objections—and the still-raging main channel a little more than a quarter mile away.

Before the water began emitting steam, a thundering guttural roar began bouncing between the canyon walls. I looked to the cliff's edge where it met the sky, expecting a low-flying military jet to zoom past us overhead. The rumble boomed louder and louder.

My friend Terry Gunn had emailed me a few days before we launched. In his note, he instructed me to watch for two things while on the lake:

1. When the high-temperature forecast changes by ten or more degrees for two consecutive days.
2. When low-surface "scuddy" clouds form then disappear then reappear.

"When these two things are in place, listen for jets to get loud… this is very important," he wrote. "They will get really loud just before BIG winds hit the surface…usually within 30 min. before they arrive. Normally you cannot hear jets at 38,000 feet. But just before a big wind, you *can*, and they make a loud HUGGHHH_UHHH sound."

I scanned the sky for an airplane, cringing. How could these winds get worse for us? All I could see overhead was a thin layer of grey with a few cloud puffs here and there. The roar increased. What was I missing? Where was the plane? Was it even a plane I was looking for?

I tilted my head toward the mouth of Forgotten Canyon. Out of the corner of my right eye, I spotted a shiny glint of light on the surface of the water near the mouth of the bay. It disappeared for a second, then reappeared and sparkled. The rumble intensified. It wasn't an airplane. It wasn't the wind either.

"Oh my god." I climbed on top of the nearest rock like a meerkat to make sure what I saw was no mirage.

Mom perked up. "Oh my god, it's a fishing boat."

"No way," I said, shaking my head. "No. Fucking. Way."

Mom scrambled next to me on the rocks. We waved our arms. The boat's bow angled toward us. My eyes widened. "That's no fishing boat."

As the boat approached us, familiar green lettering on the grey side bumper flaunted its owner: "National Park Service." The words "Police Rescue" shimmered on the front of its silver metal cabin.

My whole body melted. Tears started to fall. I took off my winter hat and ran my aching fingers through my uncombed hair. "How is this even possible? How is this happening right now?" I looked at Mom and pointed at the boat. "Do you see this? Is this real?"

The craft idled as it neared the talus slope. A spry twenty-something-year-old man wearing a bright orange life vest over his pressed green National Park Service uniform unzipped the plastic cabin door. He leaned over the railing, studying us and surveying our gear strewn across the rocks.

I spoke first. "Did someone send you to get us? Or are you just making your rounds?" It was plausible someone like Dad or Terry might have seen a revised weather forecast and asked a ranger to check on us.

"I'm just out making my rounds," he said. "I've got about 600 miles of terrain to patrol."

"We need help," I muttered through my sniffles. Saying the words shocked me. My stubborn independence rarely asked anyone for help.

Mom and I alternated recapping our intentions to float the entire length of the lake and recalled the recent dramatic events at a disorderly and frenzied pace. Four-foot swells. *Sob.* Crosswinds. *Sob.* Steep cliffs with no place to exit. *Sob.* Almost fell in. *Sob.* Smashing against the rocks. *Sob.* Almost died. *Sob.* He nodded now and then in an impressive show of patience and empathy to two hysterical women.

"It was supposed to be calm today. No wind. Not this," I said with barely enough composure.

"Yeah, that's what the forecast said. But the storm coming from California dropped further south than they expected. Which is why we have these winds now," he said, adjusting the top of his olive-green knit beanie. "A new storm will blow in tonight or tomorrow. There's another one behind it."

"So, conditions are not going to get any better out there?" I asked, knowing the answer.

"No." He laughed. "They are probably going to get worse for at least the next five or six days. We may get snow tonight."

I could endure hard conditions. I could endure improving conditions. I could not endure worse. Nor could I—or would I—put Mom through worse either. Watching Mom almost die, strike one. Not finding a camp, strike two. Two more storms and worsening weather over the next five or six days, strike three.

"I can take you to Bullfrog or Halls Crossing," he offered.

"Can you take us to Halls Crossing?" My voice quivered. "We'll have my dad pick us up there."

"Sure. But, give me a minute. I need to use the restroom," he said. "I'll be right back."

"What's your name?" I asked, remembering we had skipped pleasantries.

"Anthony."

"Hi Anthony, I'm Colleen. This is my mom, Jacque. Nice to meet you. Thank you so much for helping us."

I eyed him apprehensively as he returned to his cabin and motored off to the floating toilet, irrationally worrying he wouldn't return to pick us up. Was he an illusion? Even though the water had not yet

Mom and I packing up and feeling relieved as Anthony, in a National Park Service police rescue boat, returned from the floating toilet (visible to the right of the boat against the whitewashed cliffs in the top photo) before bringing us to Halls Crossing.

boiled—and we had still not eaten our lunch—I turned off the stove burner and started collecting our mess of gear strewn across the rocks. Without rhyme or reason, I shoved several packed dry bags into the depths of Mom's kayak and tucked others underneath the bungee cords on my SUP. We would have time to unclutter it all at Halls Crossing.

I stood up, crossed my arms across my chest, and stared at the empty boat docked across the bay. I watched Anthony step out of the bathroom. "So let me get this straight. Mother Nature hands us our asses. We wave the white flag on a pathetic excuse of a landing against a steep talus slope in one of Lake Powell's countless side canyons, where we happen to be within sight of one of the lake's eight floating toilets. A park ranger patrolling 600 miles magically appears out of the wind in the canyon we took refuge in...all because he needed to take a crap."

I dropped my arms to my side. "I knew it. I *knew* we had to be near that floating toilet."

I had not yet internalized how Tapestry Wall had changed the fabric of our trip nor what hitching a ride back to Halls Crossing meant in terms of completing my goal to paddle the length of Lake Powell. But I was not turning down a free ticket to safety. When the universe handed you a gift like this one, you didn't refuse it. You dropped to your knees and bowed to kiss its feet. Which was what I wanted to do when Anthony returned from answering nature's call. Instead, I stood motionless, still shell-shocked by his unexpected arrival.

"Let's pull those over here," he said, pointing to our vessels and motioning to the bow resting against the rocky shoreline.

"Should we unload our gear?" Mom asked him.

I rolled my eyes. I had just repacked all our stuff back into and onto our vessels minutes before. In my haste to help, it hadn't occurred to me that I probably shouldn't have.

"No. I need the weight," he said. My shoulders dropped in redemption.

Anthony leaned over the railing at the bow, grabbed the front of Mom's kayak, and started dragging it in the water along the port to the stern. I had expected him to tie our boats to the back and tow them to

Halls Crossing. Before he reached the tail, though, he strong-armed the kayak in the water until he angled it perpendicular to the rescue boat. He took a single deep breath and yanked the loaded kayak up four feet into the mouth of a wide squared notch on the side of his ship. He heaved hard backward several times but paused when something barred the kayak from moving with him.

"Would you…like a hand?" I asked sheepishly from the shore, wanting to offer help without insulting him.

"Sure," he said. "Jump on and grab the back end."

I followed his instructions. With two coordinated tugs, we slid the kayak across the back of the boat. Assuming we were to do the same with my much lighter and more flexible SUP, I jumped back onto shore to retrieve it. Anthony lifted the SUP on top of the kayak through the convenient square opening on the side. He strapped the kayak and Lir together and then tied both vessels to his boat.

After he finished, the three of us leaned over the railing and scanned the beach for any remaining belongings. Seeing nothing but rocks on the shore, he invited Mom and me into the warm cabin, zipping the transparent door shut behind us.

He spoke into the radio to park dispatch, "I've taken two aboard. Heading to Halls Crossing."

Less than an hour after we had entered the canyon, less than an hour after I wasn't sure if Mom or I would die, the Coast Guard-style boat jetted out of Forgotten Canyon and exploded into the frenetic swells and onslaught of thundering winds. Anthony throttled through the chop. One second, we felt freeing weightlessness. The next, a jarring thud. Mom and I pressed our hands against the cabin's ceiling to prevent our heads from banging against it.

"How big would you estimate these waves are?" I asked, wanting to compare his expert assessment with my novice one.

"Eh, about five to six feet," he said.

"Whoa! Five to six feet? We guessed about four," I said, impressed that, amid the craziness, we had underestimated—not overestimated—our nemesis.

"There are two places on the lake where you can see waves this size," he continued. "Where you were at and at Lake Canyon just beyond Halls Crossing. In both spots, you can get these crosswinds where the waves run into each other."

He paused, then added a few seconds later out of the right corner of his mouth, "I've seen it get worse than this."

Mom and I exchanged a brief glance with raised eyebrows.

"Worse than this?" Mom asked but didn't stop to get additional confirmation. "Do you normally check out all these canyons on your patrols?"

"No. I didn't check on that one," Anthony said while pointing at Hansen Creek Canyon to the north.

"Or that one," he said while nodding his head toward Crystal Springs Canyon on the south side.

"But you went into Forgotten?" Mom asked. "Why?"

"I don't know," Anthony said with a little smirk. "Something just said I should check on Forgotten."

That "something" translated into "I had to take a dump and the floating toilet at Forgotten was the closest bathroom." I burst out in laughter at the absurdity of it all. Mom and Anthony looked at me. I shook my head. "I can't believe you showed up right when we needed you to. It's unbelievable."

"This boat was obviously made to pick up paddlers with gear. Could you have helped us if you saw us in the main channel?" I asked, thinking about how the National Park Service picked up stricken paddlers so often that they had created a boat to do just that.

"Yeah, I could have pulled you up out of the water on your kayak without you getting out of it," he said.

"Fully loaded? In these waves?"

"Sure, we've done it before," he said. "I could have pulled you up on your board, too. This is one of the newest boats in the Glen Canyon fleet, but it's been in the shop for maintenance. Today is its first day back in the water."

Anthony turned around, I presumed to check that our two vessels remained attached to his boat. I followed his gaze and noticed my box of Black Box cabernet sauvignon getting drenched and bouncing against the top of Mom's kayak despite the bungee cords trying to hold it into place.

"Hey, it's like Wilson," Mom said of the soggy cardboard box. "Like the volleyball in that Tom Hanks movie *Cast Away*."

Just like Hanks' character, Chuck Nolan, we could not afford to lose our Wilson. First off, I did not want it to litter the lake. Second, in naming it, Mom had now just elevated this prized possession into an icon. Third, but most critically, I would be out of wine when we hit the shore. No doubt I would need copious amounts of alcohol to calm my nerves and come to terms with the unexpected end of our trip. Then I remembered I still had Guy's tequila.

Mom started up a casual conversation with Anthony as if she was striking up a chat with the guy behind her at the grocery store checkout line. I pretended to listen as I analyzed the unfamiliar landscape zooming past us and looked for a place we could have taken refuge or camped had we not done so in Forgotten. In thirteen miles, I hadn't seen even a blip of sand. Cliffs on the right. Even more cliffs on the left. It would have been a long, arduous paddle to Halls Crossing, with or without the wind and waves.

As the boat cruised into the south side of the expansive Bullfrog Bay, Anthony pointed out the marina store on the left where we needed to pick up the solar battery Dad had shipped to us. Past another bay and sandstone peninsula, we idled into the No Wake zone. After traveling a distance that would have taken us at least a half-day or longer with our kayak and SUP, Anthony powered the boat onto the shore less than twenty minutes after picking us up. We had arrived at Halls Crossing on the exact date we had planned on my spreadsheet: November 27.

"I'll drop you off here," Anthony said, pointing at the gravel beach ahead and to the west of the formal concrete boat ramp. "The campground is just up the hill."

"Can we pay you for this?" Mom asked. She reached into her pocket for the plastic baggie holding her driver's license and $125 in cash.

"No," Anthony said.

"Can we tip you then?" she asked, offering him a wad of bunched up money with both hands.

Anthony departs after dropping us off at the protected beach at Halls Crossing.

"No," he said with equal sharpness to his first answer but this time while shaking his head from side to side.

"I'd give you every penny I have on me for this," Mom said.

"Me too," I chimed in. If I could have dug my cash out of one of my buried dry bags, I would have added another $100 to the kitty. I would have also handed him my credit card and told him to buy anything he wanted with it.

Before he could continue discouraging us from paying him for an act provided by a public servant (your tax dollars hard at work!), Mom said with tears welling up in her eyes, "Thank you so much. You have no idea how thankful we are for your help. Thank goodness you came into that canyon."

We began an assembly line on the sandy beach to unload our loose equipment: my cameras, tripod, anchor, water shoes, and dry bags. Anthony untied and unloaded the SUP from the back and dragged it alongside the boat. Wading in a foot or so of water, I grabbed the handle from him and pulled it onto the beach. Mom walked behind me to unload the kayak next.

Once we cleaned his boat of our gear, he squatted down on the deck and pulled out a pen and a small pocket-sized notebook. "Can I get your full name, date of birth, and your state of residence?" Mom answered for both of us while standing knee-high in the lake. He scribbled the information into the middle of his notepad. We were not the first troublemakers he had recorded.

"Thanks. You're all set," Anthony said. He stood up and shoved the pen back into his pocket. He disappeared behind his cabin's plastic door.

Mom waved and yelled, "Thank you! Be safe out there." With a smile, but no words, Anthony shifted his boat into reverse, spun around, and disappeared into the bay.

Mom shouted at his wake, "We'll never forget you!"

I restrained myself from pointing out the irony of her final goodbye: Anthony would be unforgotten for finding Mom and me—and not forgetting about us after taking a crap—in Forgotten Canyon. I joined in with a reticent wave. I knew how it felt to be left behind.

Except, this time, I hadn't been. We had been rescued. As the boat vanished around a sandstone mound, I wondered from what I had been saved. Or whether I had been saved at all.

12
THE SPACE BETWEEN

Days 4-6: November 27-29, 2015
From Halls Crossing to home

I sat next to my dirty board and the carnage of gear scattered across the shore, stunned at how the day had transpired. When I woke up this morning, this was not what I had planned. In the months of typing up spreadsheets and packing dry bags, this was not at all what I had scheduled. In all the "what if" scenarios we had outlined, "What if you don't finish" had never crossed my mind.

I chucked a small rock into the lake. I sunk into the sand. My shoulders slumped over my bent knees. I whispered the last line of Guy's meditation: "Don't be afraid to cry."

My dry, cracked hands cradled my head as the flood gates opened. I was relieved we were safe. I was pissed off at the guidebooks that said there were camps in Forgotten Canyon. I was thankful for being in the right place at the right time for Anthony to find us. I was sorry for getting us into those dangerous conditions, all because I wanted to paddle more miles yesterday.

Dammit, it is always more, more, always more with you, isn't it?

I was crushed we were stopped in our tracks one hundred miles short of our goal and that we would not see the rest of the lake. Not Cathedral Canyon, where I could have prayed for a different future. Not Secret Canyon, where the answers would stop hiding. Not Friendship Canyon. Not even Last Chance Bay. Furious. Grateful. Humiliated. The seesaw of emotions made me as seasick as the waves we had just escaped.

I wanted to do just one thing, just for me. In just four days—and for the second time in eight months—I had failed. A gust of wind rustled my hair and hissed into my ear, "Winners never quit, and quitters never win."

"FUCK THIS!" I threw another rock hard enough to strain my right shoulder. I winced in pain.

While Mom busied herself by organizing our gear, I dialed Dad on my cell phone without bothering to ask her what she wanted to do next. We could have waited out one storm here and then continued but not two more over the next five or six days.

Dad picked up on the second ring. "Colleen?"

"Hi Dad. We're fine," I said quickly, hoping to calm the anxiety he likely felt when he saw my name come up on the screen unexpectedly. "Mom and I are at Halls Crossing right now. We've had a change in plans. We're done."

I paused and looked up at the sky to hold back tears. "Could you pick us up here tomorrow?"

"Yes. Of course. I can leave in ten minutes."

"Thanks so much, Dad," I said, rolling a small rock in my hand. "Let us figure out where we're going to sleep tonight, and we'll call you back later to settle on where to meet you."

"Sounds good. Let me talk with Mom," Dad said.

I handed the phone to Mom. "Oh my god, you won't believe what we've been through." She started spouting out the day's events.

"Hey, can we go through the details later?" I asked, talking over her. "I'm worried about losing power on my phone. Right now, I have no way to charge it."

That was true. It was also true that I simply didn't want to hear the story of me failing to finish. Mom handed the phone back to me.

"We're fine," I said to wrap up our conversation with Dad, wondering whether I did so to convince him or myself.

I hung up.

The trip was over.

A gust of wind cut my pity party short. Despite it being only a little after one in the afternoon, Mom and I needed to find a home for the night before the next storm came in. I tied the kayak and SUP together and buried the anchor into the sand on the beach where Anthony said we could leave them overnight. For a minute, I considered setting up camp here.

"I doubt they would let us stay here," I said, referring to an unknown cadre of National Park Service rangers patrolling Halls Crossing.

Watching my misbehaving classmates kneel on hot pavement at recess during my two years of Catholic school had impressed the consequences of not following rules, so much so that I tended to strictly adhere to regulations, even in extenuating circumstances like ours, even when I had no idea what the rules were and regardless of whether anyone was around to enforce them. I hadn't seen a sign that said we couldn't, but I hadn't read anything that said we could. I just assumed we could not sleep at the boat launch.

I looked up at the long, empty concrete ramp. On both sides of it, reddened, flat-topped plateaus rose into the horizon. The barren and rocky landscape looked like the surface of Mars—and seemed to contain the same amount of human life, too. According to the map, a car ferry to Bullfrog Crossing and other visitor services existed here somewhere, maybe by the marina we saw coming into the bay, but certainly not here. It didn't matter. We only needed to find the campground.

We grabbed a few of the black carts provided at the end of the concrete slipway. We peeled our gear from the rocks and filled not one, not two, but *three* bins. Each one resembled Santa's overflowing sleigh. I sized up our gear, then the steep, 400-yard uphill climb on the ramp. I rubbed my forehead. "I thought we had packed light. But, man, we have a ton of stuff."

We kept leapfrogging each other as we lugged the carts up the slope. We each rolled one cart up the ramp about twenty-five yards until we tired. One of us rested for a few seconds before continuing with our own cart for another twenty-five yards or so. The other descended to grab the third cart lagging behind and pulled it uphill about fifty yards.

When we were over three-quarters of the way up the ramp, a truck towing a speedboat raced down the ramp. A few minutes later, it sped back up, its empty trailer bouncing and rattling across the bumpy concrete. The driver slowed and pulled up next to Mom. She had gone back for the third cart while I rested higher on the slope with my hands on my knees.

I heard a muffled manly voice ask, "Do you need a ride somewhere?"

"No, thanks. We're just going to the top of the hill," she said.

I shook my head.

Dude, if only you could have been here a half an hour ago.

The truck pulled away with a quick wave from the driver. Near the top of the hill, he turned right and out of sight. I reached the same turnoff a few minutes later with my cart. I couldn't tell what it was or where it went. Piles of sand obscured my view. My stomach growled. We had consumed only one energy bar each since breakfast at 7:30. I pulled out my phone. It was now after two.

"So, where's this campground?" I asked of no one.

The main road appeared to continue straight ahead to the southeast. To my right, to the south, a tall set of stairs climbed up a burgundy-colored mound. It led to a fish cleaning station and a large cinder block bathroom—and I hoped an elevated perspective to gain our bearings. I grabbed the handrail. As I shifted my weight onto my left leg to rest for a second, my right leg cramped and started bobbing up and down like a sewing machine needle. I sighed, then marched up the steps. I turned around at the top and noticed a sign at the head of the gravel lot: "14-Day Parking. No Camping." The turnoff we had reached was a parking lot for trucks and trailers. It was a dead end.

"Then where is it? Anthony said it was just up the hill."

In the distance to the southwest, I spotted a clump of trees sporting vibrant yellow leaves poking out of the desert landscape. Cottonwoods? Ornamental shade trees? I couldn't tell. Trees typically grow in lush riparian areas, not in barren sandstone atop a flat plateau. Humans had planted them.

Mom called up to me as she rubbed her forehead free of sweat, "Can you see it? Is it up there?"

"Oh yeah. It's up here alright. It's at least another mile away."

My legs strained to hold my own weight as I trotted down one stair at a time. I needed the clouds to part, the birds to sing, and other small miracles to come together before I had any chance of walking another mile with all our gear in tow.

"Let's go to that picnic table across this parking lot and just sit for a few minutes," I said after I reached the bottom of the stairs. "I can't do this anymore. I need a break."

I grabbed a cart and staggered across the flat pavement for another 500 feet. When we reached the table, I shed my Catholic guilt and spouted in defiance, "We'll just sleep here. If a ranger comes by and asks what we're doing setting up camp behind a 'No Camping' sign, I'll have no problem explaining our situation to them."

Darkening clouds grumbled overhead. A light pitter-patter of rain started to ping against the metal picnic table. "Here, help me put this over our stuff," Mom said as she offered me one corner of our blue tarp to drape over our three carts.

I plunked onto the bench and let my body slump into despair. My dam of emotions exploded. "I can't do anything right!" I exclaimed and then started sobbing.

"What do you mean, you can't do anything right?" Mom asked while firing up the stove to hydrate our freeze-dried food for lunch. "You've literally done everything right your whole life."

I ignored her sentiments and spewed anything that came to mind: the trip ending, the weight of the cart, my legs shaking, the weather, Mom almost dying, my failed marriage, me not being good enough for anyone, being alone, and everything in between. I closed my eyes, the cold air of disappointment stinging them. "I just keep screwing everything up."

I suddenly sensed movement in my peripheral vision. The sight of a man dressed in the traditional green NPS uniform stopped me from slipping further down my self-indulgent slide. His stocky profile crested the eastern horizon like an action hero rising out of flames. He swaggered toward us and looked everywhere except right at us. Even so, we knew once he came into view at the head of the parking lot, he was coming for us. We were the only people in an area the size of three football fields. I straightened my back, but my legs shook and my stomach tightened. I prayed he would at least let us finish our lunch before prodding us to make the long march to the campground up and over the hill.

"Hi ladies. How are we doing?" he asked when it became too awkward to continue avoiding us.

Mom burst into tears. I started laughing. How are we doing? I looked down at my rehydrated lasagna.

How are we doing? We're doing awesome. But we are wondering where our lobster thermidor is. Are you with the staff? Tell the chefs we demand it now. And it better be hot when it gets here.

I restrained myself. The only place sarcasm would get us with an authority figure was trouble, not sympathy.

"We were just rescued by Anthony," Mom wailed.

"We're a mess, can you tell?" I said, hoping to hide my red eyes and sniffles behind the pretense of a smile. I recounted the day's events, then of our grand plans to paddle from Hite to Wahweap.

"You do know that's over 140 miles, right?" he asked slowly.

"Yeah. And we were so prepared to do the whole thing too," I said *sotto voce*, shaking my head and adjusting my winter hat.

He hesitated as if to offer me a moment of silence to deal with my grief. He then responded with a take-charge attitude. "Here's what we're going to do. I just got on duty, so I haven't cleaned out my van yet. I'm going to go get my truck. We'll load up your gear, and we'll find you a good campsite. We need to get you in your bags and warm."

He surveyed our three bins of gear. "You *do* have a tent and sleeping bags, yes?"

"Yep. They're in there somewhere," I said, pointing to the blue tarp.

"Great. I'll be right back," he said.

"Thank you so much," I said. I was not accustomed to accepting help from strangers, especially in a strange place, but as we used to say at Intel, this was a "win-win" scenario. We needed a place to spend the night—and that designated place was too far for us to walk with our gear. He did not want vagabonds sleeping in the "No Camping" area.

By the time we ate the last of our meals and cleaned up the picnic table, he had returned with a white National Park Service pickup truck. We unloaded all the gear from the black carts and dumped bag after bag into the bed of his truck as if we were throwing garbage into a dumpster.

"Leave the black carts here. I'll come back tomorrow morning to pick them up," the man said. "It'll give me something to do."

Mom and I squished into the front seat of the truck cab. Hunched on the awkward middle bump, I asked his name without turning my head.

"Marty," he answered.

"Colleen," I said, extending my hand to him. "This is my mom, Jacque."

"Would you like to stay at my house for the night?" he said, pointing up the road beyond the trees.

"Oh no, we won't trouble you with that," I said. The dirty, distressed, and independent introvert in me could only take so much generosity at once.

"We have everything we need to camp," Mom chimed in.

"At least come up for dinner then?" he continued.

"So nice of you," I said. "But after what we've been through today, we aren't feeling terribly social right now."

"Plus, we just ate," Mom said while looking out the window. "I'm exhausted. I just want to crawl into my sleeping bag and sleep."

Mom and I were almost on the same page regarding our plans for the night. I too was exhausted. But I also wanted to crawl into a dark cave, curl into the fetal position, and die of shame.

We made small talk as Marty wound his way toward the campground. He had retired years ago and now spent part of his time volunteering at Halls Crossing. He spent the other part chilling in

Costa Rica. He was currently wrestling with whether he should stay in Utah or head back to Latin America to soak in the sun for the winter. I understood this dilemma from my experience as a freelancer and wanderer. Decisions, decisions. So many places to see, so little time. Freedom could be so grueling sometimes.

He used to make his home on the high seas while sailing all over the world. Once, he had traced the shoreline from Canada to Mexico. With little emotion, he recounted tales of surviving two hurricanes. His sailboat sank in Hurricane Odile when the Category 4 storm plowed into Baja California in Mexico in September 2014.

"So, you've seen a bit worse than what we experienced?" I asked.

"On this lake? Maybe. Maybe not," he said. "I've seen this lake get pretty wild. But there's nothing like sitting in the middle of a hurricane in a sailboat."

As exciting as Marty's life story was, I couldn't help but notice how long it was taking us to get to the campground. I couldn't estimate the distance any more than I could estimate the size of the waves we had just endured, but the lake behind us kept getting smaller and smaller in the rearview mirror as we meandered along the deserted, paved, undulating road. No way would we have made it this far with our shaky legs and three carts of gear. So much for "just up the hill."

The right-hand turn into the empty campground finally appeared, and we began the painstaking process of picking a campsite from forty-three open choices. Marty launched into his sales pitch about the campsites like a used car salesman.

"These have a good view but are more exposed to the elements," he said of the ones on the east side of the graveled road, then pointed to the middle ones on an island within the loop. "These are tucked behind the bathrooms, more protected."

The ones on the west side of the road: "These are out of the wind next to the berm but don't have as good of a view."

Marty stopped in front of the bathrooms. "These should be open," he said. He jumped out of the truck, walked twenty steps, and disappeared into the men's shower room. Mom and I shrugged at each other. A few seconds later, he returned with a smile. "Yep, they're open and you have hot water to shower."

He completed the loop and stopped his truck at the first set of campsites on the east side. He shifted his body in his seat and turned toward us. "So, what do you think?"

Research shows that stress—and analysis paralysis called the "Paradox of Choice"—follows when customers face too many choices in a buying decision. No doubt, the decision-making process is even more difficult when all the options are nearly identical.

What did I think? It's not like we were picking out wedding rings or curtains for the kitchen, for chrissakes. We were evaluating a vast, vacant, contiguous flat piece of dirt separated arbitrarily by silver metal picnic tables and brown fiberglass stakes with numbers on them. We only needed a spot large enough to fit the tent. And then drink wine. And then cry. And then sleep. And then cry some more until Dad picked us up tomorrow. I was certain any and all of these campsites would support my lofty aspirations.

Mom and I stared in silence out the windshield. Marty finally asked, "How about that one?"

"Yes, that one is perfect," I said. I would have had the same response for any site he pointed at.

The three of us walked around the spot pretending to survey it like a new home site to ensure this piece of dirt—and not that one ten feet away—was really, really, *really* the spot we wanted.

I happened to glance at the number on the brown site marker at the head of the gravel driveway. I called back to Mom, "Look Ma, we're going to stay in lucky number 13. How funny is that?"

"We can change to the next one over if that's too, well, weird," Marty said.

"After today, the number 13 seems totally appropriate," Mom said out of the corner of her mouth.

Marty helped us unload our gear from his truck. "Get settled then. I'll check on you a little later," he said, then drove off.

Mom and I piled our gear onto a blanket of burnt yellow leaves at the bases of beige-trunked trees. We formed three piles: one for showering and enjoying the evening, one for sleeping, and one for everything else. We scurried to set up the tent and our sleeping quarters, knowing that we would be too exhausted to do so later. We shoved the rest of the gear under the campsite's picnic table. Even though we kept most of what we had in dry bags, we still covered the mound with our tarp. The rain had stopped, the wind had calmed, and the clouds had started breaking up once we hopped into Marty's truck. That said, more silver-bottomed storm clouds loomed on the western horizon. I worried those might bring the snow Anthony had warned us about earlier.

Once we organized our camp, we headed to the bathhouse across the one-lane dirt road. Mom ventured into the women's shower room. I settled in on the bench in the separate heated bathroom next door. I sent Dad a text to let him know which campsite to meet us at tomorrow, then started writing about the day's events.

"Ugh!" Mom's voice echoed through the wall a few minutes later. "There's no hot water."

I put my pen and paper down, then walked out of the women's bathroom and into the men's room. I turned the water on and stuck my hand beneath the powerful stream to check. Hot water. Scorching, in fact. Just like Marty said.

I turned the water off and walked across to the women's shower. I rapped on the door with the back of my knuckles. "Ma? There's hot water in the men's shower."

"Alright, thanks."

"Can I help you move your stuff?" I stared at the brown door.

She didn't answer. A few seconds later, she walked out naked, clutching her black fleece to her chest, soap suds whitening her hair. I grabbed her toiletries, clothes, and duffle bag as she tip-toed barefoot to the men's shower.

I dumped her belongings into an unorganized heap onto the slatted bench in the tiled closet-sized room. "Check it again to be sure," I said.

She turned on the faucet while clinging to her fleece and reached her hand out to test the water. She dropped her black jacket on top of the rest of her clothes on the bench and stepped into the stream. She let out a loud "ahhhhh."

I returned to my writing—and my own warmth—on the bench in the women's restroom. Twenty minutes later, Mom opened the door.

"That felt so good," she said. She dropped an unkempt pile of clothes next to me, then pushed the hand dryer, bent over, and started drying her hair beneath it.

"I'll shower in the morning," I shouted over the loud hum. "As divine as it sounds, I don't have the energy. Plus, I don't want my wet hair to freeze and break off in the middle of the night."

While she dried her hair, I noticed an electrical outlet beneath one of the two sinks. I followed her back to camp to grab my iPhone and the small dry bag containing all our cords, chargers, batteries, and gadgets for the trip. Mom snuggled into her sleeping bag while I poured a generous glass of cabernet sauvignon from Wilson to take with me back to the bathroom to charge my electronics.

I sat cross-legged on the gray floor. My iPhone only had a 9% charge left. I dumped the contents of my electronics dry bag and began sifting through the tangled mess as if I were searching for gold in a pan of gravel. I tried every cord, but none fit my iPhone or the battery pack I had attached to it.

I sat back on my heels. "Ugh. The cord must be in my camera bag."

I pulled myself up and left my mess strewn across the bathroom floor. As I rounded the corner of the bathroom, a pair of headlights beamed at me. A white van pulled up. I knew who it was.

"Hi, Marty."

"How are things going with you and your mom?" he asked, stepping out of the vehicle.

"My Mom's bundled up in the tent, fast asleep. I'm grabbing my cord to charge my phone."

"Good to hear," Marty said. "Here, I brought you both a bottle of wine."

"So nice of you. Thank you," I said with a smile. "We'll sure appreciate this after what we've been through."

"Need anything?"

"Nah, we're set for the night."

"I'll check on you again in the morning," Marty said.

"Perfect. Thanks again for everything, Marty," I said, giving him a thumbs up. "Have a great night."

"You too," he said with a friendly grin and wave. He tucked back into his van, circled around the campground, and vanished into the now clear and windless night.

I navigated across the gravel road to our camp, guided by the beam of my headlamp. I grabbed my cord, stashed the wine bottle in the pile of bags, used Wilson to refill my wine glass to within millimeters of the rim, and headed back to the warm bathroom. I had plenty of red wine to go with my write whine now.

I sent Guy a text. "We're at Halls Crossing. Bad windstorm. Got rescued. We're done."

He texted back immediately. After a few back-and-forths, he called me. "How are you?" he asked casually.

"We're done. I'm done," I said. I spewed the same verbal vomit I had spilled out earlier at the picnic table about the day's traumatic events, about how I was such a disaster, about the flood of disappointment ravaging through the canyon of my life.

I started sobbing so hard, I couldn't breathe. My nose was so raw from blowing it so many times that the bathroom's soft and thin toilet paper grated against my skin like sandpaper. The tops of my eyelids chaffed so badly from rubbing them, they burned to the touch.

After several minutes of curling over the speakerphone and pouring out my emotions to Guy, the bathroom door opened. I straightened my back and tried to stop sobbing, thinking Mom would appear. Instead, a short brunette woman peeked her head around the door.

"Are you…okay?" she asked while creasing her eyebrows.

I asked Guy to hold on so I could answer her. "Yeah, I'm fine. We had a rough day today, and I'm a bit shaken from it."

"Were you the ones on the kayak and paddleboard we saw out there yesterday?" she asked.

"Yeah, that was us," I said. "You must have been the couple fishing up near Good Hope Bay? We waved to each other."

She hadn't been close enough to smell me on the lake yesterday, but I bet she could smell me now. I pressed my arms closer to my side. Now I wished I had showered earlier.

"Yeah, that was us," she said with more enthusiasm than I had answered her same question.

"You know, you were the first people we had seen on the lake for two days, since we had started," I said. "We were so excited to see you."

"We saw you and were so worried about you," she said. "Especially today. The winds were horrible."

"Oh, we know all about that," I said.

I gave her a quick recap of the day's events, talking loudly enough so that Guy, who waited on the speakerphone, could overhear the conversation. I did not need to express my sadness; I had disappointment already written all over my flushed face.

"So glad you're alive." She started to move toward the bathroom stall. With her hand on the bathroom door, she stopped and turned to me. "So, the rescue boat just randomly showed up?"

"Yeah. No more than ten minutes after we beached in Forgotten. It was a miracle."

"Incredible," she said, shaking her head.

I returned to my conversation with Guy. She finished her business, washed her hands in the other sink, and then asked, "Do you or your mom need anything?"

"I don't think so, but thank you."

"If you do, we're in the campsite right here," she said, pointing to the door. Through my sobs, I had not heard her and her husband roll into their camp across from the bathhouse.

"So nice of you, thank you," I said. "What's your name?"

"Tammy."

"Hi, Tammy, I'm Colleen. Thanks so much for your help."

"Hi, Colleen, nice to meet you. Have a good night."

I wished her the same, then resumed talking Guy's ear off. Four or five minutes later, the bathroom door opened again. Tammy stood in the doorway holding a box of Black Box merlot in pristine condition, unlike my weathered Wilson. She smiled, raised the box up, and without words, nodded to ask if I wanted—or perhaps, needed—a refill.

I kneeled on the floor and offered my almost empty wine glass. The remnants of my cabernet sauvignon swirled around the bottom of the glass, but I was never one to turn wine down, especially considering I was checking off drinking and crying from my ambitious to-do list. I thanked her again.

She laughed. "Have a good night."

I raised my glass to her. "I will now, thanks to you."

I went back to my emotional exchange with Guy, albeit with less reckless abandon and a softer voice now that I knew we had neighbors.

"Go home, unpack, and then come join me in Escalante for a few days," Guy said, trying his best to soothe my sunken spirit, as he had done so many times over the last eight months. "You're not done."

"I sure feel done," I said. "But, that'd be good."

After we said our goodbyes, I collected my belongings scattered across the floor. I left my iPhone to charge overnight under the sink. Normally, I would guard my possessions in a public place closely. We were miles away from any civilization, though, with only two other people in the campground. I climbed into my sleeping bag feeling confident my phone would still be there tomorrow morning.

I woke from my wine-encouraged coma the next morning as Mom unzipped the tent. Civil twilight and a waning moon in a clear sky provided enough light for us to maneuver around the tent without our headlamps. "How are you doing?" I asked her as I rubbed my raw eyelids.

"Good. I'm going to the bathroom. Do you need to go?"

"Nah, I'm good," I said. I fell back onto my Thermarest, rolled over, and closed my eyes as Mom re-zipped the tent door.

I woke up in a glowing, but empty, tent. I had no idea how much time had passed since Mom had left. Two minutes? Two hours? I sat up in my mummy bag and shivered in the unexpected chill in the air. I slid

Morning view from campsite #13 in the Halls Crossing Campground. The marina appears on the distant horizon to the left of the tent (but to the right of the trees).

into my fleece, down jacket, and gloves. I flipped the hood of my coat over my wool hat and curled the fabric around my neck.

The morning's sun echoing off the yellow tent walls illuminated a thin layer of frost inside. I shook my three water bottles, which I had left in the vestibule overnight. Two of them had frozen solid. One of them, which was only half-full of water and touching the side of the tent, had a thin layer of feather ice on the surface and sides of the bottle. I moved all three of them, one by one, in a swath of sunlight gathered around our tent. It hadn't snowed overnight like Anthony said it might, but winter had certainly arrived in the desert.

I trudged to the bathroom in my usual pre-caffeinated, zombie mode, walking against a stream of dry leaves driven across the sand by a gentle easterly draft. After only a couple of steps, I heard the murmur of conversation and a burst of laughter coming from inside the bathroom. Mom had made a friend. In the restroom in a campground. At Halls Crossing, Utah. Year-round population six. Overnight population four.

Mom filtering drinking water from the sink in the campground bathroom in preparation for the ride home.

I poked my head into the heated bathroom to see Tammy at the sink washing dishes. Mom sat on the bench, legs crossed casually as if she were in a coffee shop having a chitchat with her best friend. "Oh good. You're OK," I interrupted.

"Oh yeah, I'm telling her all about our adventure from yesterday," Mom said with a proud smile.

"She's heard plenty about it already, Mom." I glanced at Tammy in an apologetic way, feeling bad we had subjected her to not one but two rounds of our trip details.

"Did you hear?" Tammy turned her head toward me. "The boat dock at the marina here moved twelve feet in the wind yesterday. Twelve feet!"

"Whoa. That's unreal," I said while rubbing the sleep from my eyes.

I was not awake enough to relive the death-defying tale yet again—nor had my lifelong introversion turned to extroversion overnight—so I heeded nature's call, grabbed my fully charged phone from beneath the sink, thanked Tammy for her hospitality, and wished her safe and happy travels. I left the two new BFFs to chat. I pushed the door open, shuddering at the contrast between the heated bathroom and winter's arrival.

I returned to campsite 13 to boil water for tea. I poured the supercooled water from one of the now-thawed Nalgene bottles into our cooking pot. Ice crystals formed the instant the water touched the aluminum. The lighter we had left on the picnic table overnight froze as well. I dug out a second lighter buried in one of the bags packed under the picnic table and tarp. The fuel sputtered and then caught a flame.

A lull in the wind and the bluebird sky overhead made me wonder if we had given up too soon. As if the universe was privy to my inner thoughts, a strong gust of wind swirled leaves around the picnic table. A ring of cumulonimbus clouds on the horizon reminded me that two more storms were brewing. Besides, Dad was already on his way to pick us up. I rocked from side to side. "Accept it, the trip is over," I said aloud to the pot as if the water cared about my grievances.

Mom showed up in camp just as the water began boiling. "You

know, Ma. Yesterday was tough, and the decision to pull the plug on this trip was even tougher," I said with tears filling my eyes. "But I do not care what anyone says, I am proud of us for trying."

The perfectionist in me didn't believe the words coming out of my mouth. I said them to comfort my mother nonetheless. She had put her life on the line for me. It was the least I could do.

Mom walked around the table and gave me a bear hug. "I'm so proud of us too," she said, her voice muffled by our fluffy down jackets. "Thanks so much for this adventure."

"Thank you, Ma." I faked a smile and blew on the steam rising from my tea mug.

We gathered our bags into a tidy pile ahead of Dad's arrival. My brother had sent a text indicating that Dad hoped to reach us around noon. Mom and I bet he would show up around eleven at the latest. Mom looked at her phone. That left us about two hours to clean up and pack up.

I grabbed my toiletries and fresh clothes—sans bra—and headed to the men's shower. The hot water stung my frozen hands and feet at first but eventually felt like soft silk. I lingered and stretched in the steam. A loud "beep-beep" gave me pause. I knew that sound. Dad had arrived.

I dried off quickly. I rushed out into the cold and across the street to our camp, where my parent's SUV sat in the dirt parking space.

"Hi Dad." I hugged him tight—and long. "Thanks for coming to get us."

Within twenty minutes, we departed leaving no trace of our existence at camp 13. I wanted to say farewell to Marty, but we couldn't find him.

We drove down to the end of the boat ramp to pick up our SUP and kayak and then headed to the marina's store. Our new solar battery had been delivered, not to Halls Crossing, but rather to the Bullfrog Marina across the bay. Still, no one could find it. I scribbled my credit card number and mailing address on a scrap piece of paper and left it with the attendant so they could mail it to me.

(The package showed up at my house two months later.)

Time slowed once we started the eight-hour drive home. I snuggled

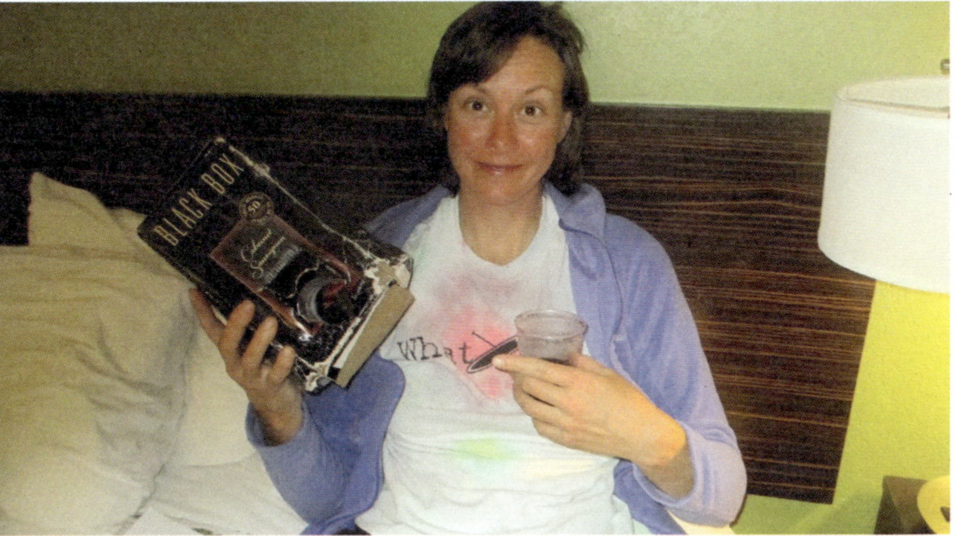

Holding Wilson in our hotel room in Flagstaff, Arizona. Photo by Jacque Miniuk.

into the front seat, the weight of failure resting heavy in my chest. I stared out the window and let the blur of my memory of the water fade into the landscape whizzing by.

We were in no rush to get home, so we stayed overnight in Flagstaff, Arizona. In our hotel room, I resorted to the previous night's to-do list: drink, cry, drink, cry, drink, cry, drink—but not necessarily in that order. Somewhere in between drink and cry, or maybe it was between cry and drink, I finally passed out.

In the middle of the night, I sat up in a panic. The heater rattled. The darkness smelled of bleach. I pulled the covers up to my chest. Where was I? Why was I not in my tent? Why was I not on a sandy beach on Lake Powell? Was this a bad dream?

I fell back into my pillow and stared into the black. I gasped for air, choking on the phlegm collected in my throat from lying prone after crying for hours. "Oh stop," the voice in my head said. "How embarrassing would it be to die gagging in a hotel room after just surviving a harrowing paddle in the wild?"

We arrived at my house in Chandler around noon the following day. After unloading my gear in the garage and hugging my parents one last time, I walked into my house with my head down. My cat, Nolan, trotted to the door and greeted me with the same meow he always did: "Hi, great, you're home. Could I have a treat now? Now? Now? Meowwwww." He could not have cared less that I had returned ten days early.

I meowed back at him, as I often did, and then followed him to his food bowl in the laundry room. I bent down to scratch his head. "Do I ever have a story for you, Nolan baby."

I sauntered into my den. I stared at the sofa, the kitchen table, and the pictures on the wall—all artifacts of the good life I had collected here, the life I was once promised, the life I had lost. Nothing here had changed since Craig walked out of our home in April. Nothing had changed from six days ago when I left for our paddle trip on Lake Powell.

Yet, everything had.

The winds and waves had only just begun.

13
REENTRY

I unpacked, bringing in one bag at a time from the garage, emptying the contents on the tile, and returning each piece of gear to its respective shelf, closet, or drawer. Leftover food to the kitchen cabinet. Dirty clothes to the washing machine. Sand to the decorative gravel in my backyard. The tasks kept my emotional baggage stashed in an orderly pile in the back of my mind.

As I ran out of daylight and bags to unload, an unsettling but familiar silence dawned. I turned to the same remedy that had pacified me after Craig left in April: a tall glass of wine and a hot bath.

Water swirled back and forth as the tub filled. I stirred in two softball-sized lumps of lavender Epsom salts, hoping the aroma of calmness would take the edge off. My white terrycloth robe fell off my shoulders. I collapsed to my knees. I grabbed the side of the tub with both hands as if a higher power forced me to pray at an altar. Tears of unfulfilled expectations soaked my cheeks.

"Failed again. First your marriage. Now this trip. What a joke."

I picked myself off the floor and stepped into the warmth one foot at a time. I recited my initials, "C.M.S. See a mess. You're such a disaster."

I shook my head and took a consoling sip of wine. "Be nice," I said aloud, feeling the chill swirl and tingle in my mouth as if to remind me to watch my tongue. "Remember your birthday? Be nice to yourself."

"Whatever," the voice in my head responded. "You're a train wreck."

Wine and warmth soothed me into stillness. The surrogate waters for the Colorado River covered my shoulders and coddled me as a concerned parent would console a dejected child. A few minutes later, I sat up, wrapped my hand around one of the small pale green unlit candles adorning the tub's edge, and hurled it across the bathroom as hard as I could. It ricocheted off my closet door and landed on the tile in front of the tub. I screamed in sudden rage, "I'M SO FUCKING TIRED OF NOT BEING GOOD ENOUGH!"

I recoiled against the back wall of the tub in horror at such an uncharacteristic and violent outburst. My eyes widened. "Oh my god. What are you doing to yourself?"

I slid my body into the water and stared at the blank white ceiling overhead, floating motionless like a corpse. I closed my eyes and yelled into the darkness, "What am I doing wrong?"

When, *when*, would it all be enough?

When would striving for unattainable perfection end?

When would I stop looking down on a laundry list of spectacular accomplishments many only dreamed of and stop dumping them in my reeking "not good enough" pile in hopes of achieving more, more, always more?

How many more achievements did I need to finally feel satisfied? Let's face it: if my first forty years of extraordinary achievements did not fulfill me then more of it never would.

Success hadn't delivered happiness. Money and love hadn't either. What, then, would?

For forty years, I had believed that success in academics, athletics, corporate America, marriage, and even paddling across Lake Powell would crown me "the Queen of Perfection." It's what I always did: tried to achieve something to prove my worth. For forty years, I had expected happiness to appear magically—like Anthony did for us in Forgotten Canyon—after working relentlessly to reach predefined goals. Happiness was nowhere to be found. Not when I succeeded. Certainly not when I had now failed not once but twice. Not ever.

I hated my life.

I hated myself.

I heard Craig's voice from eight months ago echo off the bathroom walls: "I can't do *this* anymore."

"For the love of god, *I* can't do this anymore," I said. "I'd leave me too if I could."

Remember your birthday? Be nice. Stop fighting yourself.

Striving for success was not my problem. Believing that *only* success would create contentment and then beating myself up with cruel and destructive self-talk and an unproductive judgmental attitude, whether success or failure occurred, was my problem. Believing I was therefore not good enough, and did not deserve happiness, was my problem. Letting my hungry heart control and consume my every beat, thought, and breath like a mad, seething cannibal in pursuit of perfection, accomplishment, and happiness at all costs, including the cost of actual happiness itself, was my problem.

"Why, *why*, am I not enough?" I sat up in the tub and started chewing on my fingernail. My eyes looked up at the ceiling, as if that's where the bully who had relentlessly taunted me for four decades lived. Then I finally delivered the gift I had promised myself in Moab: I stood up to my inner demon. "Leave me alone. I'm doing the best I can, dammit."

I paused, waiting for a response. My tormentor said nothing. I continued, "And that has to be good enough..."

I paused again. Nothing. I floated in silence until my fingers and toes pruned and the bath cooled. I pulled the drain plug and watched the retreating water take away residual bits of disappointment. I stared at the empty tub. "...because I have nothing, *nothing*, left to give."

I slipped back into my robe and walked into my home office to face my community. Many had watched our path via our Garmin InReach map, so I felt compelled to explain why the tracking had stopped and then disappeared after Forgotten Canyon two days ago.

My index finger tapped the keyboard as I tried to decide how to share my sentiments about our trip—and explain why we didn't finish it.

Humiliation crept up my throat with each typed word. I worried people would say, "See, I told you so. That was so stupid." I rubbed my forehead. I wanted to melt into the floor.

I managed to spin a message behind the same bubbly mask that had veiled my true feelings about my life. On Facebook, I recapped our adventure and rescue on the lake, then added:

> As we work through a swirl of emotions—relief, disappointment, immense joy, sadness, pride, and everything in between—we are so grateful for a number of things:
>
> 1. Our lives!
> 2. Our glorious four-day, 41-mile adventure through gorgeous canyons—no exaggeration, we had some of the best times of our lives out there together. Might have been shorter than expected, but it was certainly no less epic!
> 3. Help from complete strangers, especially NPS rangers Anthony and Marty, when we needed it most.
> 4. The amazing love, support, and encouragement from our family and all of you as we took on this journey.

While copying and pasting the same text to my blog on a different tab in my internet browser, my computer started making noises. Ping. Ping. Ping. Responses to my post came through one by one.

"I'm so glad you and your mom are okay."

"Wow, sure glad you are safe and sound."

"There is no shame in being safe…"

"You two made a good decision; what good is the experience if you don't live through it?"

"I am grateful for your courageous decision to let this one go…for a while."

"The adventure still awaits."

I smiled bigger and bigger after each one. Not a single negative comment. I blew out a relieved, "Whew."

I stared at my supporters gathered virtually on the screen. I realized that no one cared whether we succeeded or failed. Sure, our friends cared about our well-being as fellow human beings. But their affirmations proved that true friendship did not hinge on my achievements—or a lack thereof.

Besides, as soon as they clicked the "Like" button or finished typing their comment, they continued wading through an endless stream of political commentary, food porn photos, and videos of dogs doing cute human-like tricks. In other words, they had moved on. People were too busy attending to their own tangle of life, too worried about whether *they* were succeeding, to hold any concern about whether I had.

Who would remember whether we paddled across Lake Powell in five, ten, or fifty years besides my mom and me? Honestly, not many. Nobody gave a shit. Like, in a good way, nobody gave a shit. Which meant I could do whatever I wanted without worrying about what anybody else thought. To bastardize the idiom, I could paddle as if no one was watching, because, it turns out, no one actually was.

No one was giving us a score, a grade, or a performance review for our time on Lake Powell. Even if they had, hadn't all my ribbons, newspaper clippings, and award plaques ended up in a plastic Tupperware storage box collecting dust in my garage anyhow? No one had ever asked to see these. Hell, even I never looked at them. It's not like we get a score, a grade, or a performance review at the end of our lives. And even if we did, by that point, who cared?

To whom was I constantly trying to prove my worth? And why? Why did I need other people's approval? Why did their opinion matter more than my own? No one could possibly know me as well as I knew myself. No one could possibly know what was best or right for me better than I. The only person who mattered in evaluating whether I was good enough should be me.

You know what? I was tired of listening to other people. I was tired of lying to myself. There was enough judgment in the world. I didn't need to be my own worst enemy.

So long as I could figure out how to stop sparring with the evil spirits in my head, I could finally lay down the sword of perfection dripping with my own blood and accept that I was good enough just the way I was. I didn't have to base my perception of myself on my progress—or lack thereof—on meeting arbitrary goals or on my relationship status or on other people's acceptance. If my accomplishments didn't define me or my worth, then neither did my failures.

I pushed my chair away from my desk and turned the computer off. I clapped my hands together over my head and shook my hips from side to side in jubilation over the unexpected release from the chokehold of expectations. "Yes! I'm free!"

Three days later, a rogue wave hit.

14
THE SINJIN TEST

Confronting yourself after you've become mindful of the unsettled state of your being is not for the timid or weak. Thoughts buzzed around my head like a swarm of mosquitoes. Swatting away at them required some serious ninja-like skills. This superpower apparently takes more than three days to develop because I had not yet come to possess it when the rogue wave hit.

While scientists say it takes only three days in the wild to feel relaxed, it took only three days at home to start itching in my self-imposed solitary confinement. My ego kept telling me I *had* to retry this Lake Powell trip, start to finish, 141-miles, self-supported, on my SUP. Instead of squashing the idea, I started scratching at it.

On the morning of December 2, I cut short my peaceful coffee-in-bed morning routine to jump on my computer. My calendar showed a three-week time block in late May. Spring would offer pleasant temperatures and low boat traffic but high winds. No way would I write such an open invitation to disaster. I could also squeeze out two weeks in late June and four in July between work commitments. Scorching temperatures, boat traffic, and biting bugs did not sound ideal. Over the next year, November and December were the only other available time. Winter is often the wettest—and coldest—season in the desert. I shook my head. Nothing worked. Nothing felt right.

I had more than a timing issue. I didn't have anyone to go with me. Mom refused to get back in a kayak. Few of my friends paddled, let alone standup paddleboarded. I wasn't afraid to do the trip on my own, but when I had hinted at the possibility of attempting a solo crossing, Dad called the notion suicidal.

Adrift in a sea of questions, I turned to The Almighty Library of Life Wisdom—the internet—for answers as I had done before. I searched for "kayak guides on Lake Powell." The results spit out an article titled "Expedition to a Haunted Landscape" written by Sinjin Eberle on the American Rivers blog.

I quickly looked up Sinjin's profile on Facebook. He worked for American Rivers, a non-profit organization focused on "protecting wild rivers, restoring damaged rivers, and conserving clean water for people and nature." He was the Intermountain West Communications Director, which included the Colorado River watershed. He'd certainly be one to know about Lake Powell.

I looked back at the blog. The post started off by highlighting the ongoing management challenges with the Colorado River and Lake Powell. Then, halfway through, I read, "...a team of five adventurers is setting out this week to experience, contemplate, and capture on film some of the broad horizons and hidden wonders being revealed as water levels drop."

"This week?" I scrolled back up to the top of the article to check the post's date. November 29, 2015.

"That means..." my voice quivered. Some guy named Sinjin and a team of four other kayakers planned to travel ninety-five miles from Halls Crossing to Antelope Point on Lake Powell in December. This December. "Like...right now."

Without hesitation, I did something I had never done before with a stranger: I typed Sinjin a private message. I explained how I learned of his trip, offered him unsolicited advice about the potentially dangerous windy conditions on the reservoir, and asked if he'd be willing to share more information about the logistical support he was receiving. I rolled my eyes after hitting the send button. It sounded desperate. I didn't expect a response.

Four days later, on the morning of December 6, I checked my Facebook messages one last time before heading to Escalante, Utah, to meet up with Guy. A short reply from Sinjin appeared at the top of the list:

> Colleen. Thank you for your note. We are currently at mile 40—just west of Dangling Rope and 47 miles into our trip. So far so good. Will give a more complete update when we are out. We plan to be in Page Tuesday night.

I feigned a smile and typed, "Excellent, Sinjin! I look forward to hearing and reading more about your trip. Continued safe and happy journey!"

I shut down my computer and stared at the black screen.

What. The. Hell.

Did he just send me a message from the lake?

That I was supposed to be on right now?

I dug the palm of my hands into my eye sockets and rubbed them in circles. Had all gone according to our plans, we would have seen them out there. We would have been paddling right next to them at some point.

Like right now.

I remembered reading a stack of mountaineering books in my younger years and wondering what it would feel like to be a mountaineer who had paid $65,000, or more, to climb Mount Everest, only to decide to turn back one hundred yards shy of the summit because of weather or other extenuating circumstances. I visualized how it would feel to sit in basecamp afterward, watching other climbers reach the top in the hours and days that followed. Could I believe that it took more courage to call off an attempt in deteriorating conditions than it did to keep going in perfect ones? Or would the decision feel like someone was dousing rubbing alcohol into the thousand paper cuts of failure and then setting the disappointment on fire?

After twenty-some years—and without spending $65,000 to find out—I finally had my answers: yes and yes. I held a new respect for those adventurers who had cut their dream short to stay safe. They lived another day to climb another mountain. At the same time, I wanted to roar like a lion trying to scare off a clan of hyenas stealing its hard-earned kill. Sinjin and his friends were finishing *my* trip on *my* Lake Powell without me. And Craig was living his life without me.

My hands curled into fists. My jaw clenched. The idea infuriated me. So much so, I vomited a little in my mouth.

"Breathe. It's just a wave. It's just a patch of rough water," I said, closing my eyes and rocking back in my chair. I had to find a way to eddy out of this rapid. I needed a distraction.

I punched out a quick text to Guy: "All packed and loaded."

I should warn him about my current state of being, I thought.

I tapped out another message:

> Know that I will arrive as a body and mind of broken glass shards held together precariously by leopard-print duct tape (nice aesthetic choice, huh?). I may entertain; I may fall apart. But regardless, I know I'm better off 'out there' than I am here right now. Meet you at Hole in the Rock Road tomorrow around 3?

I did not actually own leopard-print duct tape. I couldn't figure out why I kept overcommitting to things for no reason and then made myself swim like hell to make them happen. Who cared what kind of duct tape it was? Guy didn't. I didn't.

Seconds later, I received a response in his characteristic E.E. Cummings, sans-capital-letters, texting style, "that's what i'm here for. i'll help you pick up the pieces and put them back together. the ones worth keeping, anyhow. and this is not time out. this is life!"

I left for Utah at first light. During the first five hours of the eight-hour drive, I stared at the highway lines in numbing silence. Then I saw her again.

As I passed through Page, Arizona, and crossed over the bridge at the Glen Canyon Dam, the passenger window framed the placid pool of Lake Powell. I stole a hesitant glance. Seeing the reservoir felt like seeing Craig at dinner before I left on my trip. Like looking into his resolute green eyes and craving to feel loved but only feeling a wall of rejection. Like being denied, shut out, and knowing full well he—and the lake—didn't want me no matter who I was or what I did. I turned away, not able to bear those thoughts, and traced the feisty Colorado River flowing deep in a sandstone chasm on my left until it disappeared into the distant converging cliffs.

A couple of miles later, I pulled over on the side of the road to give Wahweap Bay and the marina a once-over. A demure sun smiled over the landscape from behind a polka-dot pattern of cumulonimbus clouds. Mid-afternoon shadows draped over the sensual skin of rounded sandstone formations. Two small speedboats tickled the water's surface as they moved in opposite directions between the cliffs and sand.

The halcyon scene stirred sediment from the bottom of my soul. I gripped my steering wheel and pushed my body into the back of my seat. "That was supposed to be me, goddammit!" I snarled at the windshield. I exploded into tears with Lake Powell staring back at me and the memory of Sinjin's message singed on my psyche.

What if we had left a few days later? What if we had started earlier? What if we had kept going another few miles on that glorious Thanksgiving Day? What if we had kept going after Forgotten Canyon? What if we had continued after resting at Halls Crossing? What if we had waited out the storm for a couple more days? What if we had trained more? Packed lighter? Studied the maps longer?

What if I had been a better wife? What if I hadn't traveled so much? What if I had stayed home more often? What if I hadn't been so damn miserable about everything all the time?

"What if...you left me alone?" It wasn't a question, but rather a command, for my inner bully. I shifted into drive and pressed on the accelerator, hoping to leave second guessing in the dust. "I gotta get out of here."

In the three-hour jaunt to Escalante, I wrestled with whether I had gleaned enough wisdom and strength from the Colorado River to overthrow the voracious internal demon trying to bleed me of the contentment I had started to feel about my trip and my life. After all,

Sinjin hadn't judged me for not finishing my trip. He didn't know me from a rock. Lake Powell hadn't judged me either. Neither had the Colorado River. Or Craig or any of my friends or family. I was creating my own resentment, my own inner storm through my own jealousy, my own inane competitiveness, my own ruinous attitude about external things, events, and people over which I had no control.

To hold someone else's efforts in higher regard than my own when their efforts, in most cases, had no effect on my own, was as useful as irrational fear. It was a waste of time and energy. It only served to dismiss the value of *my* opportunities, *my* growth, *my* life. There would always be someone else out there doing something more than me. That didn't mean their channel was the better one…or mine less so.

The forty-one-mile paddle had pushed Mom and me to our physical limits, but learning about Sinjin and his trip felt like my final mental exam to salvation. Was I strong enough to pass? To drown the monsters in my head once and for all? To believe in my self-worth even as others achieved in their own ways? To live according to my own interests and standards? To hold myself together as I stepped out of the flow of societal and personal expectations?

If only I could find that duct tape somewhere.

15
FINGERS IN THE WATER

I stopped for gas in the small, sleepy town of Escalante. I went inside the convenience store to search for leopard-patterned duct tape. This was my last chance. I had already stopped at three other gas stations.

The store had plenty of duct tape, just not in any animal print styles. Even though I had regular duct tape buried in my camper somewhere, I bought two gray twenty-foot-long rolls. Before I jumped back into my truck, I wrapped the tape around my left foot and leg, my mid-section, my neck, and my right arm as carefully as I would string holiday lights around a Christmas tree. Ten minutes later, I arrived at the Hole in the Rock Road, mostly as I had promised: as an emotional train wreck held together by duct tape.

I waved out the window to Guy as I parked next to his truck at our designated meeting spot. I stepped out of my rig and raised both my arms to the side. "Here ya go. Here's what you have to work with."

He said nothing at first, which made me proud. It's hard to render Guy speechless. Then he looked me up and down and shook his head while smiling big enough to show his teeth. "Good to see you," he said.

"Good to see you too." We gave each other a friendly hug. "Thanks so much for meeting up with me. I really needed this."

He held his index finger up as if to indicate I should wait for something. He ducked into his muddied truck and emerged with his

Trying to keep it together with duct tape when meeting Guy in the Grand Staircase-Escalante National Monument in Utah on December 7, 2015. Photo by Guy Tal.

iPhone in hand. As he pointed it at me to snap a photograph, I struck a how-do-you-like-me-now pose.

"Another one for the blackmail file," he said after clicking a couple of frames—a mischievous threat but an empty one, I knew. I kept posing until he put the phone away in his pocket and started giving me directions to the camp we hoped to snag. "Let's go. Follow me," he said with an inviting wave.

Over the next couple of days, we hiked within the soothing embrace of several sinuous sandstone canyons, following fingers unfurling from the treed Kaiparowits Plateau until they reached the Escalante River flowing in the east. In the evenings, at our camp at the base of a small white-washed alcove, we sat around the campfire sipping on expensive tequila poured from a hand-painted decorative bottle, something Guy had picked up for the momentous occasion. The box promised "Very Special Tequila," and it was every bit that and more. We toasted repeatedly to being alive, to the good lives and fortunate freedom we enjoyed—and to our unlikely friendship, which, since the Moab Photo Symposium in April, had held true to what Everett Ruess wrote, "I've done things alone chiefly because I never found people who cared about the things I've cared for enough to suffer the attendant hardships. But a true companion halves the misery and doubles the joy."*

The next morning, after a few rounds of gritty coffee, we set off on another adventure down another dusty dirt road. We moved through an unnamed dry wash like a flash flood, bounding from rock to rock, gliding effortlessly over ledges and dried mud, following the twisted contours of the canyon walls, and gaining momentum as we traveled downhill. Within a mile or so, we came upon a knee-high cascade trickling its way over a sculpted white Navajo Sandstone ledge. Caustic water patterns danced in a small ankle-deep pool below, its circular rim crusted with razor-thin triangular ice formations.

"That's incredible." The motion hypnotized me. "I have to stop to photograph this."

Guy and I alternated pointing at different visual elements at play in the scene: rock blending with water blending with rock, ice melting into water melting onto ice. With as much enthusiasm as two excited six-year-olds frolicking in a ball crawl at a Chuck E. Cheese, we exchanged impassioned comments, starting with "Look at this! How cool is that?"

---

* *Ruess' thoughts were likely influenced by Marcus Tullius Cicero, a Roman statesman born in 106 B.C. who wrote in his "On Friendship" essay: "Such friendship enhances prosperity, and relieves adversity of its burden by halving and sharing it." Ruess was a writer, printmaker, and solo traveler. In November 1934, at the age of twenty, he disappeared in the Utah desert near Escalante. His body has not yet been found.*

(Some photographers refer to this state of uncontainable and overwhelming joy while making an image as a "photogasm.")

I dropped my pack to the side of the stream and started to set up my macro lens. My eye fixated on the changing water patterns crisscrossing on top of a decaying leaf submerged just beneath the surface. I leaned left and then right, searching for the best angle. Above the leaf, an overly bright space, snow white in color, kept distracting my eye. I needed something to fill that void. I couldn't figure out how I'd fix it, though, to make an effective image.

Guy pulled out his iPhone. "Here, this should help," he said.

He tapped his screen. *Cantus - Song of the Spirit* by Karl Jenkins erupted at full volume, filling the canyon with the dramatic and intense New Age song. "Oh yes, that will certainly do," I said. I straightened my spine, lengthened my neck, and pushed my shoulders back—standing as proper as a ballroom dancer—and started moving my feet to the beat using my extended tripod as my partner.

One-two-three. One-two-three. One-two-three.

I waltzed around the water, bringing my camera up to my eye to evaluate a potential angle now and then. As I hummed, I grabbed a different leaf in the sand nearby and tried to place it near the one already in the water. The leaf floated away. I grabbed it and repositioned it. It floated away. I grabbed it and repositioned it. It floated away again. It felt like getting a two-year-old to sit still for a family photo.

After several attempts to get the leaf to stay put, each paired with ineffective coaxing words, it escaped my grasp and drifted downstream a few feet before coming to rest on a sandstone ledge along the stream's left bank.

"Gah! Total bummer!" I laughed at my feeble set-designing skills.

Guy stood motionless on the other side of the creek with his arms crossed loosely against his chest. Watching and waiting for another photographer's photograph to unfold was only slightly more exciting than watching concrete cure.

"Sorry this is taking me so long," I said, still studying the scene.

"Don't apologize," Guy said without moving. "I have nothing else to do today."

I didn't want to walk away from such a beautiful subject, but it seemed like there were only so many ways I could put together the photograph effectively—and none of them were working. I stared blankly at the rivulet.

A few minutes later, I realized that I could not control the positioning of the leaf, but I could affect its surroundings. I stripped my mitten off my left hand and plunged the back of two fingers into the shallow water to create a new water ripple. It caused a small stream of ribbons across the otherwise blank and bright white space. I wiggled my hand until I got the pattern above the leaf just right. I snapped a couple shots with my cable release in my other hand without looking through the viewfinder.

Guy dropped his arms to his sides. "That's one of the most creative things I've ever seen someone do," he said.

"What do you mean?" I asked while continuing to click the shutter. Even though I kept my fingers still, the structure and direction of the streaming patterns changed every second.

"I mean, putting your fingers in the water like that…"

"I needed to do something. I needed more texture in the water right…" I pointed to the white spot on the sandstone slab. "...here."

"I know, but I would have never thought to do that."

"Well, *now* you will!" I beamed with pride from receiving high praise from my talented friend. "I'm not sure it's working. So, we'll see."

"But are you having fun?" Guy asked.

"Of course! So much fun."

"Then it's worth it regardless of whether it turns out," he said, crossing his arms again.

I snapped another frame, then leaned back, keeping both hands on my tripod to stay balanced on my toes. "Is it? Is it still worth it if I don't make a photograph?"

From the time I had picked up a camera in 2001, I had applied my tightly controlled, achievement-focused approach religiously to my image-making. Things had changed for my professional photography, though, thanks to my three artist-in-residencies at Acadia National

The photograph I made after putting my fingers in the water to create a ripple in the upper right corner.

Park in Maine. During my second residency, in October 2010, I had helped establish a photojournalism class for the Schoodic Education Adventure. SEA is a residential education program for middle schoolers where they learn about art and science in Acadia's natural classroom.

On the first trial run, I led a group of fourth graders through the forest. A young boy took off down the dirt trail, then suddenly stopped. He started pointing at the ground and kept repeating, "You guys, come here! Look at this mushroom!"

I approached him and commended his choice of mushrooms. (It was, indeed, a fine specimen.) Before he took his camera out of his pocket, he looked up at me and said matter-of-factly, "I think I want to be a photographer just like you when I grow up." Then he aimed his point-and-shoot camera at the mushroom, clicked the shutter once, and skipped off.

It did not occur to me until three years later, during my third residency in 2013, that the little boy thought, that as a photographer, I did what he did. That I ran around the forest with unbridled joy all the time, photographing whatever it was that sparked my emotions. I hadn't been doing anything of the sort. After photographing for more than nine years, I had become a robot controlled by my perfectionism, much as I had as a student, gymnast, volleyball player, probably even a wife. I'd arrive at scenic locations, always and only at sunrise or sunset, with my wide-angle lens, find a rock or stick to put in the foreground, then press the right buttons on my camera to produce a technically perfect, but completely emotionless, picture. I never liked the images I produced in Acadia or elsewhere. And I was bored out of my mind. To the point I no longer wanted to photograph *anything*.

For the remainder of my third residency, I decided to play like that fourth grader. I set out to a small bay one morning with my camera—and expectations for making an image—tucked away in my backpack. I noticed the patterns of air bubbles embedded in a thin translucent ice shelf. I lost all two marbles in my brain. I might have even squealed aloud. (Which begs the question: If a photographer squeals on the shore and no one is around to hear it, does she make a sound?)

I studied that ice sheet for hours—although it felt like only seconds had passed. Arguably, I made the worst photographs I had ever made. It didn't matter. I felt refreshed, euphoric even. I had never had more fun "photographing" while not caring about photographing before.

I had unknowingly tapped into what's called an autotelic approach and tasted "flow." Renowned psychologist Mihaly Csikszentmihályi described this mental state in his book *Flow: The Psychology of the Optimal Experience* as "a state in which people are so involved in an activity that nothing else seems to matter; the experience is so enjoyable that people will continue to do it even at great cost, for the sheer sake of doing it."

Since 2013, I have dedicated my artistic endeavors, as Guy already had, to playing and acting curious instead of forcing myself to make a photograph, let alone a good or sellable one. If a photograph materialized out of the experience, great. If it didn't, great. Spending meaningful time in a meaningful place mattered more.

Practicing this approach until it became second nature set me free in my photography. I no longer felt pressure to perform—or frustrated when I didn't get results. Much to my surprise, not worrying about my productivity made me *more* productive. I finally liked the photographs I made. Photography was no longer just an escape; it was a deliberate celebration of discovery and self-expression. I had found my creative flow.

As I stood over the creek now, contemplating Guy's statement, it occurred to me that I had not yet found my flow in my everyday existence. My perpetual self-flagellation in the service of achievement over the years had prevented me from not only enjoying the scenery along the way but also from noticing it existed at all. In focusing my attention on executing plans, working hard, and pursuing dreams in academics, athletics, work, photography, and even my marriage, I had overlooked the joy of the experience. The joy of trying. The joy of the moment. The joy period.

The recipe I had followed for most of my life, however well-intentioned, suddenly felt misguided. I looked at the leaf and its serrated blade wavering underwater. I wondered, what if I started approaching my life as I did my photography? What if I ditched achievement and replaced it with curiosity? What if I made choices because I enjoyed the experience and did not care about the results? What if not worrying about my happiness led to more happiness?

Decoupling joy from accomplishment and adopting an autotelic personality sounded like a refreshing direction. There was only one problem: to an overachieving perfectionist, doing things purely for intrinsic pleasure sounded sinfully self-indulgent. But was it? Was paddling across a reservoir selfish? Was photographing leaves in a desert stream self-absorbed? Was splashing in puddles to celebrate a rare desert rainstorm immature?

Who cared?

I had developed into a functional, independent adult. I ran two companies—my photography and book publishing businesses. I took care of my basic needs like food, water, and shelter. I paid all my bills on time. I paid my fair share of taxes. On good weeks, I even managed to set my garbage can out on the curb on time.

So long as I wasn't a burden on society, what prevented me from having unadulterated fun? I don't remember getting a memo that said adulting had to be a slog through the mud of responsibility while dragging a lifetime of baggage along the way. I mumbled under my breath, "I bet I'm capable of being a hard-working, responsible adult and having a roaring good time at it."

And a "roaring good time" need not be extravagant or expensive. Fun for me entailed discovering a new view in the wild, reading about a novel idea, dancing in my truck to 80s music, and helping people learn how to become better and more creative photographers—experiences that cost nothing more than time and led to well-roundedness, fulfillment, even purpose.

As long as I filled my time with endeavors I deemed consequential and didn't disregard other people's feelings or otherwise negatively impact others, I couldn't see how assuming responsibility for piecing my own happiness together could be classified as self-centered. It sounded more like integral self-care. Besides, I couldn't imagine how my constant self-abnegation was making anyone's life better.

I looked down at the water trickling by my feet. Guy was right.

Losing my mind over water patterns and a leaf in the company of one of my best friends was worth doing whether I made an image or not.

I moved my tripod, pretending to focus on snapping another frame of the leaf. Instead, I started formulating a way to simplify my life "recipe" to asking myself, "What would be fun to do right now?"

In other words, in a salute to that fourth-grade boy in Acadia, I'd make forty the new ten. And I'd have a roaring good time doing it, too.

"Now imagine what that leaf just went through and what it's thinking right now?" Guy said with a sardonic, theatrical flair, his voice snapping me out of my silent musings. "Here it was minding its own business, having a great day. Then, someone comes by, sticks their fingers in the water, and messes *everything* up."

I spilled into laughter, choking on my own breath while pulling my eye away from my viewfinder. I said with mocking desperation, "It sure sucks to be the leaf now, doesn't it?"

"Sure does," Guy said.

"Whatever. Look where it gets to be," I said with a sweeping motion of my hand across the landscape.

I moved my tripod a few inches to the left. "You know, that's a pretty profound metaphor for life. You should write a poem or something about that."

"I could," he said. He placed one hand on his hip, stroked his chin with the other, and then tilted his head toward the sun with his eyes closed as if he were a Shakespearean actor on stage beneath a melodramatic spotlight. He improvised several lines of superficial poetic rhetoric littered with unrecognizable big words one would only find on the SAT. I rolled my eyes and laughed.

Once I made a photograph I liked, I packed up my camera gear so we could continue exploring the canyon. Guy pivoted on his heels to turn downstream. Before following him down the narrowing canyon, I squatted next to the creek. To make things copacetic with Mother Nature, I discreetly apologized to the leaf for messing things up for it on this sunny and crisp morning. "I understand how it is. I was minding my own business, trying to do what I thought I should do, until last April, when it all got screwed up for me too. Then, just ten days ago, it got messed up again," I whispered to it. "Now what?"

I scrunched my nose and cheeks to prevent a flood, but the tears started streaming down my face, leaving thin trails on my skin as if it were desert varnish streaking down the aged and polished sandstone cliffs around me. I turned my head to look over my left shoulder toward the trailhead and dirt parking area. My past. I couldn't live there anymore. I shifted my gaze over my right shoulder and traced the meandering creek disappearing into an unfamiliar and darkening chasm of the canyon. My future. I didn't know what was in store for me there. I looked down at the leaf resting in the trickling water. My present. I couldn't put the leaf back on the tree. I couldn't resurrect the Colorado River from Lake Powell. I couldn't rejoin a relationship my husband didn't want. I could, however, put my fingers in the water, into the void of the blank, white space and make something from the situation at hand.

I stood up and put my hands on my hips. I already knew how to keep my paddle in the water. That was only skimming the surface. If I wanted to create my own fulfillment, I'd have to start creating my own ripples.

A rambling breeze rustled the nearby cottonwood trees into an encouraging applause, their silvery leaves of late autumn seemingly cheering me on. In a single gust, the shallow water loosened its grip on the leaf, and it floated downstream. Without releasing my gaze on the leaf disappearing into the unknown, I offered my final goodbye: "Maybe things haven't fallen apart. Maybe they aren't messed up. Maybe they are just coming together. Maybe you've just been set free into the grandest journey of your life."

16

CHOICES AT LONE ROCK

I stopped at the Lone Rock Beach Campground along the shores of Lake Powell to camp overnight on my way home from Escalante. I settled into an isolated stretch of sand twenty feet from the water's edge on the far northwestern end. Winter had chased away visitors save for two small white trailers on the far side of the beach and a couple of ravens scavenging for dropped potato chips and other food scraps in a charred fire pit.

I sat on my dropped tailgate, then checked my phone for service. I noticed the date. December 9. Had nothing else prevented our progress, Mom and I would have finished our paddle across Lake Powell near here, around the corner at Wahweap Marina, today.

I dangled my legs back and forth and noticed how different Mother Nature's mood seemed compared to two weeks ago. An opaque shade over the sun softened her glare across the landscape. Thin trails of blue-grey corduroy clouds reflected in the glassy lake. Winter's callous breath cantered in the occasional light breeze, stroking the sculpted shoulders of countless buttes, knobs, and mesas and turning the water's surface into a waving silk sheet. A frosting of snow capped the little sliver of Navajo Mountain peaking over Castle Butte in the distance. Three consecutive storm fronts—the first of which we had paddled though—had carried in nature's next season.

Juno (my truck and Alaskan Camper) dispersed camping at Lone Rock Beach Campground along Lake Powell. Castle Rock in Wahweap Bay is visible on the horizon.

The calmness hypnotized me. What a storybook day it would have been to land. I raised a full glass of lukewarm leftover chardonnay to my lips, gulping half of it in one sip, drinking in stillness. I imagined what today would have been like had we finished our trip as intended.

I envisioned waving to Dad—and perhaps Guy and a few interested friends—in between strokes as we approached Wahweap Marina. I pictured us arriving relieved, overwhelmed, and exhausted as we pulled our vessels onto the shore. I imagined hugging my mom and dad while jumping up and down in jubilation. I visualized raising my paddle over my head while hooting and hollering, "Whoohoo! We did it!" After these few moments of elation, we would have stacked our gear into my parents' SUV and headed to the Dam Bar and Grill in Page to gorge our thinned stomachs on fat, juicy hamburgers and french fries. Restaurant food would have dropped our freeze-dried-food-conditioned bodies into paralyzing food comas faster than we could have spelled "Lake Powell."

A curious raven swooped in front of me. Its sharp "Caw! Caw! Caw!" jolted me out of my reverie. I closed my wet eyes as the splendid fantasy of us completing our trip and standing on top of the world faded into the wind.

A part of me still wanted to be upset with Mother Nature for dipping her fingers in our waters and for screwing up our plans. A part of me still wanted to blame Craig for damming our marriage and stopping my life in its tracks without my permission. The other part of me—the part that the Colorado River had taken a hold of and started shaping into something else—knew that I could no longer stay stagnant in a reservoir of disappointment. I couldn't do *this* anymore.

At Guy's encouragement, I had just started rereading *Man's Search for Meaning* by Austrian psychiatrist and Holocaust survivor Viktor Frankl. In it, he wrote: "Everything can be taken from a man but one thing: the last of the human freedoms—to choose one's attitude in any given set of circumstances, to choose one's own way."

Let's be clear: I wasn't trying to escape genocide. If Viktor Frankl could take on his attitude, given his horrifying Holocaust experience, I could, too, when facing my problems. I refused to be a casualty of my circumstances just because my perfect and privileged life got a little hard.

I now sat on the beach at Lone Rock at a "T" intersection with the chance to choose my own way. How I viewed the four-day trip came down to a simple choice: I could remain upset it did not work out as planned or feel proud that it happened.

How I viewed the first forty years of my life also came down to a choice. I could keep draining my well of self-worth with more degrading "shoulda, coulda, woulda" thoughts. Or I could fill it to the brim with excitement and appreciation for my growth along the way.

How I viewed my separation from Craig came down to a choice, too. Had he impeded my flow by building a dam on my river? Or had he sent me into the grandest journey of my life?

Given these disparate options, how were these even decisions? Why would I—or anyone—*choose* to feel dissatisfied and lonely if contentment and freedom were curled up in my lap like a sleeping kitten?

(That's called "purrr-fection.")

"Did Mom and I finish the crossing?" was the wrong question to ask about our Lake Powell trip. Instead, the more appropriate queries were, "Did we start? Did we get value out of the process of planning the journey? Did we find meaning in the experience? Did we learn about our surroundings, ourselves, and each other?"

We did.

"Did the fairy tale last forever?" wasn't the right question to ask of my marriage either. Did we do our best for each other during the times we had together? Did we share meaningful and memorable experiences in our twenty-two years together? Did we help each other grow into the people we are today?

We did.

I would never forget spending part of my life with Craig. How lucky I was to have shared all those years with someone who loved me, who laughed with me, adventured with me, and took better care of me than I did at times. Some people never find a person like that to be with. I had enjoyed it for over half of my existence.

For two weeks, I had cried a river about our incomplete voyage across Lake Powell. Over the past eight months, I had done the same about the unexpected bend in my relationship. But I had the power to reframe the narrative of past events. I could define the meaning of my experience however I wanted.

I stood up from the tailgate, picked up a flat rock from the shore, and chucked it into the water. The reflections shimmering on the lake's surface shattered. Each ripple carried the memory of waves with a different truth of how things happened on Lake Powell.

I thought about falling asleep to the lullaby of sloshing water tickling the sand. I thought about seeing the smoky clouds consume the nearly full moon in the middle of the night. I thought about our surreal fifteen-mile paddle on our third day, when the entire day unfolded into a heavenly dream. I thought about sitting on our little beach eating freeze-dried Thanksgiving dinner, where I made a promise to my mother that I'd return to Lake Powell on my 64th Thanksgiving to have a big feast in her honor—she would be a lively eighty-seven then. I thought about how comforting it was to see my mother's smile as she turned to me to ask how I was doing so many times. I thought about how I watched in amazement as Mom—straining with all her might—repetitively pushed her kayak through pounding waves and away from cliff walls because she loved me and was determined to stay alive. I thought about how fortunate we were to have paddled forty-one miles together through some of the most majestic canyon scenery I had ever witnessed. I thought about how much life we had packed into four days.

I thought about us arriving relieved, overwhelmed, and exhausted as Anthony dropped us off on the shore. I thought about how we waved to my dad as he pulled into the Halls Crossing campground. I thought about how I hugged my mom and dad after the trip ended.

Exactly, *exactly*, as I would have done had we finished the crossing today at Wahweap Marina.

Mom and I would never forget sharing this life-changing journey. We could never duplicate the memories we held not only from our four-day experience but also the entire months-long process of dreaming and preparing that led up to our adventure. I refused to take our trip (or my marriage or my life) for granted anymore.

I raised my arms to the sky and yelled out to the lake, "Whoohoo! We did it!"

I had still made it to the end of Lake Powell on the day I planned. December 9. Who cares how I got here, whether by paddling my board or by driving my truck?

More importantly, I was still alive. Mom was still alive. Had either of us died near Forgotten Canyon—or ironically, had we finished our paddle today at Wahweap Marina as planned—I would have missed *this* exact moment. This ephemeral moment where the sky celebrated the day's end with a resplendent palette of cotton candy pinks, blood oranges, and lipstick reds across its cloudy canvas all around me. Where squawking American coots bobbed in a commotion. Where the wisdom of the Colorado River dripped from my fingers. I would have missed all this. For a food coma. Or worse yet, for a funeral.

The glorious sunset at Lone Rock Beach Campground along Lake Powell on December 9, 2015.

"What a glorious place I'm in," I said, raising my almost empty glass to the sky.

It was now as clear to me as a saint's conscience that it did not matter whether Mom and I went forty-one miles or 141 miles. It did not matter whether Craig and I spent twenty-two years or forever together. This, *this*, was what contentment felt like.

When the first star appeared on the night's blank page, I walked down to the water's edge and sank my hand into the lake. I was ready for my next season. I was ready to choose more wisely.

"We must be willing to get rid of the life we've planned, so as to have the life that is waiting for us."

-Joseph Campbell

PART III: DOWNSTREAM

17

ON THE FLATWATER

A Chinese proverb suggests, "Don't push a river; it flows by itself."

That might be true for a wild river. But a dammed one does *not* flow by itself. No matter how hard you try to get a river that has become a reservoir to flow, pushing her only leads to banging her head against the wall of a concrete dam.

In the months that followed my Lake Powell trip, I didn't push Craig. I stopped believing that initiating communication with him—the only way we had talked since our separation—could or would deliver any answers beyond the one I didn't want to hear. The silence between us went on long enough that I could sense a storm developing on the horizon. I couldn't tell how far away it was or how much time I had before it hit. Even so, the waters kept rising.

When facing a threat, we respond with fight or flight. *So they say.*

I did neither.

Clinging to the idea that I could somehow escape the squall ahead seemed futile. Misplaced hope was nothing more than unreasonable expectations for a different future. It was an attempt to exert control over uncontrollable situations, a mirage, an ignis fatuus.

Rather than try to redirect the storm, for the first time in my life, I abandoned spreadsheets, Gantt charts, and plans—including the idea of trying to cross Lake Powell again and trying to save my marriage.

I didn't rush downstream into the dam. I didn't try to swim upstream pretending I would somehow find the ocean.

Instead, I anchored to my reality. I gave *in* to my situation. But I didn't give *up* on myself. I explored the calm reservoir of time and space my ongoing separation offered me with a mix of patience, acceptance, and determination. You might not be able to push life any more than you can push a dammed river, but you can push yourself to discover new places while you are floating on the provisional lake.

Instead of asking Craig and others, "What do you want from me?" I asked myself, "What do you want for yourself?"

I started by cleansing and reshaping the only thing I had control over: my psyche. One by one, I picked up each thought, habit, expectation, and assumption as they crossed my brain and studied each with curiosity as if it were a piece of gear. Was it serving me well? Would it provide me support on the journey ahead? If not, I thanked it for its service and left it behind. In life, as on a river trip, you do not need much to get by. And what you do need, but do not have, is easier than you think to improvise. Besides, extra baggage does not fit on your board if you pack enough courage.

Drifting alone in my mental wilderness spawned possibilities as a matter of conscious choice. I *chose* to drown unsupportive thoughts. I *chose* to see opportunities, not despair, in the uncertainty ahead. I *chose* to find balance in breathing and existing—and not in achieving or chasing. I *chose* to find peace, purpose, and rhythm in the present moment. I *chose* to notice the reflections of life's highlights and shadows gleaming on the surface. I *chose* to admire breathtaking canyons and powerful waves and an optimistic sun coloring the landscape, even on the coldest days. I *chose* to see my solitude as a gift, not a condemnation. I *chose* how I wanted to live my big Life with a capital L each and every day, regardless of how my separation might end and regardless of what I thought "they"—society—thought I should do.

Sitting stagnate in a pool of victimhood changes or fixes nothing. Simply letting time pass does not heal all wounds. Neither does running away to the great outdoors. Self-awareness and inner growth do. Fulfillment emerges from our internal attitude to our circumstances and in the individual decisions we make in our everyday lives. Not just in good times but in hard ones too.

Over the next few months, while at home, I kept my paddle in my life's current, taking one stroke at a time, trusting I'd somehow, someway, however slowly, find my way across the flatwater on this reservoir.

I soon realized that the storm looming on my horizon was no longer something to fear or to run from but rather something I could paddle into with confidence. For storms are what birth the Colorado River. Storms are what return her to her true color after the dam strips her of her sediment. Storms are what give her strength and vitality in her journey to the sea.

Storms are, in fact, what push a river to flow by herself.

~ ~ ~

I threw the covers aside and sprung out of bed as the sky outside my bedroom window rioted in reds and oranges, my room glowing with the fire of new beginnings. I walked into my bathroom and paused in front of the full-length mirror on my closet door. I looked myself up and down but avoided eye contact. My crumpled nightshirt was tucked into the corner of my underwear, revealing plump thighs and rounded hips that had been carrying fifteen extra pounds, likely from eating too much macaroni and cheese—one of the few things I knew how to cook for myself.

(It came from a box, so calling it "cooking" might be a stretch.)

I brushed the short, straight strands of greying hair away from my forehead, then rubbed my sleepy, crusty eyes. I had posed in front of this mirror countless times, sucking in my gut, jiggling the flab beneath my triceps, and measuring the gap between my thighs, eventually walking away in disgust.

The past whispered, "If monsters remain hidden beneath the surface, they won't exist."

I stretched my neck from side to side, pushed my shoulders down, then peered straight into my eyes. I spoke to the reflection, "I see you. You exist."

I burst into tears. The beasts beneath my water's surface finally existed. The exhausted, beaten-down little girl desperate for acceptance finally existed. The controlling perfectionist wanting to live like an unfettered river finally existed.

A calm voice, mimicking my therapist, encouraged, "Go on. Tell Colleen something you like about her."

"This is ridiculous," I said, looking away.

I shook my arms out and straightened my back. "Come on, do it. Be nice to yourself like you said you would."

"I like those crow's feet around your eyes. They give your face texture and shape. There."

"Ugh!" I laughed and turned away. "How lame."

I felt like I had just been cast for the revival of the "Daily Affirmations with Stuart Smalley" comedy skit on Saturday Night Live where he says, "I'm good enough, I'm smart enough, and doggone it, people like me."

I put both hands on the mirror and leaned into my reflection to study my crow's feet. I hadn't ever paid attention to the sand-colored ridgelines, the contrast in the creases, and the lines flaring from the corner of my eyes forming butterfly wings. As I squinted and studied, I wondered, what awful things would happen if I treated myself with love, respect, and dignity? What if I appreciated myself just as I was right now without trying to change me? What was I afraid of? Embarrassing myself in front of no one? Turning into a lazy, egotistical asshole? Becoming mediocre?

We mistake thoughts for truths. Thoughts are not facts. They are malleable. If I believed the negative thoughts, which my brain had made up, then I could believe the positive ones, which my brain would also make up, just the same.

I stepped back, then said, sans sarcasm, "They light up when you laugh. They hold the flash floods when you cry. One who is not afraid of feeling as deeply as you do is bound to have those kinds of wrinkles.

They are a testament to your strength and character over forty years—and especially right now. You've earned every single one of those beautiful lines."

I smiled. "And those?" I turned sideways and grabbed the back of my thigh. "Those big old things are strong as a bull. How do you think you're still standing through all this, princess?"

I pulled my nightshirt out of my underwear. "You know what? I think you deserve better than mac and cheese from a box every night."

~ ~ ~

I stood paralyzed in the grocery store aisle, staring at twenty-three different types of canned black beans and pondering what I could make for dinner besides macaroni and cheese. Craig had always done the grocery shopping—and all the cooking. I was a paddleboarder out of water here.

I tapped my finger to my lips. If today were my birthday, what would I request for dinner?

"Chicken fajitas!" I said to no one.

Craig and I had made the meal together enough over the years with me serving as his sous chef. I could figure this out on my own.

I rounded up the necessary ingredients. On the way to the flour tortillas, I scooped up half an apple pie and ice cream. After all, if it were actually my birthday, I'd have dessert. Oh! And flowers too. A bouquet of brilliant yellow roses jumped into my basket.

At home, I made up a pitcher of mean margaritas and poured myself a drink in one of my fancy glasses. I blasted Jimmy Buffet and used a bunch of cilantro as a microphone to belt out the lyrics to "Boat Drinks." I danced the salsa while making some. To spice things up, I pulled an unopened bottle of Dave's Gourmet Insanity Sauce out of the pantry. Sauces like Tabasco and Cholula were staples in our Arizona diet. Over the years, I had tasted my fair share of other hot sauces with Mexican and Latin American foods, gradually increasing my tolerance for hotter, spicier flavors.

I should try this. How hot could it be?

I took the cap off, removed the safety seal, and turned the glass bottle on its head, intending to splash only a drop or two onto my finger. Nothing happened. I flipped it right-side up, replaced the cap, shook it hard from side to side, then turned it again. Nothing happened. I shook it hard upside down a couple more times. Suddenly, half the bottle spilled into the cooking pan.

I gawked at what looked like a pool of blood. I would have normally cried and scorned myself. I just laughed. And laughed. And laughed so hard, I snorted. Twice. The ruckus scared my cat into the next room.

I fished the cap out with one hand and swirled the hot sauce into the chicken and vegetables with a spoon with the other. I licked a drop of the sauce from my finger. At first, I thought, eh, this isn't too bad.

A few seconds later, I had a five-alarm fire in my mouth. My eyes watered. My nose started dripping. I stuck my tongue out like a panting dog and waved my hand across my open mouth—which was as effective as pouring water on a grease fire.

(Important public service announcement: NEVER pour water on a grease fire.)

I had consumed enough hot sauce over the years to know that consuming dairy products, which contained casein, neutralized the burning sensation caused by capsaicin. I didn't have any milk on hand, and I wasn't going to drink the sour cream from the container or shove a stick of butter in my mouth.

(Arguably, I wouldn't have been able to taste either, so in hindsight, maybe I should have.)

I did the only thing I could think of in the moment: I ran to the freezer and pulled out the quart of vanilla ice cream I had bought earlier to go with my apple pie. After devouring a few scoops, my dragon mouth eventually cooled, and I stopped sweating.

I looked down at my first batch of fajitas. I might have ruined dinner and burned my mouth to hell and back, but at least I hadn't burned the house down in one of my first attempts to cook for myself. I decided that alone was worth celebrating.

So, I ate ice cream and apple pie for dinner. And again for breakfast.

~ ~ ~

I sat at my kitchen table, sipping coffee and thumbing through social media and news outlets on my phone. An older article from *Psychology Today* happened to pop up in my feed. It suggested if a person could name just three things a day for which they were thankful, researchers believed you could rewire your brain to feel more determined, energetic, and optimistic in as little as four to six weeks. For it to work, though, you couldn't spew a bunch of random items. You couldn't "fake it till you make it." You had to genuinely fill your soul with appreciation.

I set my phone down. If I were to seek more of anything, it would be more determination, energy, and optimism. Besides, my analytical and curious brain liked a good nonscientific experiment. I'll bite.

I started by recognizing that not one of us chooses to be born and not one of us chooses the circumstances into which we are born. I had hit the jackpot in the birth lottery with two loving parents and a stable family. Being white and middle class gave me advantages and opportunities that not everyone enjoyed while sparing me hardships that others have had to endure. I felt grateful for my brother, my extended family, my dear friends, and my supportive community who cheered for me during my darkest—and brightest—hours. And for strangers, like Anthony and Marty and Tammy, who extended kindness on Lake Powell when Mom and I needed it most. Love from so many, not just from one person, surrounded me like canyon walls.

I felt thankful for every opportunity I had to participate in dance, gymnastics, cheerleading, volleyball, and so many school activities during my upbringing. How lucky I was for the rare chance to attend not one, but two, world-renowned institutions for my higher education. For receiving financial support to do so and coming out of school with no debt. For working with incredible talents in my almost ten years at Intel. For my photography career and my clients who helped enable it. For every trial and tribulation that had shaped me into the person I was right here, right now.

I considered how much I had learned over the years from my

teachers, coaches, teammates, and peers who had taught me new skills and enabled my many successes. From authors, photographers, painters, musicians, and other artists who had inspired me to experience novel concepts. From friends, family, and strangers who had helped refine my principles.

I even appreciated the chair I sat on. The table I sat at. The roof over my head. Heat during Arizona's winter. My cozy pajamas. The person who made my cozy pajamas. My soft blankets that had kept me warm at night. My coffee. The taste of my breakfast. The taste of apple pie and ice cream. The people who grew the coffee I drank and the food I ate. The people who trucked these goods to the grocery store. The water coming out of my faucet. The Colorado River. Snow. Rain. Storms in the desert. My truck, Juno. My standup paddleboard, Lir. The ability to standup paddleboard. The freedom as a freelancer to wake up every morning and decide how I would spend every minute of the time given to me.

Jeez, I had more than enough. And I was just getting warmed up. Why had I believed otherwise?

Society tells us we can be anything we want to be. Except when we try to be ourselves, they say we need to do more, be more, give more, have more to adhere to their norms. They say we don't have enough time, money, talent, fancy cars, square footage, or sexy looks. They say who we are, just as we are, isn't good enough. *So they say.*

But who are "they?" And why do they get any say in how we live our lives? They—anyone with an opinion who gains enough power behind their voice to create implicit or explicit pressure on the rest of us to conform—hold us in this mentality, not out of concern for our well-being but rather for their own power and profit.* They capitalize on our fears of not belonging, of not being accepted, of not being loved.

This constant bombardment of negative messaging triggers a

---

* *A case in point: according to Statistica, global revenue in the cosmetic industry in 2022 equaled $93 billion. (Source: www.statista.com/forecasts/1272313/worldwide-revenue-cosmetics-market-by-segment). Imagine what would happen if we—you, me—decided our eye wrinkles looked beautiful without concealer, botox, and chemical peels? Because they do look beautiful as they are. And I'm tired of being told they don't.*

scarcity mindset, an empty feeling that causes us to do anything and everything, including swimming upstream and doing things like working hard in jobs we don't like in order to make money to acquire things we might not truly want, to backfill that gap—one that may or may not truly exist. It's even worse when we forgo appreciating these external possessions once we acquire them because we, and society, expected us to have them in the first place.

When I read the article about gratitude, it hit me like a wall of water. A scarcity mindset acts like a dam. Society's relentless and omnipresent "so they say's" pool up behind it, causing stagnation and suppression of our own spirit. We turn into the people "they" want us to be with stuff "they" think we should have. We turn into the people we aren't.

Buying into the idea that I lived in scarcity—when I clearly did not—had caused years of anxiety, overthinking, jealousy, and a misplaced sense of entitlement. It had drowned joy. It had twisted me into someone I no longer wanted to be.

It seemed the way to break the dam of a scarcity mindset was by expressing thanks. Appreciation leads to an abundance mindset. Acknowledging and valuing our present gifts reveals just how plentiful our lives are already without needing more, more, always more. This attitude enables us to find our flow in our own desires.

To be sure, it wasn't society's fault for having a flood of opinions. It was mine for blindly listening to and adopting ones that didn't align with my own values.

Over the years, I had read countless self-help articles touting "10 ways to get any guy you want" (followed by another article on "how to get rid of crow's feet"). I had watched Disney princes rescue princesses like Cinderella and Snow White from dire situations in movies. I had listened to countless love songs that yearned for settling down with "The One." So many voices perpetuate the myth that external sources, like buying material goods, changing your appearance in response to beauty trends, and finding a partner "who completes you," will automatically deliver happiness.

Over those same years, though, I had also read countless self-help articles, like the one I had just read, touting "7 scientifically proven benefits of gratitude" (followed by another article on "how to create peace through life's storms"). I had watched female Disney characters like Mulan and Elsa exhibit bravery, strength, and determination in movies. I had listened to countless songs motivating me to keep going during hard times. Plenty of encouraging voices suggested that connecting with community and place, as well as appreciating your unique appearance and finding ways to complete yourself, leads to more lasting fulfillment.

"They" are not monolithic or absolute. While some voices might mislead us, other "they's" express positive notions worth embracing that help us grow and expand our understanding of our existence. Which ones do you believe? Whichever ones you wish. Choose wisely. Voices shape us like a river shapes her shores along its course. We become what we listen to.

I sincerely wanted to be a better human being—and I couldn't do that living in a bubble. I wanted to learn and challenge myself with fresh perspectives. I wanted to produce excellent work to the best of my abilities. I wanted less judgment and more love and kindness in the world. I wanted to help more people feel safe and confident in living their best Life with a capital L, however they defined it for themselves.

I wanted to spend my remaining time on Earth pursuing more of these ideas and being a positive influence. I had knowledge, resources, privileges, and opportunities that I shouldn't take for granted, that I shouldn't waste, that I could put to good use—and would enjoy doing so, too. I had a voice of my own that I could—and wanted to—contribute to help make the world a better place. Knowing how much my life meant to me, if only to me, signified I should keep investing in it.

I drank the last sip of my coffee. The scientists were right. Just thinking about gratitude made me feel rich and happy. I laughed. As a child, that's all I ever wanted to be when I grew up. All it took was being thankful for what I had and not sad for what I lacked.

That said, I realized wanting more, more, always more for ourselves was not necessarily foolish. Wanting to live in a house, excel in a career, feel healthy, travel the world, and thrive in relationships were not unreasonable desires. Having dreams and goals puts a rudder on our lives. So long as they evolve from our own agency and not from fear, ego, comparisons, or other people's expectations. Ambition and appreciation could coexist when they came from satisfaction with oneself, confidence in one's own chosen ideals, and a genuine motivation to fill one's life with purpose.

Learning about gratitude also made me realize that I had birthdays wrong all along. Celebrating your birthday—and your "unbirthdays" on every other day of the year—wasn't about being the center of attention, getting showered with presents, taking trips, or even eating pie or otherwise doing more, being more, giving more, having more, more, more, always more. It was about taking a moment to acknowledge the miracle of our existence, our progress through the sometimes overwhelming chaos, and our individual worth right here, right now, no matter how the journey ahead would unfold.

Life itself was the gift.

~ ~ ~

"Girl, you look damn fine in that dress," I said to the mirror on my closet door while trying on an old dress to see if it still fit me. I spun around in a slinky, sleeveless teal maxi dress, then wrapped a matching scarf around my neck. I curtsied to myself and smiled.

In less than a month of practicing gratitude, I went from scraping three things together to making a long Academy Awards-style acceptance speech to my life every morning. By pushing through the foolishness of stroking my own bruised ego, I found that treating myself nicely did not turn me into an indolent bum or an arrogant asshole, as I had initially feared it would. It not only silenced the untamed critic who ran amok in my brain for way too long, but it also redecorated the inner workings of my being with optimism, passion, and vitality. I became the captain of my own cheerleading squad. My biggest fan. My own best friend. It didn't make my problems disappear. But it stopped me from creating new ones that had no reason to exist. It stopped me from taking my life—including the hardships—for granted. Self-pity transformed into compassion, compassion into confidence and empowerment, empowerment into resilience and courage. Contentment didn't stunt my progress; it emboldened my spirit in meaningful-to-me ways.

"You look so good, I'd take you on a date!"

So, I did.

I went online to look up events around Phoenix. I found a musical performance by a singer I admired scheduled at a nearby concert hall for the following week. I bought one ticket online, then strutted back to my closet to decide which shoes I'd wear out on the town.

A week later, the lady behind the will call desk at the Musical Instrument Museum sifted through the standard white envelope with my last name listed on the front. I wasn't sure what she was looking for. As she became more frantic moving her arms around the tabletop, I said, "There should be only one ticket."

"Oh! Oh good!" she said, putting her hand to her chest. She slid the envelope across the tabletop. "Then you're all set. Enjoy the show."

I shyly snuggled into my aisle seat on the left side of the theater, one I chose intentionally. If I wanted to make a quick exit, I could. A few minutes after I settled in, a well-dressed, grey-haired woman took the chair next to me. A string of empty seats extended beyond her on the right. I assumed she was half of a doting couple. I kept to myself and thumbed through the program.

She propped herself up on our shared armrest. When she adjusted her program in her hand, her soft white translucent wrap gently fell away from her left forearm, revealing a tattoo on the inside of her wrist. Written in flowery cursive lettering, it read, "Control your destiny." Below that, "One decision at a time."

Before I could say something, the lights dimmed. As the theater went dark, a group of eight people, whom she did not seem to know, filed in from the other side of the row and filled all the seats next to her. She was alone too.

We sang. We clapped. We stood with the crowd to dance.

After the show, I walked out into the dark night alone. Inspired by the entertainment and the experience of sitting next to another single woman—one who was possibly trying to take a similar brave step in her life—I found myself singing, swaying, and shining as bright as the moon peering down on me from above. I gathered the skirt of my dress with a twirl to get into my truck. I sat behind my steering wheel and thought, you've figured this life out when you realize there's nothing to figure out about life. The big Life with a capital L comes not from planning out your entire life but rather by controlling your destiny one decision at a time. One moment, one rapid, one paddle at a time.

I grinned. That's it. That's the secret to life.

~ ~ ~

"Table for one, please," I said to the teenaged girl behind the hostess stand at a bustling local restaurant. I chose my words carefully. I no longer reduced myself by saying, "Just one."

"Would you like to sit at the bar?" she asked.

I bit my tongue. It was a question asked often of me as a solo diner. Although I had become more accustomed to hearing it, the implication irked me. No, I didn't want to talk with the bartender or other random strangers. No, I didn't care what onlookers would say under their breath if I sat alone. Yes, I was good enough company for me for an hour of my life.

"No, I'd like a table, please. On the patio, if it's available," I said, lifting my sunglasses.

I followed her outside to a corner table set for four beneath a wooden pergola. She cleared three sets of utensils, leaving one, and walked off. "Have a nice meal," she said in a polite, but reserved, tone.

A few minutes later, a bouncy curly-haired woman greeted me with a swagger in her step, a welcoming smile, and water. "Hi there. How are we doing today?"

"Fabulous. I'm celebrating!"

"How exciting!" She relaxed into her hip. "What are we celebrating?"

"Today! Life!" I grinned and clasped my hands together on the table.

She cocked her head back. It wasn't the answer she expected. "Oh.

Okay. Okay. I got you, girlfriend. What can I bring us to drink then? A martini? A glass of wine? What are we feeling right now?"

"I'm feeling a little bubbly. Do you have any prosecco or champagne?" I asked, flipping the drink menu over to scan it.

"We do. A tasty prosecco."

"Perfect, I'll go with that."

She took the drink menu from my hand. "Would we like to kick this party off with an appetizer?"

I picked up the main menu but couldn't find what I was looking for. "Actually, could you bring the dessert menu?"

"Now? Or after your dinner?"

"Now, please."

"Are we doing dessert for dinner, then?"

"No, I'm going to have dessert *before* dinner," I said. "What if I croak in the middle of my meal and miss out? I can't let that happen."

"Girl! Come on now. We can't die on my shift!" She choked on her own laugh.

"Okay, okay, I'll try not to!" After our laughter subsided, I asked, "Do you have any pie?"

"We don't. Would we like to try our Big Daddy Chocolate Cake instead? It's my favorite. Comes with ice cream."

"Sold!"

I savored my prosecco and chocolate cake—which was as large and divine as it sounded. I then ate a salad for, you know, balance, and paid my bill.

On my way out, I stopped at the hostess stand. "Could I speak with the manager on duty?" I asked of the young lady who checked me in.

"Was everything okay with your meal, ma'am?"

"Yes. That's why I'd like to speak with your manager."

She disappeared into the dining area and returned with a stout gentleman dressed in a black suit and tie in tow. "Thanks for dining with us tonight," he said as he held out his hand to shake mine. "How can I help you?"

"I've never done this before. I'm not sure it's even possible. I'd like to buy my server a Big Daddy Chocolate Cake."

I had noticed halfway through our conversation that my server had used "we" instead of "you" to address me. It hadn't bothered me. I never sensed she was doing so to be patronizing. In fact, I appreciated sharing joy, laughs, and a positive connection with her, if only for an hour of our lives. She reminded me that we're never truly alone even when we eat (or live) alone. So, since she and I were the only "we" at the table, I figured "we" should also share dessert.

"I don't see why not," he shrugged his shoulders and led me over to the bar to settle the deal. "I'll make sure she gets it when her shift ends."

"Excellent, thank you."

"Thank you. I'm certain she'll appreciate it very much."

"Hope so! She said it was her favorite."

He ripped the receipt from the register and handed it to me. At the bottom of it, below my signature, I wrote: "Happy today! Here's to life and to eating chocolate cake before dinner."

I walked out the door and into the sunset, smiling. Through a simple gesture, I had finally learned the difference between being a people-pleaser and being kind to people—and which one I wanted to be.

~ ~ ~

While tidying up my house one afternoon, I noticed a small, framed photo of Craig and me. I wasn't sure why the photograph had caught my eye now. It had been sitting on the same shelf in my den for close to twenty years.

I plopped onto the couch and cradled the frame. In it, Craig and I were embracing in a dimly lit one-room condo at the Purgatory Ski Resort in Durango, Colorado. I was sitting on his lap. He had one arm around my back, the other on my thigh. I had one arm wrapped around his shoulder, the other flat against his chest, flashing my shiny new engagement ring.

We looked happy. Why wouldn't we be? We were doing what society expected us to do after dating for a couple of years: promising to marry each other.

Craig had tried his best to make our engagement a surprise for me.

We had talked about the idea of spending our life together, so much so, that we chased any possibility of spontaneity out of it. It wasn't a matter of if but when. In January 1999, he had booked a getaway for us during Durango's annual Snowdown festival, but he hadn't revealed the location until we were in the car driving away from our house. I had packed my sexy blue nightie anyhow. I knew where we were going—wink, wink—even if I had no idea where we were going.

Too much time had passed for me to recall how we spent the weekend once we arrived there. We didn't ski—which now seemed odd for a couple who enjoyed skiing elsewhere across the West. I remembered sampling steak and elk medallions during a romantic dinner at the Ore House Restaurant on the final night of our stay. I had fidgeted in my chair during most of the meal, making trite conversation to fill the empty spaces. He had planned this trip to seal our future together, but two days had passed, and he hadn't popped the question yet. Had he gotten cold feet?

We spoke little on the drive back to the ski resort a half an hour north of town. He must have sensed my impatience, possibly even my disappointment, when we crawled into the Murphy bed and turned off the light. An almost full moon illuminated the snow-covered mountain. The tree-lined hillside glowed through our floor-to-ceiling windows. Silvery-blue light filled the studio. With little formality, he rolled over and asked me to be his wife. The casualness of the life-changing conversation fit our relationship perfectly. Instead of holding onto that beautiful moment, though, I made him turn on the lights and persuaded him to redress in our dinner clothes so we could take a formal picture. It was a perfectly choreographed charade.

Why? And for who?

I had never stopped to think whether marriage was right for me, for us. As a young girl, I had never fantasized about walking down the aisle with Prince Charming. That said, I wasn't against the wedding. On the contrary, I couldn't wait to slide a flashy diamond ring on my finger, wear a princess-like white ball gown with an oversized bow on the back, curl my hair, and throw a party for my friends and family where I sparkled as the center of attention. Even better, I couldn't wait to go on my extravagant honeymoon in St. Lucia and show all my friends the pictures of our private plunge pool in the back of our two-room cottage with a stunning view of the Pitons. Because all those things offered the external validation I needed to feel worthy of it all.

Beyond that, though, I couldn't see through my own naiveté to understand how to navigate within the institution of marriage. Getting hitched was just what you did once you had dated for a couple years. Craig and I had been together for almost three and had known each other for six. One of my well-meaning friends once said, "Tell him to shit or get off the pot." Even my own mother had cautioned me with the age-old adage, "Why buy the cow if he's getting the milk for free?"

Once we were engaged, I felt pressure to marry quickly. We chose to wait over two years, mainly because I had my heart set on an April date—just because I did—and I wanted enough time to plan everything to perfection in between our sixty-hour workweeks at Intel. Some scoffed at our slow crawl to the altar. "Well, at least we know you aren't pregnant," I heard more than once.

I wondered now whether Craig and I had needed a ceremony, witnesses, and a piece of paper issued by the state of Arizona to endorse our love and commitment to the life we wanted together. In hindsight, I'm not sure I did. I wasn't a cow. Or a pot.

I pulled the photograph closer. As I drifted in the limbo of our ongoing separation, I could not help but laugh at the irony that, of all the places we could have gotten engaged, we became betrothed at the *Purgatory* Ski Resort.

I rubbed the dust from the frame. The heaviness of loneliness replaced the lightness, filling my stomach, then tightening my chest and climbing into my throat until it robbed me of breath.

I missed Craig. I missed my old life. I missed laughing about my past with someone who understood it. I missed our intellectual banter. Him spontaneously shaking his butt while cooking fajitas at the kitchen stove. Drying our clothes out over a wood stove after cross-country skiing to a backcountry cabin. Toasting wine glasses after a day of exploring and misadventures. The comfort of someone having my back. Him rubbing my back.

Treating myself nicely and feeling grateful had led to marked improvements in my well-being. But I did not feel like Pollyanna every day. Holding onto or faking a positive attitude does not turn life into a skip through a field of flowers. Life is not a continuous parade of double rainbows, prancing unicorns, and eternal bliss. And to think it is, or to strive for such an unrealistic state, only leads to more anguish. There's no way around it; being a human is damn hard sometimes.

I labored through rocky aches and pains of missing Craig one minute at a time, knowing they would eventually pass if I just kept paddling. With every swell of emotion, I held onto the memory of watching Mom bob up and down on the waves in desperation near the Tapestry Wall. We could not fight or control the intensity of the waves. We could only work through them to the best of our ability.

The word "emotion" comes from "emovere," a Latin word that means to "move out or away." On a river, waves do not move downstream. Water does. Water moves through the forms of waves created by rocks, branches, and other hindrances. These sudden fluctuations—rapids, storms, and feelings—were temporary.

Even so, one cannot expect to work through the painful demise of a twenty-two-year friendship and a fourteen-year marriage—and a foiled trip across Lake Powell one took to cope with that shock—overnight. I knew trying to suppress my sorrow about either event would deny me the opportunity to embrace them, to learn and mature from the experiences, and to create meaning out of adversity. I was no longer afraid or ashamed to cry.

The separation of two intertwined lives in love *is* sad. Sadness was not bad in the same way that happiness was not good. These states of being just existed. Instead of assigning negative and unnecessary labels to how I felt, I acknowledged my reaction to my thoughts. When I found myself wanting to seek solace or emotional support from others, I gave it to myself.

"I'm sorry it hurts," the voice in my head said as I leaned my head back into the couch. "It sucks to get rejected. It's hard to lose love and live alone. But look at how far you've come. You're doing great."

I pushed myself out of the soft pocket of the cushions and set the photograph on the end table. I stirred up a gin and tonic with a hint of lime—Craig's favorite drink, one I had come to favor in his absence. I grabbed the hand of loneliness, walked to my backyard, and sat down on my fake grass. I closed my eyes, turned my face to the sun, and smiled through the tears.

I couldn't make my longing for companionship or the heartache disappear, but it comforted me to know that when a storm sets in and a ray of sunlight passes through a raindrop, it creates a rainbow. I raised my glass to the sky and said what Craig and I used to say to each other, "Love you, love me."

~ ~ ~

I spoke again at the Moab Photography Symposium in April 2016. Afterward, in honor of my 41st birthday, Guy and I paddled sixty-eight miles on the Green River through Labyrinth Canyon, he in his inflatable kayak and me on Lir. It rained for almost four days straight. Even the daily downpours and turbulent waters weren't enough to wash away the orange sand grains lingering on my board from Lake Powell.

My route home from southern Utah brought me by the North Wash/Dirty Devil Takeout for the first time since November. I intended to drive past the launch area without stopping, nervous it might trigger unwelcome feelings I had spent the last five months processing. As I approached the turnoff, I changed my mind. I figured it wouldn't do any harm to share a few words with my friend the Colly Raddy.

I pulled into the graveled parking lot just as the brooding sky began spitting raindrops. I parked, then slowly scanned the area from left to right as Juno's windshield wipers cleared my view. I ambled down the steep, now unusable, dirt boat ramp, raising the hood of my jacket.

The changes in the landscape since November were palpable. The mucky banks indicated the water level had dropped three to four feet. Mud-covered grasses adhered to the water's edge as if the river had run slick grease through her hair. Clumps of branches and foam clung to the sides of the channel like old memories.

I attempted to check the current water levels on my iPhone. No service. Before I tucked my iPhone back into my pocket, the date glowing on the screen caught my attention: May 1.

One year and one month ago, I had watched the safe and stable life I had worked so hard for spin into chaos. One year and one day ago, I had spilled my then-concealed and shameful separation into the Colorado River for the first time while paddleboarding on my birthday in Moab. One year and one day ago, I had drummed up a "silly" idea to paddle the length of Lake Powell while eating strawberry pie. Those circumstances and choices had led me here: standing alone in front of the Colorado River in the wilds of Utah.

At the water's edge, I squatted and picked up a submerged speckled stone. I rolled it around in my hand. I started talking with the river as if we were old buddies, recounting the stories of what had transpired while navigating the rapids and flatwater since Mom and I launched from this very spot just five months ago. How different my inner landscape looked now.

I grinned. "Failing" to finish our Powell trip was one of the best things that could have happened to me. Shoving off this shore helped me start to shift my unproductive lifelong beliefs about fear, control, expectations, perfectionism, and success. I was still learning and trying and practicing and evolving; I always would be. After all, waters in a river aren't static. They don't stay in the same place for very long.

The Colorado River listened to me, as it had in April, August, October, and November, as if it was the first time it had heard my spiel. Then I realized, it *was* the first time. Maybe the drops Mom, Lir, and I glided through last fall remained in Lake Powell behind the dam. Maybe some had traveled all the way to the Gulf of California more than 800 river miles away. Maybe some had come out of my faucet at home and into my drinking glass. But *these* waters and I, we had not shared a past. This wasn't the same river in the same way I wasn't the same person. These waters and I only shared the present.

When I pulled off the highway, I had worried about feeling drained by returning to the place where I had started a journey I did not finish; at least not according to plan. But I didn't. I felt fuller than ever. I felt like the vibrant river racing in front of me.

Fingers in the water—my ritual greeting and farewell—with the Colorado River at North Wash/Dirty Devil takeout in southern Utah on May 1, 2016.

I dipped my fingers into water pooling along the shore and whispered, "Thank you, Colorado River, for showing me how to be the most authentic, fulfilled, and richest version of me I've ever been, a person I didn't know I could be."

I looked up at the river curving out of sight and around the bend along the towering cliffs. Instead of fearing the uncertainty ahead, I was overflowing with excitement to see what waited for me on the other side of the dam. One month later, I had that chance.

THE GRAND CANYON

Artistic rendering only. Map not to scale and should not be used for navigational purposes.

To Kanab, UT
89
GLEN CANYON NATIONAL RECREATION AREA
Lake Powell
VERMILION CLIFFS NATIONAL MONUMENT
Paria River
Glen Canyon Dam
Lees Ferry
Page
Paria Riffle
Cliff Dwellers Lodge & Restaurant
Jacob Lake
89A
Navajo Bridge
98
Badger Creek Rapid
To Kaibito, AZ
67
Camp 1
South Canyon
NAVAJO NATION
Deer Creek Falls
Colorado River
89
Camp 2
North Rim
To Tuba City, AZ
Little Colorado River
Camp 3
Phantom Ranch
160
GRAND CANYON NATIONAL PARK
South Rim:
Grand Canyon Village
Desert View Watchtower
Tusayan
64
64
Cameron
89
N
To Williams, AZ
To Flagstaff, AZ

18
THE MOST EPIC THING

"This trip will be the most epic thing you'll ever do in your life," said the curly-haired gentleman sitting next to me on the patio at the Cliff Dwellers Restaurant in Marble Canyon, Arizona. His name was Murray. I'd known him for all of ten minutes.

It was the first day of June 2016. A group of strangers, but all friends of Terry and Wendy Gunn (who owned the Cliff Dwellers Restaurant and Lodge), had gathered for a group dinner. The sixteen of us were fueling up and getting acquainted ahead of our rafting adventure together on the Colorado River through the Grand Canyon. In the morning, we'd join two boatmen from Hatch River Expeditions, our commercial outfitter, for our single-boat private charter. They were to motor us 188 miles from Lees Ferry to Whitmore Wash in a thirty-five-foot-long raft. Assuming we lived through the world-renowned rapids, we'd get plucked out of the canyon by a helicopter and returned to Cliff Dwellers eight days later.

"Pffff...." I waved my new friend off with tactless arrogance, then swirled my glass of chardonnay. "Look, Murray. I know we've just met. I've done—and I do—a lot of incredible things in my life. To suggest this will be the *most* epic is a pretty bold declaration."

"Just wait. Wait until the second day." He flicked his head back in a nod of confidence. "You'll see."

I shook my head and laughed. This trip was my first "lap" on the river. It was Murray's thirty-something-th. Enough that he had stopped counting. "I'll admit," I said while leaning back into my chair, "it intrigues me that you've come back for more."

I had learned by now that the easiest way to meet or exceed expectations was to start by having none. So, it surprised me when Murray used a superlative to describe an experience in a place where superlatives fall short in describing it.

Early explorers called the canyon "Big Canyon" and "Great Canyon." John Wesley Powell popularized the current name in 1871 after his Colorado River expeditions. The name "Grand Canyon" now refers to not only the main—and most pronounced—chasm but also the maze of precipitous side canyons, buttes, plateaus, pyramids, and countless raised pedestals showing off thrones, temples, castles, spires, arches, and windows surrounding it. The gorge rises over a mile high above the Colorado River. The two rims sit almost eighteen miles apart at the widest point. According to the Department of the Interior, the national park, which does not contain the entire canyon system, covers more acreage than the state of Rhode Island.

The canyon's dimensions are only the start to its impressive breadth. The natural museum catalogues a billion years of the Earth's geological story of ancient dried-up seas, floodplain remnants, petrified sand dunes, and cooled lava flows. Scientists believe the Colorado River has conspired with wind and storms for at least five million years to create this discombobulating work of art in its current form. From only a few spots along the rim can you catch a glimpse of the main culprit zigzagging through the creases in the cliffs. The Colorado River's 300-foot glistening girth looks like a pencil-thin line drawn through the multi-colored rock. Her prowess might not be obvious from afar. But the beauty she's caused all around her provides evidence that even something seemingly small can have an unexpected and immense impact on their environment.

I had seen parts of the Grand Canyon before but only while standing on the rim or peering out the window on commercial airline flights—save for one exception. Over five days in late October 2009, I hiked down to the river's edge on the Thunder River/Deer Creek loop with Craig and two friends. I remembered the rush of camping along creeks under yellow-leaved cottonwood trees, seeing Deer Creek Falls plunge over 180 feet out of a sculpted sandstone slot canyon, and getting a cold beer—one of the most prized possessions by river runners—from a private rafting trip while on the beach. I also remembered my legs cramping during the 9.5-mile hike from the Upper Tapeats Campground to the North Rim, a gain of over 5,000 feet in elevation. The steep climb brought me to tears. As my excitement for this rafting trip grew, my only hope was that I could spend more time in the canyon without crying in pain when I came out of it.

Craig and I had planned for over a year to join Terry and Wendy and their crew. Given our ongoing separation, though, Craig backed out. I still wanted to go. I wanted to let the Colorado River carry me through what many humans deemed her greatest achievement. I wanted—no, *needed*—to see what was on the other side of the Glen Canyon Dam.

I faced a choice. Since Craig and I signed up as a couple, I could either pay for his vacancy—which meant I'd pay double for the trip—or I could fill his spot. I was willing to go alone, but a seven-night, all-inclusive river trip doesn't come cheap. I knew who to call: Mom.

I knew little about the river trip beyond the logistical information Hatch distributed in their paperwork. I still tried to sell Mom—who had also never rafted the Colorado River—on the idea that we'd be following in Powell's footsteps. We'd be going into what he called "the Great Unknown." While plenty of others, including Native Americans, explorers, and river runners, had experienced the river this way, we hadn't. We'd be going into our own unknown.

The adventure promised isolation from the manufactured world. No cell service, emails, news, napkins, or showers for over a week. Only real-world paradise. It would differ from our previous escapades, though, in that our itinerary was out of our control. We wouldn't know what activities we'd do, what we'd eat, where we'd go to the bathroom, or even where we'd sleep each night. Before I finished pontificating from my soapbox, Mom declared, "I'm coming with you!"

Sean (left) and Lars pack Boat 5 at Lees Ferry before launching on the Colorado River through the Grand Canyon on June 2, 2016.

So she did. We had both packed our dry bags and traveled together to Cliff Dwellers earlier in the day. She now sat next to me, nodding her head now and then as Murray and I bantered at dinner. When we stopped talking, she blurted, "I don't know about epic. But this can't be any wilder than our trip on Lake Powell last year."

The next morning, Steve Hatch (the owner of Hatch River Expeditions) and his team picked us up at Cliff Dwellers in white vans. We drove eastward along the base of flat-topped plateaus, jagged buttes, and rolling sandstone mounds known collectively as the Vermilion Cliffs. Twenty minutes later, we arrived at the concrete boat ramp at Lees Ferry.

What was once a remote ferry crossing for Mormon settlers in the 1870s was now bustling with a flotilla of small yellow oar boats, green and red wooden dories, and whitish-grey S-rig rafts like our own.

Commercial trips lined up on the gravel upstream. Private trips on the pavement downstream.

The rafts and I weren't the only things separated here. Although the river flows like any other river, Lees Ferry represented a significant split, one invisible to the human eye. It marks the dividing line between the Upper and Lower Basin states as defined by the 1922 Colorado River Compact.* To the north of this beach, the Upper Basin states—Wyoming, Colorado, Utah, and New Mexico—manage the obligatory water allocations to the Lower Basin states—Arizona, Nevada, and California—to the south of this beach. Lake Powell, which sits fifteen river miles upstream from Lees Ferry, stores the water for the two factions.

I skipped to the shore's end and offered my hand to the cold, clear water in my ritual greeting. A living, flowing river glided through my fingers. I decided I would divide my life's flow not by my separation, but rather into BC and AC: before the Colorado and after the Colorado. Because that's the law of the river. I shrugged, then giggled aloud.

Lars, our head boatman, and Sean, his assistant—called a "swamper"—introduced themselves to our group. They coached the sixteen of us to line up and shuttle our large roly-poly overnight dry bags—called "pumpkins"—one by one into a duffle pile in the center of our raft. We each grabbed an orange life vest from a tidy pile on the beach. Then, one by one, we climbed aboard Boat 5.

Mom and I bounded to the back of the oblong-shaped doughnut, loping along one of the long, torpedo-like tubes attached to the sides like an outrigger pontoon. Still on the beach, Sean pressed his back into the underside of the tubes to push us backwards into the fast-moving channel. Once the raft released from the rocks, he jumped onto the boat while Lars cranked the motor to right us downriver.

The newness of the scenery hushed the chatter on the boat and fascinated me from the start. I peered over the side and saw clear down

* *Per the 1922 Colorado River Compact, the official dividing line is called "Lee Ferry" and is located less than a mile downstream from the Lees Ferry boat ramp. Although one might believe "Lee's Ferry" is grammatically correct (since it was named after local settler John Doyle Lee), the USGS mapping group removes apostrophes from place names.*

Mom riding the side tubes to start our Colorado River rafting adventure near Lees Ferry on June 2, 2016. The reddened cliffs in the distance are the Vermilion Cliffs. The Paria Riffle begins downstream where the foliage tapers and meets the river.

to the riverbed. Piles of white pebbles rested between tan cobbles which rested between orange boulders. A panoramic reflection of the buff-and-salmon-colored Vermilion Cliffs shimmered in the water on the right. A mirror image of the smaller rust-colored Echo Cliffs reflected on the left. A great blue heron—or a "GBH" as I learned river veterans called them—fluttered from its rocky perch along the shoreline. It flapped its wings over our heads, then disappeared in a grove of tamarisks on the opposite shore. The same bliss Mom and I shared on our third day on Lake Powell swept my soul back into the hands of the river. I didn't need three days for the Three-Day Effect to kick in. I only needed three minutes.

Not even a river mile had passed before I spotted choppy water ahead. I started looking around the raft for a seat. I hesitated to claim a spot in the "Bathtub" on the bow. After all, I wasn't in control of this ship. I had no idea how big these rapids would get. And since we had just started the trip, I wasn't dirty enough yet to need a Grand Canyon "bath" in the forty-seven-degree waters.

I scooted into a seat on the right side of the raft and pressed my back against the tarped duffel pile. Sitting on the side felt safer than being up front but more daring than sitting in the back. At first, I thought people were calling the back of the boat the "Tea Room" because the ride back there was so dry and calm that you might enjoy a cup of tea through the rapids and not spill a drop. I later learned it's actually called the "T-Room" because the toilets for the trip are stored below one's feet there (even though toilets are called "groovers" in the rafting community). The sides of the raft had no formal name, but I decided that's where I was going to learn how to get my groove on in this first set of waves.

The smaller Paria River converged with her big sister on our starboard side. Muddy waters collided with clean waters. Whitecaps stirred. Mom, dressed in a pink plaid long-sleeved shirt, tan quick-dry pants, and her favorite hat straddled the side tube next to me. She grabbed the rope reins in front of her with one hand, then raised the other in the air and yelled, "Ride 'em cowboy!"[**]

We glided along the shadowed cliffs on the left. The undulating waves began peaking and frothing with bubbles. Splashes, hands, and "yahoos" flew into the air. The raft slinked over the playful whitecaps. I thought sitting on a thirty-five-foot raft would feel like an old, clunky Winnebago maneuvering through test cones without power steering or brakes. It didn't. With over 280 trips through the Grand Canyon to his name, Lars drove this beast of a boat like a spunky Corvette.

The water settled into flatwater after about twenty seconds. I stood up and called to the back of the boat, "What was that rapid rated, Lars?"

While most river ratings worldwide follow the American Whitewater Association ratings from Class I to Class VI, the Grand Canyon uses its own scale from Class 1 to Class 10, with Class 10

** *Riding the side tubes on S-rigs through rapids is no longer permitted.*

being the most difficult. This rapid reminded me of Moab's Big Bend Rapid, the Class II whitewater I faced in April 2015. But I didn't know how to translate that into the canyon's terms.

Lars' blue gingham button-up dress shirt and baggy jeans swallowed his lean, compact, and muscular body. It was an unusual outfit for a 103-degree day but one he had obviously perfected to protect him from the sun during his thirty-five years as a guide. He straightened his collar, then cupped his hand to his ear. "Whaaaaaaaat? I caaaaaan't heaaaaaar yoooooou baaaaaack heeeeeere."

I giggled like I was ten again. I liked him already. "Laaaaaaaars! What was that rapid rated?"

He gave Sean, who was sitting across from him in the motor well behind the T-Room, the side-eye. He looked back at me with a crooked smile.

"It's not," Lars said out of the corner of his mouth.

"Whaaaaaaaat?" I mocked him.

"That was the Paria Riffle, boys and girls. I guess you could call it…a point five? A half a class?" He shrugged his shoulders and revved the motor. "Sit tight. The real rapids start once we pass Navajo Bridge."

I slid down into my seat and looked downriver. How bad could these rapids get anyhow? They were already bigger than what I experienced in Moab on my paddleboard. Would they get bigger than what we saw on Powell? I laughed. It didn't matter. Mom and I were riding this raft down this one-way track until we reached Whitmore Wash. There was no turning back now.

We splashed through another small, unrated riffle at the mouth of Cathedral Wash around river mile 3 (as measured from Lees Ferry). Afterward, Lars pointed out that we were not yet in Grand Canyon proper. On his 1869 expedition, John Wesley Powell deemed this stretch of the river "Marble Canyon" for its marbled-looking rock even though no marble exists in Marble Canyon or anywhere else in the Grand Canyon landscape.

A voice from the T-Room offered the mnemonic "Know the canyon's history; study rocks made by time" to remember the different geological layers, in order, from top to bottom: Kaibab, Toroweap,

Coconino, Hermit, Supai, Redwall, Muav, Bright Angel, and Tapeats. I pointed my finger at the visible strata and kept repeating the names in hopes I'd remember them.

I pulled my camera out of my dry bag. I pointed it up, down, left, right, forwards, backwards. I photographed the house-sized boulders in repose on rock ledges. A barrel cactus clinging to the side of a terraced slope. A lone tamarisk basking in a shaft of light on a thin strip of white sand. The gleaming reflection of the now 500-foot-tall sheer walls off the bow. The circular skypools and landpools dancing in the undulating wake off the stern. The two bridges spanning the canyon's rims, which are known together as the "Navajo Bridge." I made pictures of Mom, Wendy, Murray, Lars, Sean, and all our new friends. I had one photogasm after another.

I relaxed my camera into my arms. I spent a few minutes breathing in the earthy breeze, feeling the pull of the mighty river on the raft, and trying to blend into the grandest place on the planet. We couldn't motor upstream to rerun a rapid. We couldn't see around the next bend downstream. We had no choice but to live in the present moment exactly as the canyon presented it to us, bend after bend.

I called back to Lars, "You know what, Lars? You're right. Marble Canyon is a marble-less place!"

Several of my trip mates groaned. Lars shook his head. I doubted it was the first time he had heard that line before. Nonetheless, I was content to crack myself up just like any ten-year-old would.

Eight miles south of Lees Ferry—a distance I knew only by looking at my laminated guidebook—the wide river channel disappeared into the rocky horizon. Spray spewed into the air like a bubbling caldron. The percussion of her taunting and loudening madness started echoing off the overhanging rock, the talus slopes, even the clear blue sky, and drowned all other noises in the canyon: the raven's caw, the canyon wren's trill, the rafters' sighs. Badger Creek Rapid, the first rated whitewater on our trip, was making herself known.

Water raced past the mouths of two side canyons. Badger Canyon on river right. Jackass Canyon on river left. Car-sized stones, which were scattered across the channel as if a giant had thrown his bag of marbles, constricted the water from both sides. Our S-rig was the shooter, and there were no quitsies here.

Badger Creek Rapid rated as a Class 4 to 6 on the Grand Canyon scale depending on how much water the dam releases from Lake Powell. In a little more than a tenth of a mile, the river dropped fifteen feet. Lars said it translated into about a Class III on the AWA scale. Even from a distance, I could tell I'd never faced any bigger crests or holes before, even in the windstorm on Lake Powell.

"You'll want to hold onto something for this!" Lars hollered with remarkable calmness. "Things might get a little splashy."

I curled my hands around the ropes on either side of my seat. Only when the raft started to slip down the glassy, undulating tongue, when we came face to face with the first curler, did the true enormity of the waves set in. My eyes widened. My grip tightened.

Mom, still sitting on the side tube, dropped her smile and uttered, "Oh my god."

Lars gunned the motor into the rollers at the bottom of the tongue, then cut the power. We hurtled head-on into an exploding wave. The front of the boat rocked out of sync with the back. The two halves flexed around a joint designed to allow the raft to fold like a taco—and not snap in half—under duress. The rubber side tubes rubbing against the doughnut frame brayed like donkeys.

The boat bounced into the belly of the rapid. A wall of water slammed against the nose. The wave surged over the raft, submerging the bow underwater. I howled with laughter as the piercing cold water slapped me in the face, drenched my entire body, then dripped down my back.

The sky returned overhead, but only for a few seconds, before the raft smashed into an even bigger wave. Water sucker punched me straight in the face. I howled again.

The force of the next wave picked me up out of my seat and tossed me several inches toward the back of the boat. I landed on my hands. I didn't dare release my death grip on the ropes. I howled and howled.

By the time the river returned to stillness, I was laughing so uncontrollably, I was crying. I wiped water and tears from my eyes and looked over at Mom. She was laughing so hard that she was convulsing in her seat but wasn't making a sound. The utter absurdity and naughtiness of the Colorado River walloping us with truckloads of her frigid water over and over again sent most of our group into hysterics.

Think of it this way: in everyday life, if I asked you to stand still while someone flung full five-gallon buckets of ice-cold water at you over and over again from two feet away, you might think such an idea was outlandish. You might run. You might hide. You probably wouldn't pay thousands of dollars to get such a thrashing. Here, on the river, the idea was real—it was called a rapid—we couldn't run from the boat, we couldn't hide from the waves, and we *had* paid thousands of dollars for this thrashing. Yet, I couldn't get enough of this splashing and smashing ridiculousness. It was as if the river tickled forty-some years of pent-up merriment out of me, as if to make up for all the times I had reacted with resistance instead of resilience whenever hardships hit me in the face. This rapid proved that I could get pummeled by big waves and still laugh about it afterward.

After getting another soaking—and another fit of glee—at Soap Creek Rapid, Lars docked the boat along the shore against treeless rock ledges for lunch. The 300-million-year-old Supai Group, with its orange and black and white abstract shapes embedded in the overhanging walls along the river channel, made me gasp with childlike awe. I made at least 200 photographs in less than an hour. I lost all sense of time. The moment entranced me so much that I forgot to eat. As we returned to our boat, Mom handed me a peanut butter and jelly sandwich with peanut M&Ms jammed inside. A Grand Canyon specialty, Lars said.

Back on the water, the river kept falling deeper into the embrace of the cliffs. Lars drove us through Sheer Wall and House Rock rapids. He then dashed through the flamboyant series of rapids called the Roaring Twenties. In this ten-mile stretch, nine consecutive boat-flipping rapids (some up to Class 7) dropped the river by about seventy feet—almost the height of a seven-story building. It didn't take long to learn that when Lars warned "things might get a little splashy," it was code for "hang on; we might die."

Even today, the Supai Group, with its striking shapes and abstract patterns, is one of my favorite rock formations to photograph in the Grand Canyon.

In the sweltering heat of late afternoon, we pulled up to a sprawling sand dune at the mouth of South Canyon. The sun moved into a gap in the stone ramparts. A shaft of light spotlighted a patch of beige rocks at the end of the beach, then disappeared. Reflected light from the west-facing precipices turned the placid green river into fiery liquid gold.

Our group lined up again but this time to unload the boat. The pumpkins went first, then foldable chairs, sleeping cots, kitchen tables, pots, stoves, water buckets, and the groover. We each found our own

What heaven on Earth looks like while camping at South Canyon near river mile 32 in Marble Canyon. Bottom photo by Jacque Miniuk.

little plot of sand to call our own for the night while the guides started setting up the kitchen. Sean sizzled up New York strip steaks to order on the grill. Lars made margaritas from scratch in our coffee mugs.

Once Mom and I set up our cots at the far end of the beach, I strolled, with a margarita in hand, down to where the oou-oou-hot sand met the oh-so-cold water. My toes curled into the wet grains of sand along the shoreline. My head swirled in the dizzying heights of the glowing canyon walls surrounding our camp.

If heaven on Earth existed, it was here. We were there. On a beach in the Grand Canyon along the Colorado River. Thirty-two miles from Lees Ferry. Forty-seven miles from the Glen Canyon Dam. Who knew—and who cared—how many miles away from the manufactured world.

My existence seemed trivial here, and we wouldn't reach the oldest or deepest parts of the canyon for at least another couple of days. Even to someone who had spent much of her life trying to stand out and feel big, there was a comfort and peace to blending in and feeling small—in acknowledging my place as a small drop of water in a five-million-year-old river flowing past walls of rock that are hundreds of millions of years old while traveling 67,000 miles per hour on a 4.5-billion-year-old planet in a galaxy moving 1.3 million miles per hour through a single universe expanding at a rate of 163,000 miles per hour in a multiverse made up of a trillion galaxies or more.

And we think the Grand Canyon defines grand.

And that how we load the dishwasher, or what size jeans we wear, or winning a first-place ribbon matters.

And that when we sit still, soaking in the present moment, we aren't moving in some direction.

My eyes fixated on the Colorado River and the waves of its constant motion. None of this matters. Nothing in this life or in this world means anything. Yet here I stood. By some miracle, I existed. And in my very existence in this incomprehensible and mysterious vastness, I mattered.

Why were these rocks here? Why was this river here? Why was I here?

I couldn't tell you the meaning of life or say why any of us were on this Earth to begin with. There are no universal definitions as to how we should or shouldn't live our life or how the people around us should or shouldn't live theirs. Society tries to make us believe it has all the answers. It doesn't. Everyone, *everyone*, is making this up as we go. In the excess of guesses that swirl around us day in and day out, what mattered was creating whatever meaning you wish out of your own life in however much time you are granted. We own our own answers.

Spending time with the Colorado River had taught me how to embrace feeling inconsequential to the manufactured world. In becoming irrelevant to others, I became relevant to myself. In becoming relevant to myself, I discovered how irrelevant most things in the manufactured world were and are. I learned what was relevant to me. When you stop focusing on your importance to others, the importance of living your life in your own way becomes clear. To understand your own significance in the insignificance of the grand scheme of things is to understand your own freedom.

I now comprehended that this astounding chance and remarkable privilege to exist was all I had and all I will ever have. And *I* was all I had—and all I will ever have—through it. People, money, material things, and accomplishments would all come and go. But I was the only person coming along for the entirety of my own journey. So, what I say goes for me.

I returned to the small alcove where Mom and I had set up our camp. The canyon walls had shapeshifted from understated beige and pink to neon orange and sultry magenta. Day turned to night, as light and shadow, beginnings and ends, danced around the edges of eternity. Uncountable stars and galaxies started to speckle the navy-blue canvas overhead. The sky only enlarged my sense of triviality and uncertainty. Who knew if I, or any of us, would make it through the rapids tomorrow? Even surviving through the night was not promised. I could die of a heart attack. A rockfall could crush me in my cot. A mountain lion could eat me. What mattered was that Mom and I had made another day in our lives count.

I wrapped my arms around my shoulders and gave myself a hug. I leaned back into my cot and slid my legs into my sleeping bag. I fell asleep listening to the lullaby of rushing water in the nearby unhurried riffle in front of us and the rhythmic swaying of a tamarisk scraping against the untroubled rock face behind us.

The next morning started with a cheerful cascading chorus from a canyon wren hiding in the cliffs across from our camp. A thin layer of spotted clouds had settled into our V-shaped view. Dawn still unfurled a drape of rich orange along the east-facing walls up and down the river. Tendrils of golden reflections from the cliffs intertwined with the green waters rushing by the shore.

"Good morning, Ma." I rolled onto my side in my cot and propped my head up on my elbow. The Energizer Bunny was already packing her belongings into her dry bags. "I hate to admit it, but this is definitely the most epic thing I've ever done."

"I agree. Even if the trip ended today, this has already been mind-blowing," she said, looking up at a raven whooshing by. "Can you believe we have seven days left?"

"How did we get so lucky?" I asked, then stood up and gave her a hug.

In the shrouds of cool purple shadows, I strutted down the sandy beach toward the kitchen setup. Murray was shuffling his feet toward me in a morning daze. "Good morning, Murray," I said. "Hey, look, I'm really sorry."

"For what?" he asked with nonchalance.

"For doubting you," I said with a grin. "You were right. This is THE most epic thing I've ever done in my life. And I want to do it again and again and again. And bring other people here too."

"See?" Murray put his arm around my shoulder. "Welcome to the club."

Murray and I joined Mom, Lars, Sean, and our trip mates gathered around the metal kitchen table. Lars flipped fluffy blueberry pancakes on the griddle. Sean shuffled smoky sausage links in the Dutch oven nearby. I skipped the pleasantries and got straight to the point. "Lars, I have to bring people here to meet the river. I want to put together a private charter like this but for my photography clients. Is that possible?"

In less than twenty-four hours, I realized that this experience was the culmination of everything I had come to value through my time and connection with the Colorado River. Living the big Life in the great outdoors. Being whoever I wanted to be without facing external judgments. Celebrating the spotlights and the shadows. Discovering new sources of awe and wonder. Learning and laughing with my family and friends. I had seen enough of the other side of the Glen Canyon Dam, and it flooded me with so much joy around every bend, on every ledge, and with every splash that I wanted—no, *needed*—others to experience this too.

Not just so others could check off a box on their bucket list. Instead, I wanted them to see for themselves that the ravens and the cliffs and the water didn't care who they were, where they were from, or whether their sarong matched their t-shirt. So the real world could reveal the core of who they were and remind them of the inner child they used to be before society got its hands on them. So that they could leave the minutiae behind and let the stresses of the manufactured world get carried away by the wind and waves. So they could drown the notion that they needed more, more, always more to feel like they were enough. So they too could taste a slice of their own big Life with a capital L.

In other words, my "Explorer's Syndrome" and "canyonitis" had flared, and I wanted to spread it to everyone. I no longer cared about impressing others with my best life. I wanted to help others live theirs. Like a river, I wanted to provide nourishment to my surroundings as I passed by.

I smiled. That's why I am here. That's why I exist.

Yet, I couldn't bear to become yet another voice in society telling people what they should and shouldn't do. I wanted to team up with the river and the wind and the storms to help people release their reliance upon expectations, achievement, perfectionism, external validation, and control. I wanted to give others the time and space to define their own meaning for their own life, to dance to their own music in a landscape chanting the limitless possibilities in their independence.

"I'll help," Lars said.

And he did.

Over the next seven days, we sorted through details for a photography-focused trip as we reveled in more of the canyon's treasures. One day, waterfalls splashing in side canyons cooled us in the 115-degree Fahrenheit heat. The next, Sean encouraged us to lie on our backs to examine fossilized wormholes hiding underneath rock ledges. And the next, Lars stopped the boat so we could watch bighorn sheep strike majestic poses on tall rock outcroppings. Over the course of our trip, our group told so many groan-worthy jokes, we turned into a bunch of turkeys. (And do you know what a group of domesticated turkeys is called? A rafter.)

To celebrate the day's events, our guides served up delicious desserts in camp each night. Cheesecake. Brownies. Pound cake. Yellow cake with chocolate frosting. Chocolate pudding with Oreos and whipped cream—which I deemed my favorite river treat. After cowboy camping in our cots, we ate dessert leftovers for breakfast, so long as the ringtails hadn't eaten them first.

As we moved downstream, Lars navigated even bigger and splashier rapids like Hance, Crystal, and Sockdolger (which is an archaic slang word for "knockout blow"). Hermit Rapid, around mile 95.5, featured waves over *three times* bigger than our first rapid at Badger Creek. The fifth haystack wave in its wave train rose a staggering twenty feet from trough to crest. The boat folded such that those of us sitting in the T-Room could high-five the people sitting in the Bathtub.

By the time Lava Falls came around near mile 180, I rushed to the front of the boat to sit in the Bathtub so I could get baptized by the canyon's most notorious Class 10 rapid. We boomed headfirst into the Big Kahuna wave at the bottom of the rapid. I squealed with delight, then cleaned the fish out of my ears.

Eight miles later, we arrived at our final camp at Whitmore Wash. I didn't want our trip to end. No one ever wants a river trip to end.

As we unloaded our gear from the raft for the final time, I turned to Lars and begged, "Can you please leave me here on this beach? Can I live here forever? I don't need emails or showers or napkins. Just leave me with the Oreos and the coffee, and I'll be fine."

"I have no problem leaving you here," Lars said with a mocking shoulder shrug. "But the National Park Service isn't going to like that. Besides, you already ate all the Oreos."

"Fine. Fine!" I staged a pretend tantrum while giggling. "Mark my words, I'll be back! Next time, I'm bringing my people. And I'm bringing more Oreos."

Early the next morning, I reluctantly climbed into the backseat of the helicopter. As we lifted off the beach, happy tears rolled down my cheeks. My beloved river disappeared out of view once the chopper turned inland. "I *will* be back," I whispered into the window.

Lars, Sean, and Boat 5 would travel another ninety-seven miles to the takeout at Pearce Ferry. The Colorado River kept flowing to Lake Mead. I flowed home.

The minute I arrived, I rushed upstairs to my computer to book my company's first photography-based private charter with Hatch River Expeditions. Less than a year later, in May 2017, with Lars as my head boatman, we held the first of what turned into annual photography trips. Every lap was every bit as epic as my first. Outside of the Grand Canyon, I also shifted most of my photography workshops to focus on water-based environments like coasts, lakes, and streams.

The irony was not lost on me that the person who spent the first forty years of her life terrified of water where she couldn't see her feet now found purpose and delight in connecting others with water. Water was giving me new directions, new opportunities, new ambitions. But in order for one to truly become a wild and free-flowing river, a dam must break.

This is what epic looks like. Mom and I jumping for joy after surviving a run through Lava Falls in the Grand Canyon. Photo made using the self-timer on my camera.

19
THE HAPPY BIRTHDAY RAPID

It took almost seventeen years after the construction of the Glen Canyon Dam for Lake Powell to swell into a full pool. On June 20, 1980, the water's surface reached 3,700 feet elevation above sea level. For the few years thereafter, water levels remained consistent around 3,675 feet.

Then the storms came.

In early 1983, an El Niño weather pattern caused an unusually wet winter across the vast Colorado River Basin. Spring runoff thundered down the Colorado River, scouring canyons and fields and trees and bridges and anything else in its path. The water rushed into Lake Powell and into the Glen Canyon Dam at 120,000 cubic feet per second (CFS). By July 15, 1983, the reservoir had risen to its highest point ever recorded: 3,708 feet.

Seasonal floods of this size and nature weren't uncommon in the river's pre-dam history. Humans, with their gigantic concrete plug and fancy technology, simply weren't ready to tame nature's wildness and ferocity. Despite their models and forecasts, dam engineers had not anticipated such a high run-off level and thus had not released enough water from the reservoir to accommodate the extra load. When they realized their predicament, they flung open the gates and spillways.

The river vomited rock and debris into Marble Canyon. Cavitation almost destroyed the dam's two spillway tunnels. The Colorado River—with her turbulent, but pococurante, spirit—didn't give a damn about obstacles or human progress. She demanded her freedom.

When her waters started to crest, engineers installed plywood flashboards on top of the spillway gates to hold the unruly river at bay. It worked. The dam, though battered and bruised, held. Officials later said that the water was a mere eight inches shy of breaching the dam—an incident that would have had catastrophic consequences to downstream communities.

The El Niño persisted, and the same event almost repeated itself in 1984. Forecasters estimated seasonal runoff would peak at levels about 200% above normal. The Bureau of Reclamation quickly repaired the damaged tunnels, reduced the waters in Lake Powell before the spring runoff, and kept the flashboards in place from the previous year. A late snowmelt caused the reservoir to rise to 3,602 feet. This time, officials were ready for the flood. The dam held again but with no significant damage. The artificial lake has never been full—or close to full—since. The river remains captive.

It took less than three years for my waters to rise and breach the dam Craig had built in our marriage. What can I say? Once an overachiever, always an overachiever.

My storm arrived on December 4, 2017. I was enjoying a late-night bath when I saw an email from Craig appear on my phone. We hadn't spoken in a while—five months, eleven days, eight hours, and twenty-four minutes to be precise. I had sent him a message weeks ago to wish him a happy birthday. It was an olive branch. I hadn't expected him to respond.

I sat up in the tub to read his short note. He was moving overseas permanently for his job. He might even apply for citizenship in Germany after the requisite five-year stay. Given his opportunities, our current arrangement wouldn't work anymore. He wanted a divorce.

Now, you can pay attention to the forecasts. You can drain the reservoir ahead of time. You can erect plywood flashboards. Even when you know it's coming, nothing can prepare you for the stinging pain of finality when your best friend and husband asks you for a divorce.

I remained motionless, waiting for my brain and body to implode. My eyes widened and darted from side to side. I wiggled my knees in the water. A wave of energy surged through my body with all the power of a raging river charging through a canyon. I jolted upright and whispered, "I'm free. I'm finally free from worrying, from wondering, from expectations, from trying to live up to standards I'll never be able to meet. I'm free to be free."

I glanced back at Craig's email. This time, the subject line stood out. He had responded to the message I sent weeks ago, so it read "RE: Happy Birthday." I laughed so hard at the irony, I snorted.

I waited until morning to respond. I suggested we meet up for dinner to talk about the $12,000 air conditioning repair, his belongings, the cat—all excuses to get what might be my last chance to ask all the unanswered questions I had. When we met at a local brewery a week later, I didn't bother to ask any of them. Knowing the answers wouldn't have changed anything—the divorce, his life, my life.

In the end, it was simple. He didn't want to be in a relationship now or in the future. I didn't want to be in a relationship with someone who woke up one day and decided he didn't want to be married to me anymore, who broke what I valued as a sacred, unbreakable promise. I didn't want to be with someone who gave up on me, on us. I deserved better. We had nothing more to discuss other than how to divide what we had once shared.

The etymology of the word "river" derives from the Indo-European root "rei-" which means "to tear, cut, scratch." In Old Norse, it's "rifa," or "to tear." The word is also linguistically related to the Old Norse word "ript" which translates into "breach," and the Old English word "aræfan" which means "to let loose, unwrap." I now knew how to act like a river. After all, paddling in this rapid would come easy after facing six-foot swells on a reservoir and a twenty-foot-tall standing wave in Hermit Rapid in the Grand Canyon. I let 'er rip.

I dressed in my favorite black dress and black ballet flats for my first appointment with my lawyer. When he shoved the papers across the table in front of me to start the divorce proceedings, I joked with my lawyer about life's contradictions. About how ceremonious it felt to celebrate a promising future on April 14, 2001, in front of seventy-five family members and friends and how unceremonious it felt to resign from my past sixteen years later in front of one stranger.

Before I shuffled the pages back across the table, I looked down at my signature. The thin, sharp letters of my reclaimed initials, C. J. M., spiked above the shorter rises and falls of the rest of the letters in my name. Together, they took on the shape of a heartbeat on an EKG monitor. There were so many days, hours, minutes, and seconds where I wasn't sure I would, but this was proof: I had survived.

Forty years of planning, achieving, and striving for the perfect life had led to disappointment. Two unanticipated "failures" in eight months, followed by a two-year recovery, had revealed the path to fulfillment. I had learned how to live according to my own principles and desires and convictions. I had come to know my worth and how to evolve confidently in my own uncertain channel. I now revered my life on the other side of my dam.

I would have never sacrificed my relationship with Craig to get here. But I believed his decisions, and the events and transformations they triggered, were saving me from being a miserable, ungrateful human being for the rest of my life. I could think of no bigger gift from him.

I pushed the signed papers away from me and smiled. Happy birthday, indeed.

LAKE MEAD

Artistic rendering only. Map not to scale and should not be used for navigational purposes.

Virgin River
NEVADA
ARIZONA
GRAND CANYON-PARASHANT NATIONAL MONUMENT
South Virgin Mountains
LAKE MEAD NATIONAL RECREATION AREA
Indian Hills
Colorado River
GRAND CANYON NATIONAL PARK
Powell Mountain
Sandy Point
Lunch stop
Pearce Ferry
Hiller Mountains
Temple Basin
South Cove
Pearce Ferry Road
Virgin Narrows
Camp 1
Camp 2
Lunch stop
Meadview
HUALAPAI RESERVATION
ARIZONA
N
To Kingman, AZ

20
ALL IN

"You're going to do *what*?" Mom didn't look up from her pancakes.

It was just another Tuesday in late October 2018. It was just another breakfast with Mom and Dad at a local diner. It was just another casual conversation about our upcoming plans.

"I'm going to paddle across Lake Mead." I pushed coffee mugs, water glasses, and breakfast plates out of the way. Mom helped me unfold my new map of the reservoir across the long wooden table.

"I thought you wanted to retry Powell?" she asked.

"I did, but I changed my mind after talking with Sinjin."

Sinjin and I had not only become buddies after meeting in person at an Outdoor Writers Association of America conference in June 2016, but we had also started working together on a variety of projects regarding water management issues in the Colorado River watershed. I mentioned over beers on one of his Phoenix visits that I might try crossing Powell again, possibly as soon as at the end of the month. I asked if he needed any photographs to support future American Rivers campaigns about the state of the Colorado River. "I already have enough photos from my own trip in 2015," he said.

"Right. *That* trip." I rolled my eyes. We laughed and clinked glasses.

"What I could use is photos of Lake Mead," he said. "I have nothing from there."

"That's an interesting idea," I said, rubbing my chin. "I'll think about it."

I wanted to help Sinjin help the river. If I switched gears and crossed Lake Mead instead of Lake Powell, would I be bending to Sinjin's interests and not listening to my own? Was returning to Powell something I wanted to do or something I thought I *should* do?

People who had heard about our 2015 adventure on Powell had often asked me, "Have you retried the crossing?" The consensus among friends and others was that I should return to Powell, that I shouldn't give up on that goal.

So they say.

Other than a couple-hour paddle Guy and I took on the Overton Arm in 2017, I knew little about Mead. I knew it was the United States' largest reservoir in terms of water volume even though the east-to-west mileage was about half of Powell's. I knew it pooled because of the completion of the Hoover Dam in 1936. But how its shoreline twisted and turned in the Mohave Desert along the Arizona-Nevada border was a mystery to me. I didn't even have a map of the place.

Three weeks after my conversation with Sinjin—and a week before I planned to set out on Powell—I jolted awake at three in the morning. I proclaimed in the dark, "I'm going to Mead."

So I say.

I grabbed my laptop from my nightstand, ordered a Lake Mead map to arrive overnight, and went back to sleep.

Just like that, I let Powell go. Paddling across Mead seemed like a healthy confluence of self-fulfillment and purpose. I could follow my own desires to paddle on the Colorado River while contributing to a greater good. That was more important to me than redemption.

"Like I say to my workshop participants: 'The plan is the plan until the plan changes, and the plan changes often, so plan on it.'" I leaned over to grab my coffee mug, then turned to Mom across the table. "Something about retrying Powell hasn't ever felt right to me. It'd be like trying to get back together with Craig. I've moved downstream."

Mom nodded. "Makes sense."

"Scott will paddleboard with me from South Cove to Temple Bar."

I had recruited my friend and travel buddy Scott to join me for the first part of the trip. He and I had shared adventures before. Scott was the friend who offered me his tent before I cowboy camped for the first time in 2008. He had also joined Craig and me on the Deer Creek/ Thunder River hike in the Grand Canyon in 2009. After losing touch for a few years, we had just reconnected. He was jonesing to try out his new standup paddleboard on an overnight trip.

"We'll stop at the Temple Bar Marina to drop Scott off so he can get back to work." I traced my finger over the river's course. "From there, I'll continue to Kingman Wash. Scott will meet me there when I notify him. Then we'll do the final four miles to the Hoover Dam and back to Kingman Wash together to finish the crossing."

"How far is all that?" Mom asked.

"About sixty miles if you follow the river's course and don't play in the side bays," I said, leaning back in my chair. "I want to go up the lake first from South Cove to see where the Colorado River meets Lake Mead. I'm not sure where that happens. According to Google Maps, it's somewhere around Sandy Point. If that's the case, it would add another four or so miles."

"How long will it take to get from Temple Bar to Kingman Wash?" Mom pulled the map closer to her with both hands to study it.

"I'm guessing six days, but I could do it in three if I had to," I said. I made that up. I had no idea how long it'd take. I hadn't done the math. I hadn't put together a spreadsheet. I hadn't planned where I'd camp or where I'd be day to day on the water. I figured I'd paddle however long I wanted to, camp on inviting beaches along the way, and get to Kingman Wash when I got there. "I don't want to rush this," I said. "I want to play, photograph, and explore along the way. I have the time."

I had blocked almost six weeks on my schedule. Surely, I could finish sixty-four miles in forty-two days.

"How's the camping along the way?" Mom let go of the map and took a sip of water.

"From what I can tell on Google Earth, there aren't many side canyons to pull into like Powell. Looks like terraced sand or gravel beaches along much of the main shoreline."

"What if I went with you on that stretch from Temple Bar to Kingman Wash?" she asked without looking up.

Dad dropped his fork onto his plate and slapped his hand against his forehead. "Oh god. Here we go again."

"Did you just ask to paddle with me on Lake Mead?" I cocked my head to the side. "I thought you never wanted to go kayaking again after Powell."

"Yeah, well, I've learned a lot since our trip," Mom said. She hadn't been back in her kayak since Powell. In the months afterward, though, she (along with my dad) had gained much outdoor experience while hiking over 900 miles of the Pacific Crest Trail in sections.

"Are you sure you want to do this?" I pushed my back against my chair.

"When are you leaving to do this?" Mom ran her fingers through her hair.

"Tomorrow."

Dad choked on his coffee.

"Come on, Dad!" I laughed. "Mom would have until Saturday to pack. That's four whole days."

"I'm in. What do I need to do?" Mom asked, not paying attention to my banter with Dad.

We finalized the logistics of who would be where and when, who would be bringing what, and how we would all keep in touch as things progressed. "It's settled then," I said, drinking the last of my coffee. "We'll see you on Saturday at the Temple Bar Marina."

The next afternoon, on October 31, after an easy five-hour drive from Phoenix, I pulled up to the weathered entrance sign on the road to the Temple Bar Marina. I hadn't announced anything about this trip publicly. Besides my family and Scott, only five of my closest friends knew of my intentions.

There was one more person I thought ought to know. I took a selfie with the sign and sent it to Sinjin. "Hi river buddy! So the Lake Mead paddle is happening. Like right now. Drove up today to get a shuttle in place. Put in tomorrow..."

"Girl! You're amazing!" Sinjin typed with a smiley emoji.

"For the love of the river!" I typed back.

Minutes later, I crested a hill and caught a glimpse of the sparkling blue waters I'd be calling home for who knew how long. Scott met me at Temple Bar later that evening. The next morning, we drove Juno to the launch ramp at South Cove two hours to the northeast. By ten, we were paddling up Lake Mead to greet my beloved Colorado River once again.

~ ~ ~

After the Colorado River rages through the Grand Canyon, she peeks out of the layered red rock country of the Colorado Plateau and flows into the dry, dusty volcanic mountains of the Mohave Desert, plowing into Lake Mead to the south of Iceberg Canyon—an odd name for a place that rarely drops below freezing even in the midst of winter. From there, she ebbs and flows through four main basins behind the 726-foot-tall Hoover Dam. The river swells into a reservoir at Gregg Basin, then shrinks into Virgin Canyon, then swells into Temple Basin and the even larger bay called Virgin Basin, then shrinks at Boulder Canyon, and finally swells into Boulder Basin before collecting behind the dam in Black Canyon. Near the middle of its length, the Overton Arm—a thirty-three-mile-long bay formed as the Muddy and Virgin rivers merge—discharges into the Virgin Basin from the north. On a map, the reservoir looks like a wavy, bloated upside-down T. Or the outline of a diving bird with outstretched wings, depending on how much wine you've had to drink.

Scott and I made our way along the curvaceous western shoreline at the base of Grapevine Mesa in Gregg Basin. Retreating waters had layered the ashen gravel deposits into stone bleachers. Whitewashed rock blended into darker blocky rock faces of the brown Muav Formation and the blood-orange Redwall Limestone. An occasional tamarisk or tumbleweed, burned out by the relentless dry heat, dotted the bleached hillsides. From a mile and a half away, the white stripe of Lake Mead's own version of the Bathtub Ring, rising just above the water's surface, stood out against the black layers of granite boulders at the base of the

Hiller Mountains to the southwest. The distant shoreline to the east across the expansive bay into Nevada was so far away that it was hard to tell the difference between rock crumbs and a shrub.

The water was still, the air warm. A Clark's grebe floated on the surface, then disappeared underwater in a leaping dive. Its sudden movements stirred the perfect reflections of the landscape in front of Lir.

The water was warm, the air not still. A parade of helicopters boomed across the horizon to the south of us as if this were a war zone. I later learned they originated in Las Vegas and offered tourists a half-day or day-long "Grand Canyon experience" on the western side of the national park. I lost count after thirty-eight.

A distinct delineation in the water's color came into view near Sandy Point. A visible line separating muddy-brown from emerald-green water stretched across the bay for nearly a half mile between the Arizona and Nevada shorelines. A thin rocky peninsula extending out into the wide channel pushed the river into a small chocolatey riffle.

"The Colorado is a feisty one here, isn't she?" I said to Scott, pointing my paddle at the small wave train. "Look at her go! She's not going down without a fight here."

On Powell three years ago, Mom and I watched the Colorado River submit to the reservoir quietly, meekly even, as if she didn't know what to do with her unexpected new reality. Once the river makes it to Lake Mead, she brawls against the reservoir, against the dams, against humanity, to try to stay true to herself. Her waters thrashed over rocks and sandbars and swirled in whirlpools around small piles of gravel. Plumes of sediment exploded like milk clouds in coffee. Then the silty, tenacious river gave in to her unavoidable situation. She faded into a pool of glittering green water—the turbulent Colorado River tamed by a reservoir once again. For now.

Scott and I spent almost three hours surfing the small rapids, spinning in the chains of vortices, and exploring the debris collecting into a sludge of dead trees, plastic bottles, and browned foam bubbles along the edge of the fast-moving river and the subdued lake. I didn't want to leave, but more adventures called down the lake. We eventually turned our boards south and paddled toward the mouth of Virgin Canyon.

Where the flowing Colorado River meets Lake Mead near Sandy Point, Arizona. The mountains in the background reside in Nevada.

The next two and a half days passed under the warm fall sun without incident, without clouds, and most importantly, without wind. On November 3, we pulled into the boat ramp at the Temple Bar Marina just as we had arranged with my parents. Scott and I finished packing our gear into his car and drove up to the Temple Bar Campground to find a campsite for the night. On the ride up, I switched my phone out of airplane mode.

My phone started buzzing. A string of texts from my parents flooded in: "DON'T DO THIS!!! YOU'RE GOING TO DIE!!!"

I called my parents immediately. "What's going on? Are you okay?"

My mom's muffled voice spoke first: "We can't let you do this, Colleen. This is too dangerous. We love you too much." She sniffled. She had been crying.

"This is ridiculous," Dad chimed in. "You're going to get yourself killed."

"I'm sorry you're so upset," I said. "What's going on?"

"We're about an hour away from the campground right now," Mom said. "Dad will tell you more when we get there."

I set the phone on my leg and turned to Scott. "I don't have any idea what's going on, but I think my parents are in the process of driving five hours to talk me out of continuing."

When my parents arrived at our campsite, Dad shared that he had called the Lake Mead ranger station a couple days ago to get more information about the lake's current conditions. The woman who had answered the phone admitted she had never been on the lake before but told him that high winds often tunneled through Boulder Canyon, causing deadly waves through a mountainous gorge so slim that people also referred to the canyon as the Narrows. She had declared it no place for a standup paddleboarder—although she had to first ask what a standup paddleboard was. She had also suggested that rangers did not patrol the Narrows. She explained if a boater decided to venture into the canyon, they'd be on their own for rescue. Mom and Dad understandably panicked.

Little of what the woman said was true. "We went through Virgin Canyon, which looks longer and thinner than the Narrows, yesterday with no trouble," I said while quickly pulling photographs up on my camera's LCD screen to prove it. "The water was as smooth as glass."

I couldn't argue that wind couldn't or wouldn't howl through a constricted canyon. But the wind rose charts I had studied before the trip indicated that winds rarely moved from west to east—the orientation of Boulder Canyon—at Lake Mead. They mostly originated from the northeast or southwest. I also reminded my parents that I had learned how to handle large waves in Class IV rapids during a multi-day whitewater SUP training class on the Lower Salmon River in Idaho in August 2018. I didn't want to get cocky, but I knew I wouldn't face waterfall ledges and house-sized holes no matter how hard the wind blew. If I fell in, the water temperatures were in the balmy seventies, not the chilly fifties like at Powell. I also couldn't say how many boats passed through the Narrows on a given day nor if a ranger patrolled that area regularly. On the first part of our trip, we saw over fifty helicopters pass by overhead *a day*. If I had to press the SOS button on my InReach in a life-or-death emergency, I was sure my call for help would not go ignored.

"I appreciate your concerns. But I trust myself and my own experiences more than one person's uninformed opinion," I said. "I'm going to continue."

"I can't do this," Mom said, leaning back from the picnic table. "I don't want to go."

"You don't have to do this, Ma. I'm not going to talk you into something you don't want to do," I said, reaching for her hands across the table. I imagined she was reliving the memories of the storm on Lake Powell. "It's so brave, and so important, to decide what's right for you, to choose to *not* do something, rather than to force yourself into an uncomfortable situation."

Mom dropped her head into her hands. Not only was she working through her own disappointment, but she also knew if I went alone, she'd lose the ability to protect me from harm. She'd have to let me go. She'd have to trust me. She'd also have to trust that she was making the right choice for herself—a monumental decision considering she had dedicated her heart and soul to caring for her family for most of her life. I walked around the table to hug her from behind.

"I'm so proud of you for choosing yourself, Ma," I said, squeezing her tight. "You know I'd love to share this time with you, but I am perfectly content and capable of paddling on my own."

She nodded. "Please, please be safe," she said as she hugged me.

"I'll turn on my tracking and check in with you every night on my InReach," I said. "I'll be fine. Please don't worry."

This time, I meant it.

~ ~ ~

I lost sight of Mom, Dad, and Scott waving to me from the end of the Temple Bar boat ramp as soon as I paddled around the small rock hill near Heron Point. I turned to the hushed dark green waters of Temple Basin, the unknown ahead. "Here we go, Colly Raddy. Just you, me, Lir, and the wind now."

The morning sun sparkled across the water's surface. The same musky wisdom I smelled on Powell rose into each breath. My heart raced. The rawest, most splendid form of freedom I'd ever felt tingled across every inch of my body.

Every decision would be my own, for better or worse. Every triumph would go unnoticed. Every mistake would too. I could choose to write any story I wanted to in the waves here. With no expectations. With no outside support or influence. With no limits.

This was not a gymnastics routine or a volleyball match. There would be no score or winner declared afterward. There would be no trophy or newspaper write-up. This was a dance with water, an expression of who I was, of who I had become, an ad hoc performance with no script or preconceived ending presented to an audience of one.

No matter what transpired, I knew whatever gear and food I carried on Lir, whatever path I chose, and whatever I did would have to be good enough to get me across the rest of this reservoir, however long it took. If my decisions and actions weren't good enough, I wouldn't survive.

A river of strength, confidence, and joy flowed through me and my aloneness now. My solitary inner landscape was every bit as sacred as the outer landscape around me. I was wildness incarnate.

Which both delighted and scared the shit out of me.

I smiled out of the corner of my mouth. "The big Life with a capital L should scare the shit out of you. That's how you know you've capitalized the L."

I pressed my shoulders back and dug my paddle deeper into the lake. "I'm all in!" I boomed into the big blue sky, just in case the ravens and the cliffs and the water decided to start caring.

I turned Lir north into calm waters and passed the rolling brown, tan, and yellow hills on Plane Crash and Houseboat islands. Two miles later, I rounded a large rocky headland capped with a beige rampart called The Head. Irony kicked in once Boat Wreck Point came into view on my left and a brisk headwind rustled my blue wrap skirt. One-to-two-foot undulating waves came out of nowhere.

"Already?" I teased the wind and grinned. "Really wind? We're going to do this so soon? I *just* started."

I ducked my head to my chest and paddled hard to the nearest pile of gravel. After a quarter mile, I sat down on my loveseat and anchored my left foot on land to hold steady in the bouncing waves.

"If we're going to do this, we're going to do it with a little help," I said to the next gust.

I dug out my phone from the dry bag closest to my feet and pulled up my SUP paddle playlist from Powell. First up? *The Warrior* by Scandal from 1984.

"You better believe this wild heart is going to break out of captivity and shoot at the walls of heartache." I laughed and wiggled my butt from side to side. Solitude made me so lovably dorky sometimes. As I pushed away from the safety of dry land and into the hands of the unknown, I crooned with the chorus, "I AM THE WARRIOR!"

Wind is only a problem if you're in a hurry to get somewhere. I wasn't. I had nowhere to be, anywhere to go. If I could make it to East Point, the northernmost point along this shoreline, I'd turn south, and this headwind would become an advantageous tailwind in four miles. This inconvenience—if you even wanted to call it that—was temporary.

The contours of the water's edge directed my course. When I saw a straight sandy or rocky shoreline, I paddled hard through the swells. When the shoreline bowed into a small bay, I pulled into the calmer waters to rest, stretch, snack, and drink. I moved into the wind and out of the waves, into the wind, out of the waves, into the wind, out of the waves until I reached East Point a couple of hours later.

There, the rhythmic slosh of Temple Basin met the stiller waters in Virgin Basin. The Overton Arm, formed by the Muddy and Virgin rivers, came in from the north off in the distance. The Black Mountains lined the northeast horizon, but they were far enough away across the blue expanse that I could not discern any detail along its dark-toothed ridgelines. The reservoir resembled a thinner river channel earlier, but here it was so wide and long, it looked more like an endless ocean. It occurred to me, that in four days, I hadn't seen a single mile-marking navigational buoy like the ones on Powell.

The tailwind scooted me down the shoreline around and southwest

My first solo camp near the Gypsum Reef along Lake Mead in Arizona. My tent looks out across the Virgin Basin and into the Overton Arm (on the right where the Black Mountains taper to the reservoir).

of East Point Bay. An hour after passing the peninsula, the rock at the water level changed form and color. White gravel terraces gave way to uneven chocolate-colored ledges that looked like crumbling brownies. Layers upon layers of sculpted gypsum emerged in a fantastical collection of ledges, curves, and arches mimicking dragons and elephants and sphinxes.

I beached Lir at the nearest stretch of gravel. Once on land, my hand reached down to touch the spiky top of a table-sized brown shelf. I flinched. The polished but pocked rock looked smooth. It deceived. The razor-sharp edge sliced a small cut on my finger.

I returned to my board to get a Band-Aid and to check my map, which told me I had landed on the Gypsum Reef near East Gypsum Bay. It was only two in the afternoon—early to set up camp for the

"Deliciousness" on November 4, 2018 at the Gypsum Reef along Lake Mead.

night—but I had traveled almost eleven miles already, and I *had* to stop to photograph this remarkable foreign landscape. In all my travels, I had never seen anything like it.

I paddled back to the cobble beach I'd spotted to the east. The small horseshoe-shaped cove was protected by gypsum ledges and a couple of wispy tamarisk trees. I set out my chair, unfurled my tarp, and put up my one-person tent on a flat spot on the gravel to stake my claim—although I hadn't seen another person on the water all day.

I walked off from my camp about an hour before sundown to wander aimlessly around the area with my camera. I bounded from ledge to ledge, rock to rock, carefully balancing to avoid falling and putting my hands down. I made several images I liked, ones I knew would help Sinjin showcase this area in his and American Rivers' crusade to protect the river. I also took note of other strong compositions that would benefit from tomorrow's sunrise. Even under the now mostly overcast skies, I wanted to make a series of "happy snaps" to show this wonderland to my family and friends.

The sun poked out of a hole in the clouds right before tucking behind a rugged ridgeline. The light took the wind with it. In an instant, the grey clouds erupted into a psychedelic blend of yellows, oranges, reds, and violets. The water's surface mirrored the colors. I couldn't believe my eyes—or fortune.

I started dancing while I clicked-clicked-clicked the shutter. I couldn't photograph the moment fast enough. "How delicious is it that I'm in this magnificent place witnessing this?" I stepped back from my tripod to savor the sweetness. "Also, how delicious would a fudge brownie pie be right now?"

I laughed. Pie wasn't on my menu for this trip. Still, I could imagine the rich, chocolately taste. I decided I'd title one of my frame's "Deliciousness" to commemorate the moment.

Once the sky drew its navy curtain on its evening show, I skipped back to camp. I dropped my pack and looked up at the stars emerging between the clearing clouds. I clasped my hands together and said, "Thank you for such a great day, Lir, the Colorado River, Lake Mead, and the universe. Thanks to you too, Wind."

With over eleven miles in my day's paddling log, a memory card full of sunset photographs, and dreams of dessert swirling in my head, I fell asleep almost immediately after climbing into my sleeping bag. It hadn't crossed my mind that it was only my second night sleeping alone in a tent in the wild, my first being at Lone Rock Bay at Powell with Lir right before Craig asked for the divorce. I didn't ask, "What was that?" once during the entire night.

The next morning, I heard splashes against the gravel even if I couldn't see them in the dark periwinkle twilight of dawn. I turned my headlamp on to see Lir bobbing along the shore. Overnight, white-capped waves had whipped up a puffy layer of foam along the curved shoreline in front of my camp.

I rubbed my eyes. That's odd. The InReach forecast hadn't mentioned wind. I shrugged. I was not in a rush to move on. The wind did its thing while I did mine. To pass the time, I photographed the sunrise from the brownie rocks, took my tent down, drank multiple cups of coffee, and read while reclined on my tarp.

Around ten, the winds seemed to calm. I said a reluctant goodbye to the breathtakingly beautiful Gypsum Reef with the hope of positioning myself close to the mouth of the Boulder Canyon Narrows later in the day. Instead of paddling a direct route across the middle of Virgin Bay, a pool of open water two miles wide and almost six miles long, I decided to stay closer to the shoreline in case I needed to stop. It meant paddling more miles but safer ones.

The southwesterly headwind slowed my progress as I skirted the western-most gypsum ledges and crossed the wide mouth of Bonelli Bay. After strong-arming my way for four miles in one-to-two-foot whitecaps, I stopped for lunch at the tip of a small unnamed island in Virgin Basin to the west of Bonelli Bay. I rested easily knowing that as soon as I started up again, finished crossing this cove, and turned to the northwest along the Stewart Cliffs ahead, I'd escape the wind again.

Back on the water, I settled into a regular beat as if paddling to a metronome. Drips of water fell from my paddle and tapped the surface. Mesmerizing ribbons of water streamed from the nose on both sides of my SUP.

About an hour later, I happened to notice my tripod head, which was resting on its side near the front of my board, was dragging in the water. I groaned. It was slowing me down. I kneeled, then leaned over my knee-high pile of dry bags to straighten it out. As my weight shifted to the front, Lir started rocking from side to side. My board tilted hard on its left side. I grabbed the right edge of the board with both hands out of desperation.

"No! No! No!"

My SUP flipped like an upended iceberg. I splashed into the lake butt first. I bobbed in my life jacket and reached for Lir.

"Well, here you are," I said aloud while treading water. "In the middle of Lake Mead. In the water. Alone. With Lir turned upside-down with all your gear underwater. Now what?"

I wasn't sure how deep the water was, but I couldn't touch the bottom, and I wasn't about to dive down to find out.

My food bag, which wasn't strapped in like the rest of my gear for some reason, started floating away. I released my grip on Lir to grab it. I ran my hand under my board and clipped the food bag to the first part of bungee I could find by feel. Then I swam to the middle of the board in hopes I could flip it. "One...two...three!" I pushed up and over with all my strength.

The board barely budged. I took another breath and pushed again with a prolonged grunt. Nothing moved.

"Now what?" I tapped Lir and started cackling. Laughing wasn't going to solve anything but neither was worrying or reprimanding myself. Laughing felt better, too, given the preposterousness of my situation.

"Alright, let's try this..."

I reached underneath for my biggest bag and pulled it to the side of the board. When I pushed it up and over against Lir, my board teetered onto its side at a slight angle. I quickly grabbed another bag while keeping the board propped up with my right hand. The juggling act worked. With the added weight, Lir rolled right side up. A couple of the lighter bags still dangled in the water on taut bungee cords. One-by-one, I repositioned the rest of my gear onto my board.

I pushed away from Lir again and swam to retrieve my paddle, which had floated twenty or so feet away. I threaded it under my bags. I kicked over to the middle of Lir and said, "My turn."

With a furious butterfly kick, I reached across the top and tried to pull myself across the board. Lir tipped onto his side again. Bags started sliding back into the water.

"NOOOOOOOOO!"

I let go and slumped back into the water. Lir flopped back to its upright position with all the gear intact on top.

"Thank goodness. That was close."

I howled again. Because I was still alone in the water in the middle of Lake Mead and unable to get back on top of my SUP.

"Now what?" I said in between laughs. The warm water felt soft and smooth. If there were any scary monsters underwater foaming at the mouth to eat me, I was no longer afraid of them.

I twirled around in the water. I had not noticed it earlier, but a small island with a tiny crescent-shaped beach sat only a few hundred yards away. Instead of wasting energy trying to self-rescue again—and risking overturning my board again—I decided to swim Lir to shore.

"This is *exactly* why you didn't paddle across the open waters of Virgin Bay. Smart move, princess," I said while doing the breaststroke with my free arm and legs.

Within a few minutes, I crawled up the shallow cobbles like a swamp creature and dragged Lir onto the beach. I stripped naked, laying out my top, skirt, underwear, and sports bra across the rocks, then waded back into the shallow water to bathe and wash my hair. Why not? I was already wet.

"This one's for you, Katie Lee!" I hollered into the breeze as I let myself fall backwards into the water.

I laid back into my skirt to sun myself like a lizard and started laughing and sobbing at the same time. I let the tears flow. I cried not because I fell in. I cried because I couldn't believe I had gained enough confidence to know I'd figure something out when I found myself alone in the water. That I loved myself enough to take care of myself. Growth never comes in the comfort of standing on shore but rather in the discomfort of swimming for our life.

After my skin dried and warmed, I opened each dry bag to check for water, steadied my gear by tightening the bungee cords, and strapped my tripod on top of the pile. I turned the tripod head upright, so it had no chance of dragging again. I picked up my paddle and pushed off the shore as if the event never happened. My board had no extra room to carry fear. Or self-pity. Besides, no one was coming by to listen to me whine. I hadn't seen a boat in over twenty-four hours.

I steered my board to the northwest, toward the Stewart Cliffs and Boulder Point near the mouth of the Boulder Canyon Narrows. I estimated I had about two more miles to go in open water before I reached land again. The wind calmed. I settled back into my pace. Stroke. Stroke. Stroke.

CRACK!

My body collapsed into the pile of gear. Lir tilted to the left. I

The cobble beach I swam to after capsizing in Virgin Bay. The mouth of the Boulder Canyon Narrows appear near the center of the photograph on the horizon. The ridge to the left is called the Stewart Cliffs. Later that evening, I camped at the base of the Stewart Cliffs and just to the left of the Narrows.

leaned to the right. I managed to stabilize our rocking without falling back in the water again.

"What the…" I pushed myself back to my feet, then stared at my hands, each of which held separate ends of my brand-new two-bladed paddle. It had snapped in half. I poked one of the serrated ends and gave myself a carbon fiber sliver.

"You're tired. Let's get you into a nice camp." I sat down on my loveseat. "We'll figure things out there."

I didn't need to be up shit creek—or perhaps more appropriately, shit *lake*—without a paddle right before traveling through the Narrows or for the rest of the trip. Thankfully, I had strapped a back-up paddle on the side of my board for the trip. Even still, I used one end of the broken paddle like a canoe paddle. An overnight camp wasn't far away.

About a half hour later, I hobbled into a spacious east-facing, gently sloping wash at the base of Arch Mountain. My GPS indicated I was within a mile of the mouth to the Narrows. I kicked burro excrement away from the flattest spot I could find, then set up my sleeping and cooking spaces, changed into PJs, and taped the ends of my broken paddle to avoid more carbon fiber splinters. I had already removed three in my right hand.

As I took care of camp chores, a steady stream of tourist helicopters flew overhead back to Las Vegas. One black chopper, the last one of the night, grazed my camp at such a low altitude, I thought he was going to land on my beach. I clutched my tent, tarp, and other loose gear to prevent them from blowing away. He flew off into the western horizon as abruptly as he arrived.

In the remaining serenity of the twilight, I reflected on the day's unexpected events: the wind, the capsize, the broken paddle. Laughing, I asked aloud, "Why do you do things like this? Why can't you just be content sitting at home on the couch eating bonbons?"

My freeze-dried dinner fumbled out of my chilled hands. My knees caught it upside down. I noticed typing on the bottom of the Mountain House® package, something I had never seen before in almost twenty years of eating freeze-dried food on outdoors trips.

The white lettering on the bottom of my "Chicken and Mashed Potatoes" dinner read: "We travel not to escape life, but for life not to escape us. ~Anonymous" In that moment, I knew who I was and why I was paddling across a reservoir.

Spending time in nature, as I did, was not an escape from reality. It *was* my reality. This was my life, my work, my passion, my joy. The outdoors was where I filled my insatiable curiosity and challenged my abilities while bearing witness to indescribable beauty, gathering photographs and stories that would contribute to greater causes, and feeling richly and proudly significant—if to no one other than to myself.

Fulfillment looked different here. It wasn't the hyper-energetic, over-enthusiastic, jubilant, jumping up and down or any other celebratory expressions society has labeled as "happiness." My euphoria had settled into a quiet, calming, almost Zen-like state where I felt

A message from the universe delivered on the bottom of a Mountain House meal in my second solo camp along the shores of Lake Mead on November 5, 2018.

like I paddled in step with—not against—the river flowing silently between two distant shores, the reservoir, the universe, and my own heart and soul—even as mishaps happened. I was safe, dry, overflowing with rapture, and eating a rehydrated feast while nestled on a beach with a million-dollar view. What more could a girl want?

I looked across Virgin Basin to where I had started this morning—some seven miles as the raven flew to the east—and snapped a few photographs for myself and for Sinjin. The sun dropped behind the Black Mountains, and the pinks and purples of the Earth's shadow started to rise over the summit of Bonelli Peak on the opposite horizon. I snapped a few more photographs.

"To my big Life with a capital L!" I yelled into the sky. "For the love of the river!"

I relaxed in my camp chair and texted my parents on my InReach.

"All OK. In camp at mouth of narrows. Have 2 days to watch for best weather." The weather forecast on my InReach predicted calm winds for the next two days. I slept through the night without worry—and without waking, something I rarely did at home in my own bed.

The next morning's blue twilight was as tranquil and silent as the evening before. Waves barely dawdled over the shallow cobble shelf where Lir rested. I didn't need to wait two days to attempt the Narrows. I had my window of opportunity right now. I scampered to pack my belongings, shoved an energy bar in my pocket for breakfast, and pushed away from the beach well before the birds started singing their morning songs.

"Here goes," I said after my first few strokes on the water. I shook my shoulders, arms, and legs out to wake them up.

The edges of the western and northern shorelines started to converge. A fishing boat sped out of the canyon's mouth and disappeared across the Virgin Basin. I waved and glided over the rolling wake it left behind.

The chalky Bathtub Ring along the bottom 150 feet of rock reflected in the stagnant water. The sun kissed the tops of the two triangular mountains guarding the entrance to the Narrows like Anubis when I entered the constricted corridor of rock. The steep walls of dark igneous rock on both sides of the channel stayed in a deep tunnel-like shadow. (My Rockd app called this black rock the "Tea Kettle Pass Phase of the Wilson Ridge pluton" which I hereby nominate for The Best Geological Name Ever Created Award.)

The dimmed 500-foot-wide channel snaked past a small finger called Flamingo Cove on the right. Once beyond the shallow inlet of Wishing Well Cove on the left, the precipitous bluffs started relaxing into slopes of whitewashed ridgelines scattered with boulders. Although I aimed to get through the Narrows as fast as I could, I noted several inviting beaches in James Bay tucked into the crook of Gilbert Canyon. "Next time, we should camp *in* the Narrows, Lir," I said with wide-eyed excitement.

After four miles, once I passed Sidewinder Cove to the south, the mountainous walls started falling away from each other again, the sky widening and brightening. I put my sunglasses on, then turned Lir 180 degrees to survey my path and bowed to pay tribute to the canyon for my safe passage.

"Thank you, river gods."

I had made it through the Boulder Canyon Narrows in the calmest conditions I'd experienced in five days.

I landed on a gravel beach at the base of a smaller mountain beneath Bearing Point. I texted my parents: "Through the Narrows!" I leaned up against a clump of white rock, closed my eyes, and sunned myself like a lizard while waiting for their response.

"Now what?" With the crux of the trip behind me, I had endless options for the rest of my journey.

I checked the weather forecast. A windstorm with thirty-five-mile-per-hour gusts was on the way in the next thirty-six hours. I looked across the water and debated the possibilities. I could paddle the twelve miles to Kingman Wash today to avoid the wind. Or I could find another place or two to camp and sit still if—and when—the wind arrived. A California gull flying overhead offered a high-pitched squeal. My gull-talk was a little rusty, but I interpreted that to mean "Stay out as long as you can." So that's what I did. And I didn't feel gulled into it.

I made a short overnight stop at Sandy Cove on the Nevada side, which was, not surprisingly, a treeless, arced sandy cove tucked between whitewashed rocks. I followed lizards with my camera, asked the ravens how they felt about the dam, and took another skinny dip in honor of Katie Lee. The next morning, before the sun filled the basin's shadows, I crossed the tranquil open water to meet up with the Arizona shoreline to the south.

The mountainous terrain began to flatten into rippled ridgelines riddled with washes from the tops of the Black Mountains. Hints of reddened sandstone, similar in color to the Glen Canyon Group at Powell, started to intertwine with the white-stained conglomerate and dark volcanic rocks I'd become so accustomed to seeing along Lake Mead's shore. Bulbous pillars of sculpted rock towered into the blue skyline. The stout and imposing basalt mesa of Fortification Hill rose into the sky to the southwest.

In the warming late afternoon light, I glided into a stair-stepped

The top photo shows my camp at Sandy Cove at sunset on November 6, 2018. Fortification Ridge and Fortification Hill are visible on the distant horizon on the right. The bottom photo shows my camp on an unnamed beach near Beehive Island. I waited out the windstorm here on November 7-9, 2018.

cobble beach to the south of Beehive Island—which was not a detached isle at this low water level—and called it home. I dragged Lir and my gear up to the third main gravel ledge. Four levels above that, in what I called "the penthouse," I set up my tent.

Once settled, I texted my parents and Scott to advise them that they likely wouldn't see my track move for the next two nights—and that it was nothing to worry about. A gust poked at my tent now and then, but it wasn't enough to whip the lake's surface into frothy whitecaps. Yet.

I nestled into the white rocks, not bothering to set up my chair, then ate dinner, drank wine, and watched the lights of Boulder, Nevada, twinkle on the distant southwestern horizon. I hadn't picked it out in the daytime, but a white suspension-bridge-like structure with two long metallic rods extended into the lake across the bay. During the day, it had blended into the white Bathtub Ring on the surrounding shores, but as the sun set, a collection of spotlights illuminated one of Nevada's intake pipes withdrawing its rightful allocation of water from the Colorado River. Per the Law of the River, the state pulls 300,000 acre-feet—or 97,800,000,000 gallons—of water out of Lake Mead each year. I pumped my own drinking water from the shoreline, filling my three water bottles with just over a gallon, before heading to bed. I wondered if my consumption here had been considered in the Law of the River math.

Night fell. The winds came roaring in as loud as a low-flying jet. Water slapped against the rocks and exploded into a bouquet of spray. The reservoir looked like an ocean. Just as soon as I'd fall asleep, a gust of chaos, then another, then another shoved the tent walls down against my head. Each time, I woke suddenly, thrashing and clawing at my face. I scooted to the middle of my tent and stayed curled in a ball on my side until dawn.

CRACK!

The right side of the tent draped on top of me like a blanket. I darted out of the tent in a panic, trying to avoid suffocating in a yellow nylon coffin. The jagged top of a broken tent pole quivered. I grabbed hold of the tent to keep it from flying away as I surveyed the rest of the damage. A four-inch gash in my rainfly. Another pole looked bent and slightly cracked, but it hadn't split in two. Another gust ripped the tent from my hands and flattened it against the cobble.

I jumped on top of the fabric and pondered my options. Duct tape would reinforce both poles and make them usable, but that seemed like a waste of time and energy—and duct tape—considering that the wind advisory was not set to expire until noon the next day. I kept one foot on the tent and lunged to grab the biggest rock I could reach. I set it on top of my tent with my sleeping bag and other overnight gear inside. During a lull in the wind, I grabbed another rock, then another, and another.

I collected more rocks to place on top of my SUP. Losing my tent, although inconvenient, would not lead to tragedy. Losing Lir would be disastrous. Not because I wouldn't make it to Kingman Wash—I had enough food to stay out until Christmas and wasn't particularly keen on reentering the manufactured world—but rather because I'd lose my beloved and prized travel buddy. Lir had seen me through so much in three years. I loved Lir as much as I loved the river. And I loved the river as much as I loved myself.

Leaving wasn't an option now but neither was camping in a tent. "I'll just cowboy camp tonight," I declared. It was warm and clear, not a cloud in the sky. Perfect conditions for camping under the stars. To do so, though, I needed to get my gear out of the deflated tent without it blowing away.

I slid my sleeping bag out of the collapsed tent door and onto the tarp next to my tent, placing two grapefruit-sized boulders on top of it to weigh it down. Next, my sleeping pad. Rock. Rock. Rock. Rock. Pillow. Rock. Book. Rock. Loose pants and shirt. Rock. Rock. My camp looked like a checkerboard by the time I finished. I laughed at the ridiculous sight. It didn't have to look pretty. And it didn't. It just had to work. And it did.

After securing my gear, I passed the time on the unnamed beach near Beehive Island much like I did with Mom on Gilligan's Island on Powell in 2015. Except now, I felt comfortable in my aloneness

Ready to cowboy camp! Rocks hold down my gear at an unnamed cobble beach near Beehive Island along Lake Mead.

and inner stillness. I wrote in my journal. Tinkered with my camera. Finished reading two books. Hiked up the ridgeline behind my camp to check out the view. Stared blankly at the waves for hours. Existing in chaos never felt so calming.

Enduring the windstorm all day hadn't tired me, but the prospect of cowboy camping for the first time by myself lured me to an early sleep. As the sun scampered behind the distant ridgeline dotted with houses, I started removing the rocks on top of my bed only after my body weight shifted onto it. My sleeping pad fluttered beneath my relaxed legs. My sleeping bag filled with restless air and shook from side to side. I rolled on my side, wrapped my arms around my pillow, and let the wind rock me to sleep.

A gentler breeze woke me the next morning. The water still swelled one to two feet into the air and splashed onto the first tier of gravel ledges in front of me. I rubbed the sleep out of my eyes and (in an uncharacteristic show of enthusiasm before coffee) proudly proclaimed, "I just cowboy camped all by myself for the first time!" I wiggled my hips while still in my sleeping bag.

I dug out my InReach. I checked the weather forecast. Winds calming around midday. I sent Scott a text: "Still whitecaps. If it calms just a little more, will make the hour run today."

I packed up my belongings and watched and waited and watched and waited. Around noon, the lake had settled its whitecaps into smooth rollers. I sent a text to Scott: "Going 4 it! Wish me good luck!"

One shove of the paddle was all it took to push Lir back into the flow. Backwards. A sudden gust of wind turned my board in the direction of Kingman Wash. "I love you, Wind and Waves!" I shouted. "It would not have been right to finish this journey without you."

An hour later, after nine days—six solo—and sixty miles, I arrived unscathed at Kingman Wash. Scott and two friendly RV campers with a playful black Labrador retriever welcomed me on shore. We downed a bottle of chardonnay and made the requisite celebratory photographs. The wind disappeared.

"Do you want to paddle to the dam tomorrow to complete the crossing?" Scott asked.

"Not really. I don't want to see a dam after feeling so free for the last six days," I said, looking back at the still waters. "I've just had the most remarkable adventure. I don't need more. I've had enough."

Paddling on Lake Mead had never been about achieving a goal. It was about learning about myself and a new place I had never paid attention to before. It was about following my inquisitiveness. Bonding with my beloved river in her ever-changing forms. Realizing my own ever-changing forms. Directing my course while dancing with the wind and splashing in the waves. Building confidence in paddling on my own. Helping friends. Helping the Colorado River.

After all, my middle name was not "Perfectionist." It's "Jacqueline" after my mother.

I did not complete the crossing.

I threw my gear in the back of Scott's car. We reunited with Juno at South Beach. I sent Sinjin a few iPhone photos to tease him with the types of photographs I'd later send him. I drove home. I hugged my mom and dad. I ate pie.

The river kept flowing.

Past the Hoover Dam, the Colorado River continues running south along the Arizona-California border through an intricate network of dams, reservoirs, pumping plants, canals, lifts, and tunnels. Water pools in Lake Mohave behind Davis Dam and then again in Lake Havasu behind Parker Dam, where California and Arizona siphon their legal allotment of water. She passes through five more dams for diversion or irrigation purposes, becoming less and less of a river with each mile and turning into a tightly controlled waterway by the time she reaches Mexico. What little water does make it to the border is so saline and toxic from pollutants like agrichemicals, wastewater discharge, storm water discharge, storage runoff, mining contaminants, and even fecal matter, it must be processed and treated before use. As if her condition in her final days wasn't distressing enough, an ongoing drought and population growth across the western United States insists the river works so hard that she dries up before she reaches her intended destination. The Colorado River has not reached the ocean naturally in over twenty years.

The river isn't failing. She tries to do what she's built for—meet and marry the sea—but she is stopped short by forces beyond her control. She gives everything she has even as she is overworked, mistreated, and underappreciated. Her 246,000-square-mile watershed irrigates over five million acres of agricultural lands, generates hydroelectric power, controls unexpected floods, and supports world-class recreational opportunities. She provides thousands of jobs across multiple industries. She delivers drinking water to forty million people. While the river traveled uninhibited to the Gulf of California for over five million years, she has been bound to humanity's societal expectations and unreasonable demands for over a hundred years. It's too much to ask of one river, even one as powerful and persistent as the Colorado. We continue to press her for more, more, always more, and we're draining her. By taking and taking from her, we're harming our own lifeline.

As I unpacked my dry bags at home, I thought about how, on

the surface, it seemed like a sad fate for a river to not live up to her potential as society expects—like how I did not live up to mine, being a wife until "death do us part." I hadn't failed. I had given everything I had. I had tried to be the best spouse I could be, but I was stopped short too. Yet, after spending time with the Colorado River, I was more myself than ever. Now, unlike her, I ran free.

I wondered what would happen if we let the Colorado run free. Or, at the least, we reduced her burdens and supported her in being the river she was meant to be. If we turned our mindless consumption into a healthier respect for the value the river brings to our lives, could she flourish and gain even more strength, like humans do when we give them the space and grace to live autonomously and authentically?

Maybe, just maybe, there was greater meaning to the Colorado River's existence than whether she reached the ocean like a river should in the same way there was greater meaning to my existence than whether I reached the end of my life being a wife like a woman "should." That maybe, just maybe, the river does something bigger than herself in her struggle to survive along her long and winding journey from the Rocky Mountains to the sea.

Even as gravity pushes her to the lowest part in the landscape, even as she faces obstacle after obstacle in servitude, she inspires people by simply existing, by being herself, by flowing to the best of her ability. The river shapes her surroundings without having a voice of her own. She relies entirely on the magnetism of her actions to influence others. In doing so, the river creates advocates, protectors, lovers, a chorus of individuals who use *their* voices to amplify mutually beneficial interests for her, for themselves, and for civilization. She multiplies her own power by giving power to others, and she does so without asking for attention, without seeking permission, without saying a thing.

See, the Colorado River has never uttered a word. To me. To anyone. Yet a river is far from mute. Over the last three years, I've heard everything she's had to offer. The Colorado's wisdom has rolled off her silky tongues at the beginning of rapids, boomed in the folds of her crests and troughs, giggled in her skypools and landpools, gurgled in her swirling eddies, clapped against cobble, reverberated off every sheer cliff, and soared in her silence under starry nights—and will for as long as she flows.

I still had much to learn from her, but now I understood that any sentiments I heard on my journey between her shores were my own and from the voices she had elevated. A river's guidance merely reflects the human soul but only for those who attend to her stories of patience, perseverance, and vigor with reverence. Any conversation we have with the natural world echoes instincts we already possess, either on the surface or hidden deep inside, about life, death, and the space in between.

Nature just exists. When we connect with rivers, and with nature, we form our own meaning. In other words, we hear what we want—or in my case, need—to hear. If only we are willing to listen.

From the moment I met her, the Colorado River has spoken to me—and she will continue to speak to me. My bond with her runs deep. For on her waters is where I found my own voice, my own truth. On her waters is where I became my own river.

So said the river.

21
SO I SAY

This is the point in the story where I am supposed to tell you that I found another Prince Charming, fell madly in love, and lived happily ever after. But, that's not how my current has flowed.

Two of those things did happen. I did fall in love. But with a river—the Colorado—and with myself and my life, one filled with more fulfillment, peace, and passion than I could have ever imagined. No, no knight in shining armor has crowned me as his own. But I was no longer lost. I didn't need saving. I had learned how to face and tame my own dragons.

Besides, I was already The Queen. And I already owned a tiara.

Some people may feel disappointed or sad for me that I have "failed" to find a new soulmate. Beware of falling under the spell of societal expectations. Despite the voices around us trying their best to convince us otherwise, when it comes to defining what brings us satisfaction, they—whoever "they" are—aren't an accurate judge. You are for you. I am for me.

Rest assured, this story—my story—*has* a happy ending. It's just not the one you've been told I should have.

For forty years, I listened to what "they" said and thought there was one path to happiness: that checking all the boxes and doing more, more, always more would one day pay off with my eternal bliss. In

April 2015, when life deviated from my carefully constructed plans, I reached the crest of my disappointment and unhappiness. My unexpected separation threw me into chaos and into the very things I feared most: failure, uncertainty, living alone. I thought I had been handed a life sentence of isolation and misery.

I turned to the Colorado River for solace. She delivered so much more. The river changed my course forever. After my mom and I escaped death on her waters in November 2015, the river guided me to believe that life, even with its unpredictable and beautifully messy turbulence, was still worth living.

I didn't know it at the time, but when Mom and I launched from the North Wash/Dirty Devil takeout, I stood at my own confluence. I desperately wanted to hold onto a life I once had while desperately wanting everything to be different. On Lake Powell, in the wind and waves, these sediments mixed. In the time that followed, through the Grand Canyon and across Lake Mead, the river finished dissolving the muddy person I used to be. What remained was clarity.

Through adversity, I became more than the broken remnants of my old self held together by leopard-patterned duct tape. Swells drowned out habits of controlling circumstances, chasing perfection and achievement, and seeking validation from others. Wind scrubbed and scoured my being to give me new depth. Tributaries provided strength and volume to my new channel. Reflections from my supportive surroundings painted my blues with bright and vivid colors. The waters in this channel stripped the pretense of who I thought I should be, who I planned to be, and exposed the core of who I was.

When Craig and I separated, I did not know how to navigate rapids. I didn't own a paddleboard or a paddle. I didn't even like water. Since then, I have paddled or rowed over 400 miles on nine major Western rivers. The Colorado, Yampa, Green, Salt, Lower Salmon, Snake, Deschutes, Chama, and Arkansas rivers had shifted the sands within me. I took swiftwater rescue classes. I trained to be a river guide.

Now river water flows in my blood. I seek out spontaneity for fun. I crash into waves on purpose. I no longer fear failing or falling in.

The Colorado River had helped me discover—and live—my

own big Life with a capital L. One where I live free of expectations. Live beyond the meaningless minutiae. Live one moment at a time with curiosity and conviction. Live without fear of the future. Live deliberately according to my own principles and desires. Live a life from which I do not need an escape. Live as if every day was my birthday.

The wind and waves taught me that happiness isn't something you pursue or wait for. It's something you choose to live every day. Despite what we've been told, lasting fulfillment does not come from external sources like fame, money, career, marriage, or vacations. Nor from grand accomplishments like crossing a reservoir on top of nothing more than a long inflatable flotation device.

Lasting fulfillment comes from within and comes in many flavors—just like pie. Contentment originates from self-acceptance, leveraging your talents, surrounding yourself with a community who believes in you, and expressing gratitude for all your gifts. Gratification emerges from facing big waves with confidence, creating meaning out of experiences, and learning through unexpected hardships. From self-awareness, in all its evolutions, comes true personal independence regardless of whether you are married, single, or something in between.

Out of the storms and rapids I had faced since 2015, I had found "The One" I wanted to live happily ever after with: me.

Had everything gone perfectly according to my plans—had I stayed married, had I not paddled in Moab in April 2015, and had I finished crossing Powell with my mom in November 2015—this fortunate transformation may not have happened. My life now is better than anything I could have ever dreamed up and scribbled on a spreadsheet. It is better than any fairy tale. It is sweeter and more delicious than pie.

So I say.

Big Bend Rapid on the Colorado River at low water in winter.

On August 8, 2021, I returned to the Big Bend Rapid alone with a new SUP built for whitewater (named Flora). I paddled through it, staying upright and dry. Afterward, I celebrated with a fried peach pie—gas station special—while floating on my beloved Colorado River.

EPILOGUE: MY EVER AFTER

The waves kept coming.

My divorce was finalized.

My beloved sixteen-year-old cat, Nolan, died.

Mom had more skin cancer removed.

Dad beat prostate cancer, then later fought a deadly pneumonia-turned-sepsis illness for eight months. Doctors say he should have died in three days. He survived and thrives today.

My parents, so many friends, and I fell ill during the COVID-19 pandemic. My outdoor photography and publishing businesses—along with my enriching travels—underwent significant and sudden change when the world went into lockdown for months.

The waves on the river of life don't stop. No one can say why the universe chooses us to endure the tumultuous whitewater we do, but it does. If we rise to the challenge as the waters rise, if we push off these shores seeking growth and meaning, we get more resilient at navigating through them. Even so, sometimes we stay dry; sometimes we don't.

Among so many things, water had taught me that waves are just Mother Nature's way of restoring equilibrium. When life's rapids hit, I turn to thoughts of my time with the Colorado River for comfort, for a reminder to keep flowing no matter the obstacles or hardships.

Paddleboarding showed me how to steady my board and to keep my paddle all in.

Then the biggest wave of all hit.

On September 7, 2021, while eating lunch at my kitchen table, a Facebook message popped up on my phone from a friend and former coworker, one I hadn't heard from in years.

Craig had died on September 5.

He had been hiking with friends in Phoenix. He had started complaining—Craig rarely complained—that he didn't feel well. His condition deteriorated enough that his friends left him to seek help. By the time help arrived, Craig was dead. He was a mile from the parking lot.

The initial report for the cause of death suggested he succumbed to "environmental effects." Likely heat stroke and dehydration. It was 104 degrees Fahrenheit with twenty-percent humidity that day. I couldn't imagine a more absurd and tragic fate for someone who had hiked for forty-five of his forty-six years and had lived in Phoenix for twenty-five years.

He didn't have enough water.

My world went black.

When I picked myself off the floor, I tried to choose the best line I could, scraping against rocks of pain and crashing into waves of maddening confusion. I paddled hard and without hesitation through self-care.

In addition to expressing gratitude each day, when I walked past the mirror in my bathroom, I looked into my red and puffy eyes and said, "I know this is so hard. You can do this. I love you."

One morning, I dug my engagement ring out of my jewelry case and slid it onto my ring finger. It was one of the last, and most meaningful, tangible items I had from my time with Craig, one that reminded me of abundant joy and hope for the future. Surrounding myself with a physical representation of that lightness helped keep my head above water.

It also reminded me that I had already been grieving the loss of Craig in some way for six years. Drawers had been cleaned out. Pictures had been taken down. Coffee mugs had been divided. I had already cried through all my "firsts" without him. My first trip to the hardware store to pick out paint colors on my own. Eating at our favorite restaurant alone. Changing the smoke detector battery at two in the morning by myself. None of this made Craig's passing any less painful, but it reminded me that I had a map of grief tucked into my life vest.

Some life events you can swim alone. Not this kind. Instead of wading through isolation as I did at the start of my separation, I called everybody. In the space of an afternoon, I had talked with my parents, my brother, Guy, Sinjin, college friends who knew Craig, and other connections in my contact list.

Guy reminded me, "Don't be afraid to cry." I cried and cried and cried floods, the kind that makes your head hurt and your temples pound into your head, the kind that nourishes and brings green growth to a desperate and dry desert landscape.

When I shared the news with Sinjin, he replied, "As the sole survivor in this disastrous turn of events, you get to decide how you wish to remember your time with Craig."

I chose to extend love and gratitude. For Craig. For me. For us. For all of us. At the end of each phone call, I let each of my friends know what they meant to me, what they meant to Craig if they had met, and how I appreciated them being a significant part of my—and his—life. I told them I loved them. I refused to wait until a person's obituary to express how I felt about them.

It took me a week to gather enough strength to share a public tribute for Craig. As I processed his passing and continued to hear stories about him, one thing stood out to me. In recalling their memories of him, not one person mentioned what kind of car he drove, or how big his house was, or how much money he made at Intel. Not one person brought up how he and his high school soccer team won multiple Montana state championships, how he was one of only a handful of undergraduates to graduate with a Materials Science and Engineering degree at Stanford, or how he beat me at minigolf every time. (Yes, *every* time, and often by a lot too.)

Beyond his many notable achievements, in the end, people admired

Craig for his big heart, his charming smile, and his willingness to go the extra mile to put people at ease and to enable their goals. (Except when he played minigolf.) He shined because he treated people with kindness, respect, and dignity. People looked up to him, wanted to work with and for him, wanted to learn from him. He inspired others and made the world a better place for me, my family, and everyone he interacted with.

That's success. *That's* good enough. *That's* a life well-lived. People won't remember what you accomplished. They also won't remember your shortcomings or failures either. They'll remember how you impacted their lives.

I could say Craig died unexpectedly. What that really means is those left behind weren't ready for his departure. Craig didn't plan on dying at forty-six. No one plans to die. No one puts it on a Gantt chart or spreadsheet. Yet it is the only thing certain in our lives. Death is literally the only thing we can—and should—expect.

Men are expected to live until seventy-five. Women until eighty-one. *So they say*. Some of us don't make it that far. Craig didn't. His mother didn't. My maternal grandparents didn't. My grandfather had dreamed of traveling the country in an RV with my grandmother when he retired. Except, he never retired. He died at fifty-seven of a heart attack. My grandmother died at sixty-seven from cancer, before she could retire and figure out how to wander on her own.

Age is just another human-constructed measure of achievement. Our time, like a river's journey across the land, is indeterminate yet finite. I don't mean that to be morbid or depressing. I mean it to be freeing.

If we expected death to rip us away at any time, not just in old age, maybe we would choose to celebrate every day like our birthday, to live our own individual big Life with a capital L. Maybe we would choose to eat that pie first.

Maybe we would not ask anyone for permission to love ourselves and to love our lives. Maybe we would not wait for bank holidays and so-called special occasions to wear our best dresses, drink out of our expensive glassware, and hug our loved ones. Maybe we would not waste time entertaining fear, holding on to resentment, or second-guessing our self-worth. Maybe we would stop toiling away at things we don't want to do, kowtowing to other people's judgments, and reacting to the meaningless trivialities so many of us subject ourselves to, sometimes unknowingly, day in and day out.

There will be a time when we will all meet our own oceans, where we will be absorbed back into an unknown and unknowable place from whence we came. With the time you have left, what definition of success will you embrace?

Instead of concerning yourself with how you wish to be remembered when you're gone—because it won't matter to you then—consider: how do you want to be celebrated right now? For your car, house, and salary? For the trophies, newspaper clippings, and medals in a box in the garage? Or for being an authentic human who made the world a little better, kinder place than you came into it? How will you shape your landscape? With hate, ugliness, fear, judgment, and disappointment? Or with love, beauty, courage, acceptance, and contentment?

Choose wisely.

You only get one run down this river of no return. You can't always go back upstream and rerun the rapids with faster, sleeker equipment on a better, cleaner line. You also can't always see what's around the next bend. You can, however, decide in the next second to choose your course. To pick the best line through the next rapids. To change directions.

And you don't have to be perfect at it either. Be the best paddler you can be and tumble, rumble, and ramble as you face obstacles—rocks, eddies, boils—learning lessons, growing within your true self, and embracing gratitude with each turn. No doubt you can—and will—fail at many things over the course of a lifetime, especially if you're pushing your boundaries, challenging expectations, and leaning into uncertainty. But remember, the one thing you can never fail at, no matter how hard you try, is being yourself.

Besides, would you rather try and fail or fail to try and live with regret?

According to *The Top Five Regrets of the Dying,* a book by Bronnie

Ware, if a person feels regret in their last moments, it is because they believe they worked too much, did not spent enough time with friends or family, did not have the courage to express their emotions, did not allow themselves to be happier, and led a life others expected of them, not a deliberate one.

All of us are dying.

Too few of us are deliberately living.

If you're reading this, you still have time.

You are gloriously and wildly alive.

Act like it.

~ ~ ~

In the weeks after Craig's death, I sorted through the thousands of printed and digital images I had collected from our life together. As each picture passed through my hands, I relived each memory. I saw so much laughter, togetherness, and affection as we got lost in Lost, Aberdeenshire, Scotland; recreated the American Gothic stance in front of a cabin in the ghost town of Garnet in Montana; and warmed ourselves by a campfire on the beach while houseboating on Lake Powell.

One framed photograph stood out. It was one from our backpacking trip on the North Rim of the Grand Canyon on the Deer Creek/Thunder River trails in October 2009. I hadn't noticed it before, in all the years that photograph had sat on my shelf, but there she was, the Colorado River, flowing behind Craig and me in our embrace on the beach at Deer Creek Falls. I realized that trip was the first time I had put my fingers in the Colorado River in river form.

On my next rafting trip through the Grand Canyon in August 2022—my seventh in seven years—my photography group stopped at mile 137 to see Deer Creek Falls. I settled my participants at the 150-foot-tall waterfall to make their own photographs then ambled to the river's edge with that framed photograph in one hand. I dropped to my knees and plunged my other hand into the Colorado River. Together again, but lifetimes apart.

The "'til death do us part" promise between Craig and I had now been fulfilled, albeit in a way I could have never imagined when I said "I do." Memories, both joyful and heartbreaking, would leave a residue on my being, like the Bathtub Ring along the rocks of Lake Powell and Lake Mead, like the layers of history in the Grand Canyon. My tears joined the current.

As the rapids rushed downstream through the narrowing corridor of reddened cliffs, I thanked Craig and the Colorado River, for together they had given me the gift of six years to learn how to paddle alone on my own river.

I could not say what waited for me around the next bend. But, as I stood along the shores of my beloved Colorado River, hugging a framed photograph of the life I had lost while living the life I had gained, it comforted me to know for myself that water does, in fact, give life.

In August 2022, I stood in the same spot Craig and I had posed for a photograph while backpacking in 2009 along the Colorado River near Deer Creek Falls (river mile 137) in the Grand Canyon. Photo by Josh Nelson.

OPPOSITE: The Colorado River flows along the base of sheer cliffs near Tuckup Canyon (river mile 165) in the Grand Canyon.

"Said the river: imagine everything you can imagine. Then keep on going."
-Mary Oliver

ACKNOWLEDGMENTS

While living through the adventures you have just read, I embarked on a second, parallel, yet no less arduous, journey: writing this book. Like life, this was not the narrative I planned to write when Mom and I launched from the North Wash/Dirty Devil Takeout in November 2015. What started off as a simple story of two women trying to cross a reservoir became a celebration of community, a multitude of confluences that gathered to support me with love, encouragement, guidance, and wisdom through one of the most difficult times in my life. Thanks to many, this story transformed into something much deeper and much more meaningful. We may become our own river, but we don't float on it alone—and I am better, richer, and happier because of it.

I am especially grateful to the following people:

To my parents for giving me not just a life, but also one full of love, support, opportunities, and learnings. Thank you to my mom, Jacque, for having an overflowing energy, zest for life, and enough devotion for me to proclaim, "I'm coming with you" on Lake Powell, through the Grand Canyon, and throughout my life. To my dad, Bob, for your unwavering love for your family and caring for our well-being, not just on Lake Powell but also through our various challenges and triumphs over the years. Thank you for your logistical support during all our paddling escapades. You both are my heroes!

To my one and only brother, Rob, for role modeling a carefree "going with the flow" attitude growing up, for keeping me company while devouring baskets of chips at Nando's, and for spicing up my fajitas and other meals with your homegrown green peppers and jalapeños. I don't know what I did to deserve it, but I feel incredibly fortunate the universe chose you, Mom, and Dad to be my family in this life. The adventures we have shared—and will share—mean so much to me. Long live the Maniacs! Go Team Miniuk!

To my beloved cat, Nolan. Although he's gone now, he spent too many days curled up with me on my chaise lounge while I wrote this book to not recognize his substantial contribution to my well-being and joy. He greeted me at the door every time with a cheerful "MEOW" for about sixteen years. He listened to me whine over wine, sat in the chair next to me while I ate, and slept on my chest when I rested. I never knew a heart could be so full. I miss you—and you puking on the carpet—King Nolan.

To the Sperry and Boos families for all the cherished memories we created together. Whether it was drinking pots of coffee, skiing at Big Mountain, or singing at reunions in Iowa, you always made me feel welcomed. I appreciate all the learnings and laughs.

To Guy Tal for being unapologetically you. Thanks for every drop of encouragement and all the laughs, tears, hikes, tequila toasts, banana pancakes, tater tots, Milky Ways, and poker games. I could not have asked for a better friend. I'm proud to be a finger in your solitude.

To Jen and Michael Raffaeli for our adventures, conversations, and laughs over the years. Among so many things, you have taught me how to cope with loss and pursue life afterward with grace, dignity, and strength. Hugs to you both for your endless inspiration and for providing me with a warm bed and incredibly delicious meals at "summer camp." For all the smiles they put on my face each time I see them, howls and belly rubs to the Muffins: Lucky ("my" Bubby) and Annie (Princess Annie-Bananie).

To Chris Serjak for looking after me (and Craig) at Stanford and for being one of my biggest supporters for over thirty years. Thanks to you and Susan Marx for introducing me to standup paddleboarding. Look what you started!

To Sinjin Eberle for being such a good sport about getting sucked into this story as an innocent by-stander—but such an important one. Since that one simple online exchange in 2015, you've enabled so many remarkable changes in my life. Thank you for being such a great listener as I navigated through tough transitions, for supporting my work through American Rivers, and for your dedicated efforts to keep rivers healthy and wild. Keep flowing! For the love of the river!

To Terry and Wendy Gunn for not only your friendship but also providing your expertise and guidance on Lake Powell to help keep us safe. To Anthony, who picked us up in Forgotten Canyon, and to Marty, who helped us get settled in at Halls Crossing. To Tammy for the conversation and red wine at Halls Crossing. Mom and I are alive and well because of the generosity you all extended in our time of need.

To Michael and Jeanne Falk Adams for believing in me and my work. Thank you for shaping my world in profoundly meaningful ways and for doing so with such incredible energy, wisdom, creativity, and delight. I cherish the time we spend together. Magic always seems to happen when "the river" meets "the ocean."

To my many dear friends who experienced sudden (and not-so-sudden) bouts of tears over a campfire, on a road trip, at lunch, or in a grocery store. Thank you specifically to (in no particular order) Michael Gordon, Paul Gill, Christine Peterson, Kris Millgate, Emily Stone, Tim Mead, Brett Prettyman, Phil Bloom, Bill Powell, Tim Christie, Bob and Linda Thayer, Kurt Budliger, Kelly Fine, M. Cathy Nowak, Ty Stockton, Kerry Smith, Kelly Pape, Ambika Balasubramaniyan, Vicki Uthe, Floris van Breugel, Kate Petrie, Peg Olson, Andrew MacCallum, Lee Pagni, Mike DiMeola, and my workshop participants, especially the Sheographers, for not only listening and sharing welcomed advice, but also simply giving me a hug seemingly right when I needed it most.

To those who have enabled my clients and me to explore the Colorado River through the Grand Canyon on a deeper level. Thanks to Steve Hatch and all my river guides at Hatch River Expeditions, specifically Lars Niemi, Sean Pope, Zach Zemlicka, Josh Nelson, Josh Bradford, Tanner Patty, Kelsey Pfendler, and J.P. Paszek. Thank you also to all my fellow Hatchlings for our incredible laps on the Colorado River on the Grand Canyon together.

To Paddle Moab (especially Alicia), O.A.R.S., and Canyon River Instruction for teaching me life and whitewater skills.

To Bryan Wheat and the staff at Alaskan Camper who have taken great care of Juno and me over the years.

To those who sent thoughtful notes after the rough waters of Lake Powell and during other difficult times. No act of kindness from strangers went unnoticed either. Although our encounter may have been too brief for me to learn your name or your full story, the compassion from friends and strangers alike mattered—and matters—to me. Thank you for being a bright star on some of my darkest days—and on my brightest ones too!

To my keen and patient editor, Erik Berg. There are not enough thanks in the world to account for all the ones I owe him, but I'm going to try anyway. Thank you, Erik, for not only taking on the bulk of work I abandoned after leaving Intel (I'm really sorry about that…) but also for taking on the even more difficult task of helping me be a better writer, book after book, year after year. Thank you for your extensive, thought-provoking commentary with each draft (and there were a lot of those...). With your help, it's entirely possible I may come to understand commas one day. When I do, I will count it among one of my life's greatest achievements. And you'll get full credit.

To Lori Johnson, my amazing proofreader, for going through the book with a fine-toothed comb. I don't know how you do what you do, but I'm sure glad you do it and do it so well!

To the first set of beta readers, who, even after being subjected to a horrible first draft, still provided me with honest feedback and encouragement. Thank you to Sharon Philpott, Tim Mead, Jen and Michael Raffaeli, Bob and Linda Thayer, Christine Peterson, Ambika Balasubramaniyan, Brett Prettyman, Kelly Pape, and Scott Lefler. Thank you also to the second beta readers, who, even after being subjected to draft #764, still read every word. Mom, Dad, Jen, Michael, Bruce, and Guy: thank you for your patience and insights.

To my extraordinary friend Bruce Hucko. Three cheers for him! And not just because he put together gorgeous maps for this book. (Although that didn't hurt.) This world—and my world—is a brighter place because of you, THE one and only Art Coach, as a human being, and fellow lover of Kettle Brand folded salt and pepper potato chips. I appreciate you, Bruce, for our many insightful chats, adventures, and toasts to our friendship.

To Dave Showalter, an incredibly talented photographer, writer, and speaker, who provided the inspiration for this book's title by sharing a Mary Oliver quote (which appears on page 345) during his presentation at the 2023 North American Nature Photographers Assocation (NANPA) conference. How fortunate I was, in so many ways, to cross paths with you there, Dave. Here's to continuing to flow and to putting our hands in the living waters of our beloved Colorado River.

To the Outdoor Writers Association of America (OWAA), which has helped me thrive as an outdoor communicator. In 2010, during my first time at their annual conference, a book self-publishing session planted the seed for me to write and publish books. Since then, its many talented, supportive, and kind members have taught me how to write cohesive sentences, start a book publishing business, find new outlets for my work, and more. I continue to gain endless inspiration from people I'm proud to call my dear friends. I'm honored to know you and to be a part of "the voice of the outdoors."

To Craig Childs, who taught me how to rip my heart out, slap it on a page, and watch it bleed. Thank you, Craig, for showing me how to write raw, brave, and with rhythm during various writing workshops. Also, you're right: wind definitely makes one bitchy.

To every reader for joining me on this ride and for supporting my work. Without you, I would not have the means to live my purpose. I hope in reading this tale, you have gained new courage and inspiration to put your paddle "all in" toward your own aspirations—and to always eat your pie first.

ABOUT THE AUTHOR
COLLEEN J. MINIUK

Colleen J. Miniuk (she/her/hers) is a full-time outdoor photographer, writer, publisher, instructor, and speaker. Her credits include *National Geographic* calendars, *Arizona Highways*, *AAA Via*, *National Parks Traveler*, *On Landscape*, and a variety of other publications.

After serving three times as an Artist-in-Residence with Acadia National Park, she authored the award-winning guidebook *Photographing Acadia National Park: The Essential Guide to When, Where, and How*. She is also the author of *Wild in Arizona: Photographing Arizona's Wildflowers*, *Seeing the Light in Outdoor Photography*, and *The Current Flows: Water in the Arid West*. She writes an online photography advice column called "Dear Bubbles."

Colleen leads photography workshops, women's photography retreats (called "Sheography™"), and online sessions for camera clubs, outdoor organizations, and private clients. She is the recipient of the prestigious J. Hammond Brown Memorial Award from the Outdoor Writers Association of America.

She resides in Chandler, Arizona, on the ancestral homeland of the Hohokam, in the Colorado River watershed.

To learn more about her work, including how to join a photography workshop, arrange a speaking engagement, purchase her books, or order photographic prints, please visit www.colleenminiuk.com.